e-Learning Initiat
in China

G000111268

Hong Kong University Press thanks Xu Bing for writing the Press's name in his Square Word Calligraphy for the covers of its books. For further information, see p. iv.

Education in **China**
Reform and Diversity

Wah Ching Centre of Research on Education in China
The University of Hong Kong

This series explores the dramatic changes in China's education system. By using fresh perspectives and innovative methods, each volume delves into the issues and debates that continue to challenge education in China, including cultural and linguistic diversity, regional disparity, financial decentralization, technological change, intellectual autonomy, and increased internationalization.

Series Editors

Gerard A. Postiglione and Wing-wah Law
The University of Hong Kong

Series Advisor

Kai-ming Cheng
The University of Hong Kong

Editorial Board

Hong Kong, China

Kwok-wah Cheung, The University of Hong Kong
Ho-ming Ng, The University of Hong Kong
Kam-cheung Wong, The University of Hong Kong
Jin Xiao, The Chinese University of Hong Kong
Li-fang Zhang, The University of Hong Kong

International

Emily Hannum, The University of Pennsylvania
Ruth Hayhoe, The University of Toronto
Julia Kwong, The University of Manitoba
Jing Lin, The University of Maryland
Vilma Seeberg, Kent State University
Stanley Rosen, The University of Southern California
Heidi Ross, Indiana University

e-Learning Initiatives in China

Pedagogy, Policy and Culture

Edited by Helen Spencer-Oatey

香港大學出版社

HONG KONG UNIVERSITY PRESS

Hong Kong University Press
14/F Hing Wai Centre
7 Tin Wan Praya Road
Aberdeen
Hong Kong

© Hong Kong University Press 2007

Hardback　ISBN 978-962-209-867-1
Paperback　ISBN 978-962-209-868-8

Secure On-line Ordering
http://www.hkupress.org

British Library Cataloguing-in-Publication Data
A catalogue record for this book is available from the British Library.

Printed and bound by Kings Time Printing Press Ltd. in Hong Kong, China

Hong Kong University Press is honoured that Xu Bing, whose art explores the complex
themes of language across cultures, has written the Press's name in his Square Word
Calligraphy. This signals our commitment to cross-cultural thinking and the distinctive nature
of our English-language books published in China.

"At first glance, Square Word Calligraphy appears to be nothing more unusual than Chinese
characters, but in fact it is a new way of rendering English words in the format of a square so
they resemble Chinese characters. Chinese viewers expect to be able to read Square Word
Calligraphy but cannot. Western viewers, however are surprised to find they can read it.
Delight erupts when meaning is unexpectedly revealed."

— *Britta Erickson, The Art of Xu Bing*

Contents

Figures

Tables

Contributors

Sheena BANKS is an e-learning research associate in the School of Education at the University of Sheffield and has extensive international experience of e-learning research, innovation and implementation as an e-learning course developer, e-tutor, researcher and project coordinator.

Eric BREWSTER works at the University of Cambridge Language Centre as a content developer and consultant for the *CUTE* Project. He also worked on the English at Your Fingertips projects and has been an EAP supervisor and instructor.

Nicola CAVALERI coordinates the self-access area of the Language Centre at the University of Cambridge and manages the Centre's English for Academic Purposes (EAP) courses. She was project manager for the Cambridge University *CUTE* Project team.

CHEN Zehang is a lecturer in the English Department, School of Foreign Languages and Literatures, Beijing Normal University, China. She is currently completing a PhD in the School of Education, University of Nottingham, exploring issues related to the design of online teacher training materials.

Gráinne CONOLE is professor of e-learning at the Open University, UK, researching the use, integration and evaluation of e-learning and its impact on organizational change (see http://iet.open.ac.uk/pp/g.c.conole/ for further details).

Lindsay COOPER is a member of the Centre for the Study of Human Relations at the University of Nottingham. He teaches on counselling programmes and is particularly interested in the way educators can use counselling skills in their everyday life and work.

Martin DYKE is a senior lecturer in post-compulsory education and training in the School of Education, University of Southampton, UK. His research interests include innovations in learning and teaching, the sociology of education, lifelong learning, widening participation and the use of digital technologies to support learning.

Gillian FORRESTER is a research associate in the Centre for Equity in Education at the School of Education, University of Manchester, UK. She co-ordinated the collaborative instructional design for the *DEFT* Project for the *eChina-UK Programme.*

Sue GOLDRICK is a research associate in the Centre for Equity in Education at the School of Education, University of Manchester, UK. She co-ordinated the collaborative instructional design for the *DEFT* Project for the *e-china-UK Programme.*

GU Yueguo, MA, PhD (Lancaster University), is a research professor and the head of the Contemporary Linguistics Department in the Chinese Academy of Social Sciences. He is also the executive dean of the Beiwai Institute of Online Education. His research interests include pragmatics, discourse analysis, corpus linguistics, rhetoric and online education.

Carol HALL is professor of human relations and head of the School of Education and Director of the Centre for the Study of Human Relations at the University of Nottingham. She has published widely in the field of human relations, counselling and experiential learning.

Eric HALL, a chartered counselling psychologist, was formerly a senior lecturer in the School of Education at the University of Nottingham and now works as an independent consultant in the area of human relations, with a specific interest in experiential learning and the use of imagery in education and psychotherapy.

HUANG Ronghuai is dean of the School of Educational Technology and director of the Centre for Knowledge Engineering at Beijing Normal University, China. His research focuses on e-learning, computer supported co-operative learning and artificial intelligence in education.

JIANG Xin is a PhD candidate from the School of Educational Technology at Beijing Normal University, specializing in educational informationization and knowledge assets.

Gordon JOYES is an associate professor in e-learning at the University of Nottingham. He is an accomplished director of international e-learning projects involving both research and innovation, and is an experienced online course developer and tutor.

KANG Feiyu is a full professor in the Department of Material Science and Engineering, and a vice-provost in Tsinghua University. His specialization is carbon material, e-learning, teaching evaluation and alleviation of poverty.

Vic LALLY is a senior lecturer in education in the Faculty of Education at the University of Glasgow, UK. He has directed and co-directed many e-learning research projects, and has published extensively in the fields of e-learning, education, and science education. His main research interests include human learning, its 'design', philosophy and ethics, as well as the cultural and political contexts of learning.

Anny KING is the executive director of the Language Centre at the University of Cambridge. She initiated the Cambridge University Language Programme (CULP), developed its integrated methodology and served as project director on the *CUTE* Project.

Debra MARSH works as a consultant and content developer for the Language Centre at the University of Cambridge. Her work focuses on the pedagogy of online learning and teaching and includes online facilitation, online course development, design and evaluation.

David McCONNELL is professor of education (advanced learning technology) in the Department of Educational Research, Lancaster University. His research interests are in continuing professional development, culture and pedagogy in online learning (especially groups and communities) and collaborative online assessment.

Angela McLACHLAN is a researcher in the School of Education, University of Manchester, and is currently completing a PhD on the implementation of new educational policy in primary schools.

Ian McGRATH is an associate professor in TESOL in the School of Education, University of Nottingham, and academic director of one of the university's e-learning projects. He has published widely on materials design and teacher education.

Gary MOTTERAM is a senior lecturer in education at the University of Manchester, where he teaches and works in the area of educational technology and language learning. His main research interests are in the areas of technology supported teacher education.

Barbara SINCLAIR is an associate professor in TESOL in the School of Education at Nottingham University. She has been involved in the Nottingham *eChina-UK* projects as co-bidder, academic director, researcher and materials developer.

SONG Gilsun is currently working at the Institution of Higher Education, Shanghai Jiaotong University as associate professor. She specializes in e-learning, higher education (university management and evaluation). Previously, she was a senior research fellow at the School of Continuing Education, Tsinghua University, and in charge of international research projects.

Helen SPENCER-OATEY is director of the Centre for English Language Teacher Education at the University of Warwick, and the UK manager of the *eChina-UK Programme*. Her main research interests are in the interrelationships between language, culture and rapport management. She has published widely in the area of rapport management and intercultural interaction.

TANG Min is currently pursuing a PhD in the Faculty of Psychology and Educational Sciences, Luwig-Maximilians-University (LMU) Munich, Germany. Formerly she was deputy director of the Department of International Cooperation, School of Continuing Education and Teacher Training (SCETT), Beijing Normal University.

WANG Tong is an associate professor at Beijing Foreign Studies University, China. Her research and professional interests include teaching English as a foreign language and learner/tutor support for online education. She also serves as deputy dean of the institute, responsible for learner support, tutor support, and blended training.

Caroline WINDRUM is director of development at the Learning Sciences Research Institute, University of Nottingham, UK. She has a background in intellectual property contract drafting and negotiation in higher education.

Christoph ZÄHNER is the head of IT at the Language Centre of the University of Cambridge. His background is in German philology, computational linguistics and educational technology. His main interests are in languages, logic, computation and cognitive processing.

ZHANG Haishen is an associate professor of English at the University of International Business and Economics (UIBE), Beijing, and is currently deputy director of the UIBE Centre for Self-Access Foreign Language Learning and Research. His research interests are in English language learning and technology as well as language testing. At present, he is a doctoral student at the Centre for Knowledge Engineering at Beijing Normal University.

Acknowledgements

In 2002, I took up the management of the *eChina-UK Programme* on behalf of the UK teams. Despite my interest in the post, I did not foresee what an immensely enriching experience it would be for me, both professionally and personally. Working with such a talented and dedicated team of people has been informative, challenging and fun.

First of all, I would like to express my special thanks to the Higher Education Funding Council for England (HEFCE) for establishing and funding the *eChina-UK Programme* in the UK. Without their initiative, the rich experiences of the last few years would never have happened. I would especially like to mention a few key figures. Sir Brian Fender, former Chief Executive of HEFCE and Chair of the UK Steering Committee, played a crucial role in planning the Programme in the early stages, and his vision for a truly collaborative venture helped establish the Programme's ethos. Jannette Cheong, responsible for international strategy, was an unfailing source of support, always willing to discuss issues and offer advice. Liz Beaty, Director of Learning and Teaching, took a very keen interest in the Programme, despite her very busy schedule. She believed in our abilities to achieve valuable outcomes even when we were struggling to conceptualize them ourselves, and her support and encouragement have been immense. Others at HEFCE have given excellent administrative support to the Programme, especially David Kernohan and Liz Franco. Both the teams and I are deeply grateful for the tremendous support that all these people have given.

Secondly, I would like to thank all the team members for their dedication and commitment to the Programme, and for their willingness to work so co-operatively both with me and with each other. I am only too aware that this need not have been the case. We have developed a sense of community spirit, and this has helped make the job particularly pleasurable and rewarding for me personally. We have worked closely with each other on complex tasks for an extended period, and have grown to understand and appreciate how we can complement each other in teamwork.

Thirdly, I am very grateful to Clara Ho, editor at Hong Kong University Press, for all her help and impressive efficiency. She has always answered my queries very rapidly and has been a wonderful editor to work with. I am also grateful to Gerard Postiglione and Wing-wah Law at the Wah Ching Centre of Research on Education in China, the University of Hong Kong, for their academic support for the book and for their helpful suggestions during the planning stages.

Finally, I would like thank my family for accepting without complaint my frequent absences from home and the very long hours that I have spent in front of the computer. My two young sons 'allowed' me to travel to China (hoping that I might bring them back some special presents!), and my husband unstintingly took on extra responsibilities in the home.

Helen Spencer-Oatey
December 2006

Section 1

Background

1

Introduction

Helen Spencer-Oatey

> If [Chinese] education is to serve social progress and economic development, the information technology (IT) for it must advance ahead of social progress. (Zhou 2006: 229)

These are the words of Zhou Ji, the current Chinese Minister of Education. They hint at the huge educational challenge that China is facing at present and suggest the significant role that e-learning can play in the (educational) development of the country.

Let us consider the following statistics:

- 318,783,000 people in different types of Chinese educational institutions at all levels in 2002 (Li 2004: 45)
- About 204 million children attending primary and secondary schools (Chen 2006)
- Over 20 million students enrolled in China's colleges and universities in 2004 (Huang, Jiang and Zhang this volume)
- 970,506 academic staff at China's colleges and universities in 2004 (Zhou 2006: 13)
- About 470,000 teachers of English at secondary school level in China (Chen 2006)
- 111 million Internet users in China (CNNIC 2006)

As Li Lanqing (2004), Vice-Premier of the Chinese State Council from 1993 to 2003, points out, China has the largest educational system in the world. In fact, the number of people enrolled in Chinese schools is larger than the entire population of the United States. So, he stresses that high levels of efficiency are essential:

> . . . only by achieving the highest efficiency in the world can we really come to grips with all the problems associated with education in this vast country of ours. (Li 2004: 45)

It is hoped that information technology, and e-learning opportunities in particular, will help spearhead this efficiency.

These facts form the backdrop to the *raison d'être* of this book. The book is an outcome of a major Sino-UK initiative: the *Sino-UK e-Learning Programme (eChina-UK)*. This programme was established to help promote innovation in e-learning, as well as to play a small part in addressing these massive educational challenges in China. The *eChina-UK Programme* forms part of a strategic collaboration between Britain and China in higher education, and it was set up by the Higher Education Funding Council for England (HEFCE) and the Chinese Ministry of Education (MoE), in order to promote innovative developments in e-learning for the training of teachers/lecturers at secondary and tertiary levels. Teacher education is of strategic importance in China, and as the following section explains, the MoE is bringing in a series of pedagogic reforms which are necessitating extensive in-service training for their effective implementation. The *eChina-UK Programme* was charged with the task of utilizing a new medium of learning (e-learning) to help implement these reforms.

Pedagogic Reforms in China

Over the past few years, the MoE has been carrying out a major overhaul of educational practices at primary, secondary and tertiary levels in China, including reforms of the curricula, of textbooks, of the testing and evaluation systems, and of teaching methods. Much greater emphasis is being placed on student-centred learning and self-study, and the aim is to foster greater creativity and individuality in learners through a more task-based approach, through greater use of enquiry methods, and through greater interaction between teacher and learner. Zhou explains it as follows in relation to the higher education (HE) level:

> With the deepening of reform and opening up in recent years, many universities have been exploring new modes of student training. . . . Universities . . . lay greater stress on the integration of theoretical and practical teaching. Some large, research-oriented universities have gradually implemented a mode of advisory teaching, where an advisor provides academic guidance to a number of undergraduate students. For students, it is an explorative or inspirational learning mode, different from the traditional receptive learning mode. Teachers are better prepared to teach in the form of discussion and elicitation so as to inspire initiative and enthusiasm in their students. Senior undergraduate students in many universities participate in research projects headed by professors. These universities also have research funds for students. To cultivate the students' ability to apply book knowledge in analyzing and solving practical problems, universities implement a teaching mode that combines learning, research, and industry. Students are required to do internships in laboratories, factories, and enterprises. More and more undergraduate students derive their graduation theses from industrial production and social practice. (Zhou 2006: 88–89)

The MoE is also bringing in reforms with regard to the learning of English as a foreign language. For a long time, the MoE has attached great importance to the learning of English, but they are aware that many Chinese learners are not as communicatively competent in English as they would wish. They have therefore proposed a number of reforms (MoE

2001, 2003), which Jin and Cortazzi describe as follows, in relation to the teaching of English at university level:

> At university level, there should be consistency and continuity with the English teaching from schools . . . 'College English' should develop and enhance students' English at higher levels yet be geared to students' individual or local needs (previously, mass teaching had understandably taken a fairly uniform but consistent approach across the country). This movement towards institutional flexibility is echoed in the classroom where teachers are encouraged to develop more varied learning and study strategies among students, and to use multiple modes and models for learning and teaching, including the uses of ICT in e-learning (to cater for greater student numbers). . . . The orientation towards flexibility and student-centred learning includes self and peer assessment. However, there is a gap between these aspirations and most current practice. (Jin and Cortazzi 2006: 15)

As Jin and Cortazzi (2006: 15) point out, all of these developments (including those reported by Zhou (2006)) "can be viewed as national targets for changing practices", rather than practices that are already widely-implemented.

In 2001, the MoE took another step to help develop people's communicative competence in English: they started promoting bilingual teaching. They want university academic staff to use English to teach a range of undergraduate subjects, and in fact stated that five to ten percent of courses in disciplines such as bio-technology, information technology, finance and law should be taught in English (or another foreign language) by 2004.[1] For those who are unable to reach this target, they encourage the use of English language resources (such as textbooks) as a stepping stone to bilingual teaching.

e-Learning developments go hand in hand with these reforms. The MoE has initiated a massive programme of infrastructure development (see Kang and Song this volume; Huang, Jiang and Zhang this volume), and they are encouraging the use of e-learning in on-campus education, in distance-learning education, and for educational provision in rural areas. However, a fundamental issue for effective e-learning is the availability of good quality online resources. The MoE, therefore, established the 'Project for Building State-Level Quality Courses' in 2003. This project aims to establish, within a five-year period (2003–07), 1,500 state-level quality online courses across a range of subjects.[2] The contents are to be made available free of charge to universities across the country, with a view to improving the overall quality of education through the sharing of high-quality teaching resources.

The *eChina-UK Programme*

This is the educational context in which the *eChina-UK Programme* was established. Britain, like China, was keen to learn more about e-learning, and so a collaborative programme in this area was appealing to both HEFCE and the MoE. The overarching aims of the programme were identified as follows:

a. strengthen collaboration between China and the UK by sharing experience in the use of Information and Communication Technologies (ICT), and particularly the Internet, for distance and flexible learning; and

b. develop and pilot innovative distance education courseware in selected areas.

(HEFCE 2002: 9)

It was agreed that the focus should be on teacher education, and three broad areas were identified for the first phase of the programme:

* Generic pedagogic approaches and methods
* Teaching English as a foreign language
* English for bilingual teaching and academic exchange

Key British and Chinese universities were selected to take part in this first phase of the programme (see Spencer-Oatey and Tang, this volume, for more details on this process), and the projects and partnerships shown in Table 1.1 were established.

Table 1.1

The Projects and Partnerships of the Initial Phase of the *eChina-UK Programme*

Topic Area		Project Name	Partner Universities	
			Chinese	**British**
Generic approaches and methods: teaching methodology, educational psychology and educational technology		*DEfT* (Developing e-Learning for Teachers) Project	Beijing Normal University	World Universities Network Lead: University of Manchester; Supporting: University of Sheffield, Southampton and Bristol
Teaching English as a Foreign Language	Secondary level	Secondary eELT (**e-English Language Teaching**)	Beijing Normal University	University of Nottingham
	Tertiary level	Tertiary eELT (**e-English Language Teaching**)	Beijing Foreign Studies University	University of Nottingham
English language for Chinese university lecturers of English)		*CUTE* (Chinese **University Teachers**)	Tsinghua University	Open Cambridge Lead: University of Cambridge

It was hoped that, by working together on specific tasks, the collaborative partnerships would yield a range of insights of benefit to both countries:

> In this way, lessons could be drawn from a range of pilot projects, including the benefits and issues of pedagogy, working cross-culturally, and of publishing intellectual property rights. The projects could also inform the development of national policy initiatives in distance education in both countries, particularly e-universities. (HEFCE 2002: 9)

In fact, the projects faced a complex, interacting set of challenges around these various issues. They needed to:

- train teachers via a medium of learning (e-learning) that the in-service teachers were mostly unfamiliar with;
- train teachers via a pedagogic approach that they were mostly unfamiliar with;
- train teachers to implement a different pedagogic approach in their own teaching.

Moreover, before they could do this, they needed to form effective Sino-UK collaborative partnerships that entailed mutual understanding and trust, and they needed to develop a *modus operandi* for designing and producing innovative e-learning materials. Needless to say, all this was extremely demanding, but the rewards have been immense.

The projects started in 2003 and were completed in 2005. Everyone learned very large amounts through the collaborations, and some of these insights are reported in this book. Further information about the programme as a whole, the professional learning that occurred, the online courseware that was developed, and the research insights can be found on the *eChina-UK* website, http://www.echinauk.org/.

Focus and Outline of This Book

As the title of the book indicates, the primary focus of this book is on e-learning in China. The book provides background information on e-learning policies in China, particularly at the HE level; it explores issues of e-learning design both in and for the Chinese context; and it discusses the interplay between pedagogy and technology. Like HEFCE (2005: 5), we use the term e-learning quite broadly to refer to "the use of technologies in *learning* opportunities", and thus to include the use of ICT for on-campus learning as well as for distance learning. However, much (but not all) of the policy information about e-learning in this book refers to distance learning, since so many Chinese government policies on e-learning apply only to off-campus provision (see Kang and Song this volume).

However, the book is about much more than e-learning. It is also about pedagogic beliefs and practices, educational systems and policies, international collaboration processes, as well as project management. This is because working collaboratively on the e-learning projects has entailed addressing all of these issues. The chapters of the book are thus grouped into the following sections:

1. Background
2. Designing and delivering online courses in China
3. Managing the interplay between pedagogy and technology
4. Managing collaboration processes
5. Addressing policy issues

Section 1, Background, comprises two chapters. Chapter 1 is this introductory chapter. Chapter 2, by Kang and Song, is an historical overview of e-learning in HE in China, focusing particularly on policy developments. It provides a very useful contextual backdrop against which all the other chapters need to be interpreted. Section 2 focuses on the various pedagogic issues that the project teams faced in designing and delivering their online courses, and Section 3 explores how the teams managed the interplay between pedagogy and technology. Section 4 turns to the processes of collaboration that the teams experienced, both internationally and inter-professionally. The final section, Section 5, picks up on the policy issues that Kang and Song introduce in Chapter 2. It explores the challenges that need to be addressed, both nationally and internationally, in developing and implementing e-learning policy. More specific information on each of the chapters in Sections 2 to 5 is provided in the introduction to each of the sections.

Needless to say, the theme of e-learning runs through all of the chapters in the book, but another main theme is the development of intercultural understanding. This development of intercultural understanding is vital for effective collaborative working, and it is needed at many different levels, from the micro-context of a particular activity or communicative interaction to the macro-context of educational policy and institutional structures. Many of the chapters of this book thus deal with this issue.

The development of intercultural understanding through international collaboration is a vital element in the internationalization of HE — an issue that is of growing interest and concern to both British and Chinese universities, as well as many others in the world. According to Fielden (2006), the key features of an internationalized university include the following:

- an international mix of students, either on the home campus or on offshore campuses;
- an international mix of teaching and research staff;
- curricula that are 'international' (or at least culturally independent where that is possible);
- domestic students with knowledge of other cultures and languages through study of foreign languages or study abroad;
- international teaching and research collaborations.

The insights that we have gained from the *eChina-UK Programme*, and that are discussed in this book, apply directly to many of these issues, including 'international' curricula, international teaching and research collaborations, and they apply indirectly to others, such as the development of domestic students with knowledge of other cultures and languages.

At the time of writing, we are still deepening our understanding of all of the issues associated with these two themes of e-learning and intercultural understanding. Three further projects have been approved, which are follow-ups from the initial projects that are reported in this book. Insights from these new projects will be disseminated on our website, http://www.echinauk.org/, in due course.

2

e-Learning in Higher Education in China: An Overview

Kang Feiyu and Song Gilsun

Introduction

In this chapter, we provide some background information on e-learning in China, focusing primarily on its historical development and current scope. We discuss the key factors that have shaped the present e-learning systems, and we consider how the recent massive growth in numbers of Internet and online users in China has resulted in different types of learning support and government guidance. Finally, we discuss the main problems in e-learning that have been encountered and that are now being addressed. It should be noted that the term 'e-learning' in China is very closely associated with the Chinese government's concept of modern distance education, and so the governmental policies that relate to it refer only to off-campus provision. This chapter is limited in this way.

Distance education began in China at the beginning of the 1950s, when China Renmin University and North East Normal University pioneered the establishment of correspondence education departments and institutes. This was followed by second-generation distance education in the early 1960s, when China began a programme of teaching by broadcast and TV. In 1978, the Central University of Broadcast and Television (CUBT) was established nationwide, and during the 1980s, schools, including the Agricultural Broadcast and TV School, continually added to the growth of distance education. Satellite TV education expanded the scope of higher education over the years, helping to educate huge numbers of learners and helping to establish the foundations for e-learning.

The role of e-learning is now well established in China as a means of promoting a knowledge-based society. This is the result of a sequence of Chinese policies that have stressed the role of e-learning in improving education and training. Policies such as 'Core Ideas for Promoting a Learning Society' (宣传学习型社会的理念的核心) have already been implemented, and the Chinese government has produced an e-learning action plan called 'Looking Toward the Twenty-first Century Education Promotion Action Plan'

（面向21世纪教育振兴行动计划）to help achieve its goal of a knowledge-based society (Ministry of Education 1999a). In 2000, the Ministry of Education (MoE) confirmed 'The Rule of Temporary Implemental Management of Education Websites, Internet Education and Online Temporary Management' （教育网站和网上暂行管理办法）as the key for establishing a new educational information system. At that time, external factors also came into play as the SARS (a highly contagious respiratory disease) epidemic hit China, highlighting the potential of e-learning. Educational establishments were closed, and students had either to remain on campus or to return home until the epidemic was stopped. However, students and teachers continued to work on homework, to take exams, and to participate in discussions via the Internet. As a result of these events, the important contribution that e-learning could make to education in the twenty-first century was clearly demonstrated. The successive Chinese policy developments recognize that e-learning can offer people new sources of information, improve the range and quality of education available to them, and enable all people, regardless of their physical location, to take best advantage of their learning time.

In 2003, the global economic value of e-learning was US$25.3 billion, with the number of e-learners increasing at a rate of 300 percent per year (China Invest Consultation Net 2006). An International Data Corporation report in 2001 predicted that the e-learning economy in China would reach US$100 million by 2006 (Dong Guan Learning 2006). However, the economic value of e-learning in China had already surpassed this figure in 2004 (Huang 2004), and when we consider that the Chinese population is 1.3 billion, it is apparent that e-learning has still not been brought to fruition and that its full potential has yet to be exploited.

Initial Developments (1994–98)

The development of e-learning has become a basic national policy of modern education and communication in China because its benefits are so apparent. e-Learning has surpassed traditional education in availability and in enabling people to learn anywhere and at anytime. It provides increased access to teaching resources, and it enables e-learners to take control of their own education.

The need for e-Learning

In the second half of the 1990s, rapid developments in electronic communication and increases in education information courses led to the development of an entirely new approach to education. Universities, high schools, middle schools, and the information industry in China began developing e-learning systems, delivering multimedia content via computer networks and satellite. At this time, the development of e-learning was promoted by particular events. Firstly, in February 1996, Wang Dazhong, president of Tsinghua University, proposed a tentative plan for the expansion of e-learning, and during the same year, Tsinghua University accepted and implemented a blueprint for e-learning, 'Modernization of Long-Distance Education Project Proposal' (现代化远程教育工程项目建议书). Secondly, in 1998, speeches at key political events such as the National People's Congress and the Chinese People's Political Consultative Conference called for the development of e-learning. Moreover, in that same year, You Qingquan, president of Hubei University, suggested the resolution 'Expedite e-Learning Development, Constructing an e-Learning Open System' (加快发展远程教育，构建我国远程教育的开放体系) (Ding 2002).

In fact, these events were the natural result of influences from both overseas and from within China. At that time, the international community realized that the development of a knowledge-based economic society relied on innovations in information technology, on knowledge creation, on the exploitation of human resources, and the cultivation of skills. The international community also came to realize that e-learning could be a force both in teaching and research, and importantly, that it is one of the best means of providing continuing education because of its convenience and low cost.

At the same time, people within China became aware of several facts about educational policy development, including:

- traditional education and old methods of distance education could not satisfy the demands of social development;
- the need to establish a lifelong learning system and the requirements of a learning society;
- the need to popularize higher education;
- the limited scale and resources of the traditional nine-year compulsory education system;
- the need to educate migratory workers and the need to provide new employment, as a result of economic development and reform of the economy.

As result of changes in learning patterns both internationally and domestically, e-learning is fast becoming important not only as a model in formal and informal education but also as a national policy in establishing lifelong learning systems and learning societies. In 1999, the MoE emphasized the development of e-learning, and discussed expanding degree education, non-degree education, e-learning teaching modules, e-learning management mechanisms, and the construction of network resources (Yuan 2000). Nevertheless, it is important to recognize that there is still a noticeable gap between the development of e-learning in China and that of the USA and other developed countries. This gap can be attributed to economic and educational disparities, both of which have had a definite impact on the spread of e-learning. In 2003, Chinese higher education e-learners numbered more than 800,000; however, the total population of e-learners over the age of 16 comprised only 0.08 percent. The number of adult e-learners in the USA greatly exceeded that of China, the number of students over 16 years old reaching 47.4 percent (iResearch 2003). In comparison, China can be said to have just entered the e-learning arena.

Infrastructure development

At the end of the 1950s, China broadcast black and white TV signals to capital cities in each province, and by the end of the 1970s it had established colour TV transmission through its China Central TV (CCTV). In 1979, CCTV offered 1,300 hours of educational programmes, and by the 1990s, educational programming was expanded to 30,000 hours per year through the use of three satellites. In China, there are now widely established facilities for e-learning, such as 900 education TV stations (for transmission) and 10,000 satellite education centres (for receiving).

e-Learning had its beginnings in the 1990s with these infrastructure developments, resulting in the establishment of a new generation of distance education provision that was based on the application of electronic information and communication technology (ICT). China's e-learning technology consisted of compact disk (CD) delivery, satellite transmissions, and the use of CERNET (China Education and Research Network, an Internet-based delivery system). CERNET is the world's largest education and research network, and its purpose is to promote advanced distance learning (ADL). It was established in 1994 with investment from the government. This network, which is run by the MoE, supports e-learning education, including vocational training, e-learning teaching and management, and satellite systems.

After the establishment of CERNET, the national committee delivered two important new policies. The first was the 'Information Concerning University Development of e-Learning' policy, which set out to support the development of e-learning systems. The second was the 'Blueprint of the National Committee e-Learning Education Transfer System Technology' policy. This policy supported the building of digital satellite airwave networks, computer education scientific networks and public electronic communication networks combined with network transfer systems. Under these guidelines, basic communication systems were combined with sky and ground networks that had satellite to ground transfer (microwave, cable, and fiber optics), and it resulted in three networks: a broadcast television network, electronic communication networks, and computer networks.

Four pilot universities

In September 1994, the MoE decided to invest funds totalling 400 million RMB[1] for the development of e-learning, and they appointed four universities (Tsinghua University, Hunan University, Zhejiang University, and Beijing Post and Communications University) to pilot programmes. The experimental units began operation in 1998. These universities followed four policies established by the government: (1) no enrollment limitations, plans or quotas should be implemented; (2) entrance examinations should not be the national ones but should be set by the universities; (3) the learners should be chosen by the universities; and (4) the duration of study should be flexible. It can be seen that the four government policies gave the universities comprehensive rights in determining their own goals for e-learning. The different routes taken by the universities as they commenced the introduction of e-learning programmes are well illustrated by considering these pilot programmes.

- In 1996, Tsinghua University, under the auspices of CERNET, employed satellite teleconferencing for the first time. Tsinghua University adopted satellite networks, cable TV, and the Internet to spread e-learning throughout China. The school co-operated with Xiamen Cable TV Transfer Centre in the transmission of e-learning courses via CERNET and CHINANET. Tsinghua University provided four kinds of curricula: graduate student refresher courses (degree and non-degree education); continuing education for in-post workers; professional training and certification for lawyers, engineers and accountants; and various other bachelor's and master's level engineering degrees. Tsinghua University began eight pilot classes, in the Hanhai, Shunde, Changsha, and Nanjing areas, each class comprising about 200 learners (Ding 2002). Teachers made use of ATM (the education and science information network of the Beijing Scientific and Technological Commission) to conduct online teaching, and offered opportunities for self-study and browsing online. At the same time, they provided electronic lectures, student quizzes, a teacher studio, and support through e-mail.
- e-Learning at Hunan University was established differently from that at Tsinghua University. In 1997, Hunan University's School of Multimedia Education began co-operating with Hunan Province Post and Communications Management Department in establishing e-learning programmes. Hunan University set up degree and non-degree education programmes. In 1998, through entrance examinations for e-learners, it admitted more than 1,600 undergraduate e-learners into its programme. The programme at Hunan University consisted of three majors for junior college students: computer appliances, architectural engineering, and economic management. The university also started Internet basics computer courses for students graduating that year. The Internet basics courses were established in order to give graduating students a sense of the important future of e-learning. The school recruited twice in the fall for its Internet basics courses, and accepted 1,000 graduating students.
- Zhejiang University simultaneously conducted e-learning programmes on campus and at off-campus sites. The establishment of high-speed campus networks provided technological support for the expansion of its on-campus programmes. Like Tsinghua University, Zhejiang University started its e-learning with the use of satellite teleconferencing systems, though it also employed TCP (Transmission Control Protocol)/IP (Internet Protocol) systems to transmit to its own off-campus (e-learning) teaching centres in Hangzhou, Ningbo, Jinhua, Wenzhou, and so on.

Owing to the limitations of CERNET and CHINANET at that time, Zhejiang University used the Internet for the submission of coursework, for e-mail, and for educational administration and management. In 1998, the School of Long-Distance

Education at Zhejiang University set up two undergraduate level majors for e-learning students: management engineering and computer appliances. Enrollment for the undergraduate students was taken from either two-year college students or graduating high school students.

• Beijing Post and Communications University (BPCU) successfully carried out a series of e-learning education investigations before establishing its school of e-learning. Based on those investigations, BPCU, in December 1998, signed a collaborative agreement with the Chinese Post and Telecommunications General Bureau (CPTGB) entitled 'With Regard to Co-operation in the Expansion of Long-distance Education' (开展远程教育项目的合作). This document detailed the preparation of e-learning technology, blueprints, implementation, and operations. Each partner had different responsibilities. CPTGB acted as a network provider, guaranteeing bandwidth and transfer quality for promoting e-learning. It also took charge of network equipment, teaching equipment, and the maintenance of software and hardware technology. BPCU was responsible for general management, teaching plans, training projects, teaching management, organizing examinations, issuing degrees, and so on.

   The co-operation of CPTGB and BPCU entailed establishing e-learning in two stages. The first stage consisted of setting up BPCU's learning support centres, creating an online curriculum, and improving teaching management and tutoring services. The second stage consisted of gradually expanding the recruitment of students and further establishing multimedia classrooms in cities and provinces with Internet facilities. Between 1998 and 1999, the BPCU programme consisted of two majors: communication engineering and computer communication engineering, covering three provinces (Guangdong, Fujian, and Liaoning) and two cities (Beijing and Tianjin).

In 1998, these four universities recruited 9,000 students onto degree courses. Tsinghua University recruited 1,700 master's level students and Hunan University 3,500 undergraduate students (who had completed foundation/junior college courses). In two years, Zhejiang University recruited 3,000 undergraduate students and more than 200 postgraduate students. BPCU recruited 600 undergraduate students (China Education and Research Network 2000). Most of the students were interested in obtaining degrees, and, as a result of these programmes, the government was able to set up e-learning at high-level universities and to provide communication technology through them. An important first step in the establishment of e-learning in China had clearly been reached.

Expansion of e-Learning

On 13 January 1999, the State Department approved the 'Looking toward the Twenty-first Century Education Promotion Action Plan', confirming that e-learning was identified as one of the nation's ongoing education projects. In the same year, the Chinese government announced that e-learning provided people with lifelong learning opportunities and enabled the development of a Learning Society (MoE 1999b). This declaration clearly reinforced the position of e-learning in China.

Infrastructure improvement

The development of e-learning in China cannot be understood without considering the contemporaneous development in the information technology (IT) infrastructure. While international bandwidth was better than 700Mb/s, Chinese broadband (which was originally rated at 10 Mb/s) was improved to 155 Mb/s (Ding 2002). e-Business websites at this time already numbered more than 1,000 (Ding 2002). Also, by 2000, the total number of colleges with campus networks connected to CERNET had increased to 800 (74.6 percent) (Kang 2003).

From Table 2.1 (p.18) we can see that the percentage of faculty offices connected to networks in all institutions is 81.6 percent, which is a relatively high figure. Yet the percentage of classrooms and student dormitories connected to networks throughout all institutions reaches only 41.1 percent and 36 percent respectively, and the use of Wireless LAN does not even reach 5 percent of the total number of universities. e-Learning requires new teaching tools, and Table 2.2 (p. 18) shows the ones that are used most frequently in China. Each pilot university has adopted at least three or four of the modes shown, and they are nearly always combined with traditional face-to-face instruction.

Expansion of pilot universities

Government policies to support e-learning and increase Internet users have directly influenced the spread of network education. From 1999 to 2000, the MoE confirmed the choice of 30 pilot universities plus the Central University of Broadcasting and Television (CUBT). CUBT can be considered as having the largest distance education programme in the world (see the next section, 'e-Learning in the Education Sector', pp. 19–20). It was already using satellite networks and cable TV in its adult education teaching programmes, and when later appointed by the government as one of the pilot universities, it upgraded its systems to include the use of CERNET and CHINANET. From 2000, CUBT started to use interactive teaching systems and classroom broadcast teaching systems. The scope and economic superiority of CUBT in the e-learning field has grown rapidly, as a result of both its multi-network teaching and its management systems.

By the year 2000, 31 pilot universities, established by the MoE, were in existence. These universities set up their own online institutes and offered three levels of qualification: foundation, undergraduate, and postgraduate. The courses provided by these schools mostly cover the following:

- postgraduate refresher courses, divided into two kinds: degree and non-degree;
- new, high-technology and modern management courses for lifelong learning and short-term training;
- vocational training and tutoring for professional certification examinations, such as in law, finance, accounting;
- degree-granting education, including engineering master's degree, second degree education and undergraduate courses.

Table 2.1

e-Learning Infrastructure in Chinese Universities and Colleges (Kang 2003)

e-Learning Facilities in Chinese Higher Institutions (%)	All Institutions	Ministry Universities & Colleges	Provincial Universities & Colleges	Community Colleges
Faculty Offices Connected to Network (%)	81.6	84.9	81.0	81.1
Classrooms Connected to Network (%)	41.1	40.9	41.8	39.3
Student Dormitories Connected to Network (%)	36.0	47.5	35.1	32.4
Institutions with Wireless LAN (%)	3.6	4.2	3.0	1.3

Table 2.2

Pedagogic Systems in e-Learning Pilot Universities (Kang 2003)

Teaching Tools Adopted in e-Learning Pilot Universities				%
e-Learning Tools	Internet	Curriculum Management System		100
		Video Conference System	One-way Video Conference System	89.8
			Two-way Video Conference System	84.2
		Web Courseware	Text-only Courseware	100
			Stream Media Courseware	92.5
		E-mail		100
		Chat Room		96.2
		BBS		100
	Satellite TV	Two-way Satellite TV communication		5.3
		One-way Satellite TV communication		8.1
	Others	CD-ROM (Courseware)		94.3
		Telephone, Fax		100
	Traditional Method	Face-to-Face Instruction		100
		Concentrated Exam		100

In 2000, the MoE also granted approval for the 31 online institutes in the pilot universities to establish a BA, MA, and PhD degree education system and to recruit students in the autumn of that year. Those 31 online institutes began to get involved in the higher education market and recruited not only adult learners but also students preparing to attend university. This resulted in an extended period for recruiting students into degree education through e-learning, and in a further opening up of the education market.

The 30 online institutes and CUBT can be separated into two groups, according to the requirements governing student recruitment. The first group, which included Peking University and 25 pilot universities,[2] was allowed to recruit using both the National High School Examination for Undergraduates and the National Undergraduate Examination for Adults. For instance, based on 2,000 undergraduate recruitment plans, Fudan University and Shanghai Jiaotong University each decided to expand to 150 and 200 examinees in the Shanghai area. Apart from their method of study and living situation (most Chinese formal undergraduate students live in dormitories while in university), these students were the same as traditional on-campus undergraduate students: their degree qualification was equivalent and the policies for obtaining employment, public medical treatment expenses, social security, and for obtaining scholarships through public appraisal were identical.

The second group, which included the remaining five pilot universities,[3] was allowed to recruit only from the National Undergraduate Examination for Adults. By linking recruitment to recognized entrance examinations, the pilot universities were in effect given the responsibility for popularizing e-learning as a source of good quality higher education. It can be seen that e-learning is a new mode which not only allows students to have access to a school's faculty and teaching resources and to receive higher education but also promotes reform of the higher education system.

As a result of the way in which they were established, the pilot universities were entitled to function autonomously in recruiting students, in constituting teaching proposals and teaching methods, in regulating management, and in awarding degrees and certificates. This resulted in a diversification of the traditional university education system and in the creation of a new business space.

e-Learning in the education sector

The development of e-learning in this period followed the recognition that traditional forms of education, and in particular the traditional meaning of a school, cannot limitlessly offer increased opportunities for all. Moving the educational system into the e-learning field was a response to this limitation, and so at the end of the 1990s, China began to implement its e-learning strategy. Three different frameworks for e-learning were established, in order to provide learning opportunities across a wide range of society.

One type of provision is dual provision: on-campus education and e-learning education are run independently of each other. Teaching plans, curriculum, course outlines, and teaching materials are established and managed separately, and this results in two kinds of credits and degrees. The pilot universities sanctioned by the government and key primary and secondary schools operate according to the dual provision framework. This is similar to the framework used in the Soviet Union, but is different from the Australian mode, which, during the 1990s, combined both e-learning and traditional education programmes into one system.

Another framework is single provision. CUBT, the biggest distance education university in the world, represents the industrialization of e-learning. Since CUBT already had an established distance education system, the move to e-learning did not require the addition of a separate level of educational programmes, as it did for the other pilot universities. From its main campus in Beijing, CUBT spread throughout the country. As of 1998, it had 44 provincial-level branches, 814 local city branches, 1,742 county-level learning support centres, and 17,076 basic-level teaching classes.

By 2000, some online institutes in the pilot universities had started collaborating with several different kinds of partners, and this resulted in another type of provision, the co-operation frame. Universities linked with the following types of partners to support education services: high-level enterprises, institutions, scientific research institutes and other (i.e. non-key) universities, secondary schools and high schools. For example, CUBT began the 'Aopeng' (奥鹏) project in which they co-operated with eight universities.[4] This co-operation supported multiple aspects, such as assisted learning, teaching implementation, provision of resources, service and training for certification, transfer of multimedia teaching, obtainment of employment, and so on. During this period, Chinese enterprises gradually attached increasing importance to training through e-learning, and started to establish their own management training network systems.

e-Learning was also developed in the primary and secondary education sectors. In 2000, the 'Xiao-Xiao Tong' (校校通) project,[5] run by the MoE, set out to spread e-learning in primary, middle, and high schools. This project was implemented by encouraging online institutes and enterprises to begin co-operation with high profile schools. For instance, the Beijing Fourth Middle School co-operated with TCL, an electronics company. Lian Xiang, the largest computer company in China co-operated with Beida Fuzhong, the middle school attached to Peking University. Xin Dongfang, a private academic institution, also co-operated with Beida Fuzhong. A Canadian resource company purchased OZTIME, a company specializing in e-learning for primary and secondary education, marking the beginning of foreign interest and investment in e-learning in China.[6]

Despite the rapid development in e-learning by the end of 2000, Internet-based e-learning still suffered from a series of problems. These problems were primarily related to the centralization of Internet users in just a few big cities (Beijing had one quarter of China's Internet users), slow transfer speeds, and a general lack of resources. Even today, computer and network exploitation are still imbalanced: e-learning education still relies on satellite technology, especially in the countryside and minority areas.

Management: Operational Systems

By the year 2000, online institutes were well established and had full autonomy for recruiting students and issuing degrees. As a result, most of these universities collaborated with enterprises and community institutes for the development of degree education courses. Up to the present time, the combined investment from universities and corporations working together with universities, such as China Learning Web, Aopeng, and OZTIME, is approximately 1.84 billion RMB.

The role of industrial connections in the healthy development of e-learning in China has been discussed widely. In 2000, the authoritative, high-profile magazine *Finance and Economics* published an article 'The Online School is Swimming in the Industry Market', with the subtitle 'China e-Learning Universities: Thirty-one Universities and Industrial Capital Together Build a Degree Education System' （三十一所高校与产业资本联手重造文凭教育体系）. Quite a number of universities and companies have already begun co-operation (for instance, South China University of Technology, Zhejiang University) and have even actualized enterprise management operations (Renmin University of China, Beijing University of Post and Telecommunications) (Ding 2005). As a result of these developments, e-learning is now not only focused on the higher education field but is also open to secondary education and to services associated with domestic and international organizations.

Figure 2.1 illustrates the main parties making up the e-learning sector, and indicates their function and role. They are discussed in turn below.

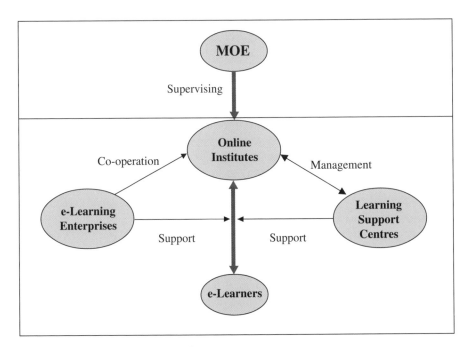

Figure 2.1　e-Learning Systems in China

MoE

The Department of Science and Technology and the Department of Higher Education in the MoE are in charge of e-learning education management. The Higher Education Department carries out most of the management, evaluation, and supervision of the entire system and the process of running each school. The e-learning management system is therefore shaped through the MoE, provincial educational administration departments, and pilot universities.

The MoE made use of the e-learning education project (现代远程教育工程) 'Looking Toward the Twenty-first Century Education Promotion Action Plan' (1999) to establish e-learning curriculum projects and to focus on the development of courses in online institutes and applications in other schools, departments, and universities for teaching and transferring credit and curriculum (MoE 1999a).

In an effort to develop an effective supervision system, the Higher Education Department of the MoE started, for the first time, a process of selective inspections and investigations by experts from the MoE and by local experts at e-learning centres in Guangdong, Fujian, Hunan, Zhejiang, Shanxi, and Sichuan provinces. These experts from the MoE evaluated the expanding work situation in online institutes and learning support centres and wrote a series of reports which discussed the problems associated with running the online institutes in universities. As a result, the MoE produced three documents in order to address the problems that were reported.

In 2003 and 2004, the MoE brought in some important e-learning policies and regulations concerning management and supervision:

1. 2003 Temporary Rules for the Management of Learning Support Centres (现代远程教育校外学习中心（点）暂行管理办法)
2. 2003 Notice on Criteria for the Management of Learning Support Centres (关于上报规范现有现代远程教育校外学习中心（点）管理工作情况的通知)
3. 2004 Notice on Standardizing the Management of Learning Support Centres (关于加快对现有现代远程教育校外学习中心（点）清理整顿工作的通知)

Through these policies and regulations, the MoE increased the standardization of management and enhanced the quality of education in the learning support centres of the online institutes. The main problem addressed by these rules and regulations is the lack of criteria for online institutes to manage their learning support centres. Since 2003, the MoE has begun to carry out formal annual quality assurance evaluations. All failing online institutes are forced to make changes and adjustments in order to meet the requirements of these new rules and regulations, or to relinquish their right to be in operation if they do not do so. The MoE has already charged five online institutes with failure to meet these required standards and has forced them to stop recruiting students. The MoE has thus recognized the need to standardize the development of online institutes, their management, their teaching quality and the issuing of e-learning degrees. Since 2003, it has been strictly enforcing relevant policy measures and controlling management supervision.

Online institutes

By August 2004, China had established a total of 68 universities with online institutes. Almost all of the expansion took place in the first two years after the establishment of the initial 31 pilot universities (2001–02). Since 2002, only one further online institute has been established. This is a consequence of the investigations by experts over the last few years, in which the Chinese government supervised and evaluated the management of online institutes and assured the standardization of e-learning quality.

Table 2.3
The Development of Online Institutes (derived from Zhang 2004a)

	1999	2000	2001	2002	2003	2004	Total
Online Institutes	5	26	14	22	1	0	68

The scale of e-learning in China is continuing to expand. Through the popularization of e-learning, the number of students engaged in it has already passed 10 percent of the total number of university students in the whole country (the number of university students in the whole country is about 19 million). In 2003, even though traditional universities carried out large-scale recruitment activities, the enrollment of e-learners constituted 17 percent of the total recruitment throughout the country during the same year (Zhang 2004a). This was the highest level of recruitment during the eight years of e-learning expansion.

At present, the online institutes in pilot universities are starting more and more master's level courses, including in subjects such as engineering, management, medicine, literature, and agriculture. There are now 18,000 courses available, covering ten fields of study and 158 different specialties (Expert Group 2003). However, in order to maintain quality at the tertiary level of education, the requirements for obtaining a degree are very strict. If students wish to obtain a degree, they must complete the national graduate level examinations. So most universities allow them to transfer their credits from their master's level modules to overseas universities, and in this way e-learners are able to obtain two certificates: (a) a postgraduate certificate in advanced studies, and (b) an overseas university master's degree, such as an MBA. Owing to the requirements for scientific research and experimentation, the number of postgraduate students studying for PhD degrees is still extremely low.

Non-degree education has also been actively promoted in recent years. At the end of 2003, 34 of the pilot universities set up non-degree education projects. In total, the 210 projects recruited 185,353 learners who made use of the resources or studied on the courses. For example, Tsinghua University and Northeast Electronic Technology University established a set of non-degree education courses. Beijing Normal University used Web and network facilities to develop innovative new courses in Yunnan Province. Fujian Normal University negotiated with the education administration department and obtained transferable credits between degree and non-degree education. Although China initially focused most of its attention on degree education through e-learning, both degree education and non-degree education are currently undergoing a major expansion.

e-Learning enterprises

During the development of e-learning, e-learning enterprises have played a special role in supporting online institutes. As early as 1998, some of these enterprises anticipated the promising future of the e-learning market in China and began co-operating with online institutes to provide technical support and management services. For instance, Zhonghua Learning Web,[7] Aopeng, and OZTIME began to co-operate with well-known universities and private academic institutes. This co-operation resulted in links between e-learning and the marketplace. In 1998, Hong Cheng, a science and technology development company, began to provide practical tools for e-learning and developed four kinds of software products that included 15 programmes ranging from e-learning curriculum to utility tools, service products, and problem-solving software for e-learning programmes. At the beginning, Hong Cheng co-operated with Renmin University Online Institute and later expanded to include five other online institutes. At the same time, 11 other online institutes adopted the Hong Cheng technology platform and 9 education institutes began to use Hong Cheng problem-solving technological software. At that time, more than 19 online institutes were already users of Hong Cheng technology.

After entering the WTO, Chinese enterprises had valuable opportunities to do business in the international market. As competition intensified, Chinese enterprises became aware of the importance of using e-learning to improve the skills of their employees as well as to enhance teamwork. At the end of the 1990s, many universities, especially famous ones, began to offer enterprise training through e-learning, providing excellent faculty and educational resources. e-Learning in China typically offered degree education, but as a result of offering enterprise training, the e-learning market gradually expanded.

Learning support centres

Learning support centres are crucial for online institutes and play a vital role in the running of the e-learning system. In practice, the learning support centres provide services such as recruitment of students, teaching services, tutoring of satellite classes, management of faculty, staff, and students, and maintenance of e-learning facilities in their local areas. Learning support centres are directly linked to the online institutes in the universities, as shown in Figure 2.1 (p. 21). The online institutes in the pilot universities and in CUBT each established their own learning support centres and directly supervised each of them.

In 2001, the number of learning support centres stood at 966. By the end of 2003, the number had increased to 2,347, which was a remarkably rapid increase of 1,381 centres (see Table 2.4, p. 25).

Table 2.4
The Growth in Learning Support Centres (taken from Zhang 2004a)

	1999	2000	2001	2002	2003	2004	Total
Learning Support Centres	–	–	966	2,012	2,347	–	2,347

The learning support centres developed along with the e-learning education market and became an indispensable part of e-learning. In March 2002, the MoE publicized the 'e-Learning Support Centres (Platform) Temporary Management Plan'. The document provides details of the procedures each centre is required to follow regarding applications, course design, examinations and awards. The learning support centres directly participated in the establishment of the e-learning system, providing a local learning site for the pilot universities.

e-Learners

A large number of e-learners engage in self-study via the Internet, satellite, teleconferencing, and networked classrooms. e-Learners often go to the learning support centres established by the online institutes or use different types of learning resources and establishments in order to carry out self-study, collaborative learning, or group discussion.

As explained in the section, *Online Institutes* (see pp. 23–24), the pilot universities established courses in 158 different specialties, offering a curriculum of 1.8 million classes. These classes are provided for in-post personnel, undergraduate students, and postgraduate e-learners. In 2003, there were 942,000 registered e-learners (master's level students, bachelor's level students with a foundation/junior college qualification, and those taking non-degree certificate courses), and of these 915,000 were in-post personnel.

Table 2.5
The Numbers of e-Learners (taken from Zhang 2004a)

Year	1999	2000	2001	2002	2003	Total
e-Learners	32,000	185,000	456,000	675,000	942,000	2,290,000
In-post Personnel	29,000	166,000	320,000	635,000	915,000	2,065,000

At the end of 2003, the online institutes in the pilot universities had recruited, with MoE approval, a total of 2,290,000 e-learners. As can be seen from Table 2.5, the number of registered e-learners increased dramatically every year from 1999 to 2003. The large increase between 1999 and 2000 was due to the high acceptance rate into the e-learning system of in-post personnel, high school leavers, and self-study learners. By 2003, nearly all of the e-learners were in-post personnel.

E-learners rapidly increased through 2003 and 2004. In 2005, the total number of e-learners (only including bachelor's level students with a foundation/junior college qualification) had reached 2,650,000, compared to 2004, when they numbered 2,370,000, showing an increase of 12.1 percent (iResearch 2006b).

The MoE, online institutes, e-learning enterprises, learning support centres, and e-learners each have a role to play in the e-learning market, but they remain dependent upon the support of each other. The MoE is continuing to invest funds, resources, and time into the e-learning system in China, in order to provide quality e-learning experiences for all learners. As a result, online institutes are continuously expanding the scope and coverage of e-learning. e-Learning enterprises continue to grow and aid in the development of hardware and software resources. Learning support centres are actively recruiting students and aiming to provide quality teachers and quality teaching support. e-Learners, the base of the e-learning system, are growing in number every year and continue to push for new developments on all levels.

Reflections on e-Learning in Higher Education in China

Computers, the Internet, and multimedia technology have become the core of electronic information technology and have spread at an immense speed throughout the world. Statistical data from CNNIC (China Network Information Centre) indicate that, in April 2006, Chinese Internet users already numbered 123 million, which is an increase of 19.4 percent over 2005 (Internet Report 2006). CNNIC also found that Internet users in China spend about 13.2 hours per week online (CNNIC 2005). At the same time, the total number of websites reached 788,400 and international exit bandwidth total gross was 24175M, which, compared with the number in 2005, was an increase of 159.2 percent (Internet Report 2006).

Since the population of China is 1.3 billion, this means that fewer than 10 percent of the total population are currently Internet users, and that there is still much room for an increase in Internet use in China. Nevertheless, the Internet is already affecting people's lives and influencing their work and their learning.

Figure 2.2 (p. 27) shows that the number of Chinese e-learners, which includes university degree students at all levels, people studying for certificates and training courses, and all other general e-learners, increased from 3,710,000 in 2001 to 6,550,000 in 2004, and it is predicted that the number will increase to 7,580,000, 8,940,000, 10,540,000 in 2005, 2006, and 2007 respectively (iResearch, 2005).

Problems identified through MoE inspections

Since the MoE established the e-learning system, it has faced many problems in all areas, including supervision, management, evaluation, and quality assurance. The assurance of e-learning quality presents especially difficult problems for the MoE. The policies directed

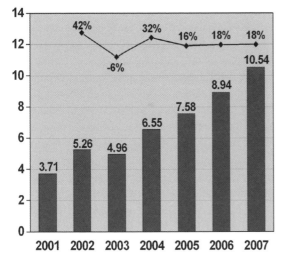

Figure 2.2   Numbers/Predicted Numbers of Chinese e-Learners and Annual Growth Rate of Chinese e-Learners (adapted from iResearch Inc. 2005)

at these problems have improved the quality of e-learning education and have given direction to the development of e-learning. Nevertheless, the MoE faces a number of problems in the development of e-learning.

- *Insufficient Connectivity.* CERNET and other commercial networks provide Internet access in big and medium-sized cities; however, Internet connections in homes, companies, and workplaces are not widespread. Moreover, there is insufficient bandwidth to transfer multimedia courseware to e-learners, so China is still not able to fulfill its 'e-learning anywhere' plan.
- *No Standards for Management.* There is a lack of standardization in management regarding issues such as student recruitment, examinations, and co-operation between enterprises and pilot universities, and this has led to many difficulties in the development of e-learning. In September 2004, the MoE inspected the learning support centres in eight provinces and 51 cities and convened informal discussions with leaders, managers, teachers, staff, and students in the support centres. The expert group sent by the MoE looked into management irregularities in the learning support centres, such as in relation to the recruitment of students, the transfer of rights to establish schools, illegal teaching support services, and so on. Moreover, some online institutes established non-approved learning support centres that ranged in size from small to large and that accepted 200,000 e-learners between 2001 and 2003. These learning support centres were unable to provide quality education, supervision, and effective management of students and of student recruitment. As a result, these pilot universities lost their rights to operate online institutes.

- *Lack of Control over Number of Degrees.* The goal of e-learners is not only the acquisition of knowledge but also the attainment of a degree. Many online institutes did not adhere to the strict policies concerning the awarding of degrees, and the promise of easily obtained degrees lured many students to registration offices. In this way, the development of e-learning in China naturally gave rise to degree management problems for the pilot universities.
- *Limited Sharing of Resources.* The problem of resource sharing is in two main areas: software and hardware. The independent nature of the online institutes did not easily lend itself to the sharing of software resources, but this failure to share led to dissatisfaction among learners. Even the Public Resource Sharing Service established by CUBT met resistance among the pilot universities over the sharing of resources. Computers and network establishments, as well as the local learning centres, were controlled individually by the online institutes, and so were not shared among the many e-learners in China. As a result, e-learners were restricted in their access to information and educational resources, which affected their learning.

Faced with these problems, as well as with the findings of the expert group's investigations carried out in 2003, the pilot universities came to terms with their situation in 2004 and made a decision to improve their e-learning quality, management, and supervision, in accordance with the MoE's requirements. The pilot universities came up with several guidelines (Expert Group 2003):

- to forbid recruitment of students without government permission;
- to give a clear indication of the national requirements for examinations at the bachelor's degree level;
- to be practical and realistic in the recruitment of students and the promotion of e-learning.

Through the MoE, the pilot universities have started to enhance their management systems, to oversee very strictly the recruitment of students, to provide quality assurance of teaching, and to standardize entry and exit examinations. These types of government-sanctioned policies to standardize educational management and quality assurance systems have helped to maintain and popularize e-learning in China. e-Learning is developing in step with the development of the Chinese economy. During this development process, governmental support has been indispensable.

The MoE's new policies for e-learning

In 2005, the MoE put forward a series of new policies for e-learning (Liu 2005):

- to use provincial education committees to evaluate existing learning support centres and to inspect and approve new support centres;

- to strictly manage entrance processing and reinforce degree requirements;
- from 2005, to ensure that e-learners at bachelor's level must take the national examination, which includes computing, English, mathematics, and Chinese;
- to introduce electronic enrollment and maintain electronic records of students who pass the national examinations;
- to establish an evaluation system in each online institute;
- to use CUBT to establish a Public Resource Sharing Service;
- to strengthen International e-learning co-operation.

In 2003, e-learning had its beginnings in China in the 'Tenth Document （10号 文件）: The Function of Economic, Social, and Cultural Rights', which identified five missions: (1) the expansion of degree education, (2) the expansion of non-degree education, (3) the exploration of e-learning teaching methods, (4) the exploration of e-learning teaching management mechanisms, and (5) the establishment of online education resources. The 'Sixteenth Big Report' （十六大报告） has definitely brought the development of e-learning to the forefront (MoE 2006). e-Learning can establish a lifelong education system, build an atmosphere of learning by all people, and help construct a learning society.

The potential of e-learning

e-Learning now includes many branches of education, especially continuing education and adult education. Even though it has already developed to a high degree, it is in much need of reform, upgraded resources, advances and innovations, as well as the establishment of a new continuing education system. e-Learning in China, which is led by the government, by social support networks and by universities, is still rapidly developing, and there are major achievements in the development of modern communication technology.

■   Using e-learning to establish a learning society

China has called for the promotion of lifelong learning and the establishment of a learning society. e-Learning is the best tool for the realization of these goals in that it provides 'anytime, anywhere, any curriculum' individualized learning. Its coverage is extensive and flexible, and it allows for the multiple transmission of education resources. Learning conditions are not reliant upon time; learners are provided with education services and resources, and they can further their education at any time. A learning society educates people according to their working or living needs; learners can learn when they want to learn and improve themselves at any time. Many kinds of education and training that make up a learning society, such as farmer education, senior citizen education, military education, and education for women, can be effectively carried out through e-learning. So, e-learning is a very effective method for establishing a learning society.

■   Using e-learning to help alleviate poverty

e-Learning in China makes use of the Internet, satellite, cable TV, digital TV, and CD-ROM. Through these technologies, e-learning can easily be transmitted to poverty-stricken areas to help spread high-quality education resources and provide certified training for skilled and unskilled workers. In this way, people who live in poor areas can receive educational opportunities through e-learning. For instance, the 'Education Aiding Poverty Project' was initiated through Tsinghua University's e-learning learning support centres. This project brought educational resources to China's agricultural communities, which make up 80 percent of China's population. The main tenet of the project was 'To Eliminate Poverty and Spread Knowledge'.

■   Using e-learning to provide enterprise training

In 2005, Tsinghua University moved from an e-learning degree system to an e-learning training system, which includes enterprise training, vocational training, and e-learning to alleviate poverty. Compared with the pilot universities, which operate degree e-learning, this move presents a tremendous change. Similarly, Renmin University has begun to consider providing enterprise training certification.

The Chinese government has also taken enterprise training through e-learning into consideration. In 2003, the Department of Small and Medium-Sized Enterprises in the National Development and Reform Commission (NDRC), in collaboration with the Foundation of Small and Medium-Sized Enterprises in the Ministry of Finance, jointly launched a small and medium-sized enterprise training project. It provided management training and support for the development of small and medium-sized enterprises through e-learning. Nowadays Shidai Guanghua, Hejun Chuangye, and Nanfang Telecom have each, in succession, participated in e-learning enterprise training. National Telecom and large electrical enterprises have established their own e-learning management platforms and provide e-learning enterprise training for their employees. Along with the expanding demand for e-learning in the Chinese market, enterprise training has extraordinary potential for further development.

■   Expansion of the Public Resource Sharing Service (PRSS)

During the last few years, online institutes have operated their own, mainly independent, learning support centres, and this has resulted in a range of problems, including courseware repetition, low utilization of resources, high management costs, and supervision difficulties. In terms of the development of a public curriculum (including general English, philosophy, basic professional classes), online institutes have always developed their own curriculum courseware, so similar curriculum courseware appeared within many online institutes. In addition, owing to an unbalanced division of work, limited human resources, material resources, and financial resources, the quality of education suffered greatly. At the end of 2001, the MoE began to set up the e-learning Public Resource Sharing System (PRSS).

After four years of operation, Aopeng e-Learning Education Centre（奥鹏远程教育中心）, an experimental unit of the PRSS, had already established a few hundred centres, similar to Internet cafés, for the sharing of resources. The Aopeng e-Learning Education Centre established a complete co-operative relationship with 15 pilot universities covering 50 specialties (Yang 2005).

In the process of public resource sharing and development, educational resources moved from self-developed resources to publicly shared resources, and they now provide for on-campus resource sharing, sharing between university and university, and enterprise co-operation. While the PRSS mode is only in its beginning stages, it has further advanced e-learning education in the development of curriculum and courseware resources in China. This mode has directly affected teaching efficiency, individual learning possibilities, and e-learners' need for independence.

As we can see, the PRSS is a kind of educational market for the dissemination of educational resources. It has broken down the independent, isolated systems of the online institutes, and has helped bring about a sharing of software and hardware among e-learners and e-learning providers. The service has brought great benefits to e-learning; however, it still needs to be expanded throughout the online institutes and e-learning enterprises in China and to be made available to all e-learners. Through this service, e-learning providers can help each other improve and further their education services.

■   **e-Learning management law**

The lifelong learning system in China does not have laws concerning the establishment of lifelong learning management organizations, lifelong learning policymaking, and lifelong learning quality guarantee mechanisms. Even though, with the help of government leadership, efforts have been made to standardize e-learning, it is still at the research stage, and rules concerning e-learning (as with the lifelong learning system) have not been completely effective. So far, all e-learning rules and statutes are based on departmental regulations. Even though the State Department clearly brought forward the concept of e-learning, its rules and regulations rely on only the goodwill of all involved in the e-learning process. e-Learning needs to conform strictly to the policies and legal regulations, in order to make e-learning truly a part of the legal system and to guarantee the quality of education.

The lifelong learning system thus needs to have a legal basis. This is the only way to standardize e-learning and the supervision mechanisms. The formulation of laws regarding e-learning is an absolute necessity for its continued development.

Concluding Remarks

Up to now, online institutes have appeared in 68 pilot universities in eight years and have established more than 2,347 learning support centres that use software and hardware in education. New educational resources, databases and electronic libraries have been created, and in expanding e-learning, many kinds of online teaching and learning support systems have been utilized. The pilot universities, the e-learning enterprises and the learning support centres have already become an important part of e-learning, and despite the slowdown in the past two years, it is likely that more universities will start offering e-learning.

The development of e-learning in China has not only occurred in higher education; it has also been rapidly adopted in primary and secondary education, through collaboration with domestic and international institutes. Currently, the e-learning market gives clear priority to degree education, but it has also expanded to include non-degree education. A key goal of e-learning in China has been to promote higher education for adults, providing them with further educational opportunities. It has already achieved a great deal in bringing education to all parts of China, and it certainly has a bright future in China, since it offers so many opportunities to help China's population.

Section 2

Designing and Delivering Online Courses in China

This section focuses on issues associated with the design and delivery of online courses in China, and explores the following crucial questions:

- What types of online courseware design are currently widespread in China, and what are their relative strengths and weaknesses?
- How can online courseware be designed so that learner autonomy (which is so important for online study) is promoted?
- Studying online can be a lonely experience, so how can the courseware be designed in order to facilitate the building of communities of online learners?
- To what extent is it feasible for foreign languages to be taught wholly online, or is it more effective if online learning is integrated with face-to-face learning opportunities?
- Effective e-learning tutors are vital to the success of an online course, so how can they best be trained?

Chapter 3, Learning by Multimedia and Multimodality, by Gu, provides very helpful background information on Web-based courseware design in the Chinese context. He identifies and illustrates six types of design that are current in China, and analyses their strengths and weaknesses from both policy and pedagogic perspectives. He presents a number of principles that can be used for evaluating courseware design, and argues that the 'Learning-process-model Design' is the most effective.

In Chapter 4, McGrath, Sinclair and Chen take up the issue of learner autonomy. They review the literature on learner autonomy from both Western and Chinese perspectives, and then demonstrate how they designed materials for a course on the methodology of English Language teaching that aimed to promote learner autonomy. They illustrate how they offered 'scaffolded' experiences in the following: making choices, assessing self, monitoring progress, consciously reflecting on learning, and making independent decisions. The authors then describe the participants' responses to the materials, which were very positive, but they emphasize the crucial importance of learners receiving excellent e-tutor support.

Successful autonomous learning does not necessarily mean learning in isolation; on the contrary, it can entail effective co-operation with others. This is the theme taken up by Hall, Hall and Cooper in Chapter 5. They argue that courseware designers need consciously to aim at promoting interactivity and social cohesion online and they then illustrate how this can be done. They describe two learning tasks that were designed to build a sense of community among learners and to promote appropriate self-disclosure, and they report how learners reacted to these activities.

Chapter 6 turns to a somewhat different yet vitally important question: whether all aspects of foreign language learning can be fostered online, or whether the online courseware needs to be integrated with face-to-face learning opportunities. Marsh et al. argue strongly for an integrated approach, and describe how they achieved this in the design of their *CUTE* (Chinese University Teacher Training in English) course.

The final chapter in this section, by Joyes and Wang, takes up the crucial issue of the training of e-learning tutors. However brilliantly a course is designed, it needs tutors to provide effective support for the learners. Yet course providers are faced with a dilemma:

should they train their e-learning tutors to operate on this specific course (e.g. familiarize them with types of learning activities included in the course, and with the technical functionality and characteristics of the technical platform being used), or should they provide them with more generic training that is more broadly applicable? Joyes and Wang grapple with this question in Chapter 7 and propose a generic framework for the training of e-learning tutors that can be used across a very wide variety of contexts.

Samples of many of the online materials described in this section can be viewed on the *eChina-UK* website: http://www.echinauk.org/. The website also provides further rationale for their design.

3

Learning by Multimedia and Multimodality:
Some Critical Reflections on Web-Based Courseware
Design in the Chinese Context[1]

Gu Yueguo

Preliminary Remarks

This chapter reports some critical reflections on Web-based courseware design in the last five years in China in general, and at the Beiwai Institute of Online Education in particular. For ease of reference, six types of design are identified:

1. Printed-textbook-transfer Design: This refers to the Web-based publication of an existing printed textbook verbatim. The design, if any, will consist of changing the print pages to Web pages plus extra navigation buttons.
2. Audio-supplement Design: This refers to the practice of adding audio clips to the printed-textbook-transfer design.
3. Video-supplement Design: This refers to the practice of adding video clips to the printed-textbook-transfer design. Note that video clips naturally include audio input.
4. Classroom-teacher-model Design: This refers to the practice of videotaping a teacher delivering a lecture and publishing online the compressed video images accompanied by PowerPoint presentations.
5. Multimedia-rich Design: This refers to the practice of integrating hypertexts with Web-based multimedia. In this design, the Web-based version is in some places considerably different from the printed textbook version.
6. Learning-process-model Design: This refers to the practice of selecting and constructing the content according to a projected learner, i.e. a default learner, who is engaged in a goal-directed learning process.

All six types of design are instructional by definition. As such, they are normally examined according to the principles governing the instructional message design. Mayer (2001), for example, presents seven such principles on the basis of the cognitive theory of multimedia learning.

A cognitive theory of multimedia learning assumes that the human information processing system includes dual channels for visual/pictorial and auditory/verbal processing, that each channel has limited capacity for processing, and that active learning entails carrying out a co-ordinated set of cognitive processes during learning. (Mayer 2001: 41)

Acting on these assumptions, he formulates seven principles as follows:

1. *Multimedia Principle*: Students learn better from words and pictures than from words alone.
2. *Spatial Contiguity Principle*: Students learn better when corresponding words and pictures are presented near to rather than far from each other on the page or screen.
3. *Temporal Contiguity Principle*: Students learn better when corresponding words and pictures are presented simultaneously rather than successively.
4. *Coherence Principle*: Students learn better when extraneous words, pictures, and sounds are excluded rather than included.
5. *Modality Principle*: Students learn better from animation and narration than from animation and on-screen text.
6. *Redundancy Principle*: Students learn better from animation and narration than from animation, narration, and on-screen text.
7. *Individual Differences Principle*: Design effects are stronger for low-knowledge learners than for high-knowledge learners and for high-spatial learners rather than for low-spatial learners. (Mayer 2001: 184, italics in original)

In distance education, however, there are other factors that have to be taken into account in instructional message design. As Shearer points out:

we have, in many ways, several critical factors that need to be reviewed prior to even considering how the course will be presented and function. *These include the audience characteristics, geographic dispersion of the audience, the technologies available to the audience, the goals of the learners, the goals and missions of the learning organization, the costs that must be recovered, the costs of delivery, the political environment at the time for the learning organization, the faculty compensation, and the market competition.* All of these factors come into play in designing a course at a distance before we even look at the learning goals and objectives of the actual course. In many instances these factors will often dictate the technologies we use to deliver a course at a distance even before one conducts content analysis or instructional analysis. While discussing technology at the beginning of the design process can appear backward to classic instructional design it tends to surface early in discussions in distance education. (Shearer 2003: 275, italics mine)

Factors such as the audience characteristics, geographic dispersion of the audience, and the goals of the learners are traditionally covered under needs analysis, which is essential to any course development. Having said this, those factors listed by Shearer such as "the goals and missions of the learning organization, the costs that must be recovered, the costs of delivery, the political environment at the time for the learning organization, the faculty compensation, and the market competition" are macro issues that normally fall outside the agenda of courseware designers, who would consider them as none of their business. For ease of reference, we shall use the term 'pedagogical dimension' to cover both Mayer's seven principles of multimedia learning and factors that fall within the traditional learners' needs analysis. The term 'policy dimension' will be used to refer to those macro issues.

An ideal procedure for courseware design and development is for specialists and senior administrators to work closely together as a team on both pedagogical and policy elements, in order to generate sound design principles and detailed specifications. In practice, however, at least in China, the ideal procedure is rarely appreciated by the parties involved, and the result is erroneous designs, misconceptions, and unhelpful products. In this chapter, I first give concrete examples of the six types of design. I then critically review them from both policy and pedagogic perspectives. Finally, I conclude with some suggestions for future development.

An Overview of Courseware Design

The global context

Let us start by briefly examining the global context of computer-assisted language learning and teaching, as this will enable us to consider what has been happening in China from a global perspective.

Ever since the first electronic digital computer came into use in 1939 (see Szymanski, Szymanski and Pulschen 1995), efforts have persistently been made to explore the use of technology in education. In 1958, Skinner, for instance, published a paper in *Science* with the title "Teaching Machines". Ten years later, in 1968, he published a book with the title *The Technology of Teaching*. He observes:

> Even in a small classroom the teacher usually knows that he is going too slowly for some students and too fast for others. Those who could go faster are penalized, and those who should go slower are poorly taught and unnecessarily punished by criticism and failure. Machine instruction would permit each student to proceed at his own rate. (Skinner 1968: 30)

A computer capable of delivering machine instructions was enthusiastically envisaged as being able eventually to 'teach' a lot of things and to replace human instructors. With hindsight, we now see clearly that he was overambitious. Even today, half a century later, with such advancement of ICT as no one had ever dreamed of, his goal of using machines to do most of the job of a human teacher is still as remote as ever.

In Skinner's case, half a century's development and practice have given us the best assessment of humans' unrealistic ambition. That the word 'assisted' was soon added to the word 'computer' signals the quick lesson that humans have learned from past experiences. Computer-assisted language learning (CALL) and computer-assisted language testing (CALT) have been with us for more than several decades now, and there has never been a shortage of both enthusiasts and sceptics.

As the use of the Internet became widespread, so Web-based CALL appeared. The relation between the now traditional CALL and the network-based language teaching (i.e. NBLT, using Kern and Warschauer's [2000: 1] term) is a delicate issue. Kern and Warschauer observe:

> Whereas CALL has traditionally been associated with self-contained, programmed applications such as tutorials, drills, simulations, instructional games, tests, and so on, NBLT represents a new and different side of CALL, where human-to-human communication is the focus. (Kern and Warschauer 2000: 1)

To facilitate a comparative study between the traditional CALL and NBLT, Chapelle (2000: 5) proposes the term 'pre-network CALL' instead of 'CALL', or 'the traditional CALL', as used in this paper. She argues that it is by no means trivial to ask: To what extent is it useful to consider network-based learning the same as pre-network CALL?

> This question is important given the tendency of work in CALL to rediscover the same instructional practices and problems with each generation of computer hardware and software — a tendency that has stifled evolutionary progress. Some of the same software designs appeared on the mainframe computers of the 1970s, the microcomputers of the 1980s, and the World Wide Web of the 1990s — not necessarily because they were shown to be effective, but because some members of each generation were satisfied to reinvent rather than determined to evolve. If NBLT is CALL, one would hope that design and evaluation of Web-based learning would productively draw on past work in CALL. If network-based activities are different from pre-network CALL, their development and study should implicate a different set of issues from those familiar in the CALL of the 1970s and 1980s. (Chapelle 2000: 5)

After some careful comparison between the two, she concludes:

> . . . given the existing themes identified in the past CALL literature and the contributions that NBLT makes, one might suggest that NBLT represents an expansion rather than a reconceptualization of CALL. (Chapelle 2000: 222)

Assuming that Chapelle's assessment of the relation between the pre-network CALL and NBLT is appropriate, which I have no reason for doubt, the situation in China is quite different. As far as I know, little or no pre-network CALL existed before NBLT was given an official nationwide launch in 1999. In 1993, I organized a mini-conference on CALL in Beijing and it was attended by only 15 enthusiasts. Between 1999 and 2002, however, 67 universities were authorized by the Ministry of Education to set up online institutes, whose avowed mission was to provide network-based teaching and learning courses (see Kang and Song this volume). In other words, China has witnessed little evolutionary progress from pre-network CALL to NBLT. The Chinese NBLT represents neither an expansion nor a reconceptualization of CALL. Unlike its Western counterpart, it came into existence and operation all of a sudden, as it were, and for the majority of the 67 universities, almost from scratch!

Reviewing the early development of online learning in the USA, Lynch observes:

> Unfortunately, anecdotal evidence also suggests that *much of this storm of development has been undertaken in haste, without expert preparation or knowledge of the process. In fact, many educational institutions and corporations have approached the development process as a reaction to perceived competition for students, instead of as a project to enhance student learning.* The attitude in much of higher education has been: "We need online courses now. I expect there to be x percent of courses by the end of the year. Oh, and by the way, there is little to no extra money to make this happen." (Lynch 2002: 1, italics mine)

Lynch's description of the USA's early situation is equally applicable to the Chinese context. Elsewhere, I characterize the Chinese situation as 'the instant return problem':

> The government has encouraged the business sectors to invest in developing ICT applications for education. They are even allowed to take part in running online education institutions. However, it has turned out that they are more interested in the number of students than in the delivery of quality education. Some institutions have ended up with more students than they could possibly cope with. Students are only given CD-ROMs of poor quality, with no other support whatsoever. Cases like this have done online education more harm than good. (Gu 2006: 105)

I (Gu 2006) further point out that the ICT initiatives taken by the central government, excellent as they may sound, created an environment in which the universities competing for Ministry of Education endorsement to set up online institutes were motivated more by fashion than by an insightful understanding of the technology. Research into the nature of what ICT can really do for education has remained superficial and anecdotal.

Bearing this background knowledge in mind, we are ready to look at the six types of design one by one.

Printed-textbook-transfer design

This Web-based courseware design, if it can be called a design at all, entails converting a bound textbook's layout into a Web-page design. The content of the former printed textbook remains intact during the transfer process. Figure 3.1 (p. 42) shows an example.

Audio-supplement design

This design is virtually the same as the previous one, except that audio clips are added, as shown in Figure 3.2 (p. 42).

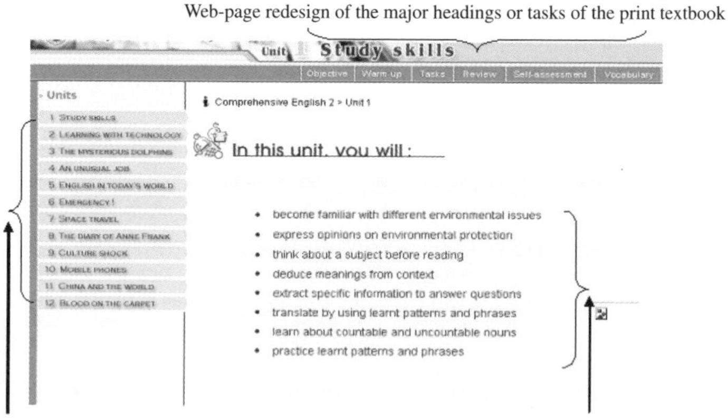

Web-page redesign of the major headings or tasks of the print textbook

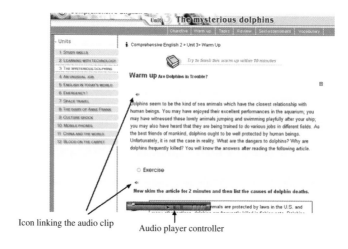

Web-page redesign of the table of contents

Verbatim transfer of the content from
the print textbook

Figure 3.1   Printed-textbook-transfer Design

Icon linking the audio clip

Audio player controller

Figure 3.2   Audio-supplement Design

Video-supplement design

This design is an improvement over the audio-supplement design in that it is enriched with video clips, as shown in Figure 3.3 (p. 43).

As it may have become apparent to the reader, all three designs illustrated so far keep the content of the printed textbook intact. Yet the printed textbook was originally written for classroom use, mediated by a human teacher, and designs like these have overlooked the fact that study with a computer is substantially different from face-to-face study with a teacher in the classroom (see the section 'Printed-textbook-transfer, audio- and video-supplement Designs' for further discussion, pp. 48–51).

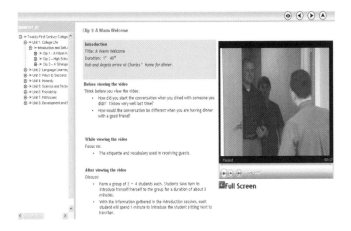

Figure 3.3 Video-supplement Design

However, it is worth noticing that, from a technological point of view, it is no small improvement to enrich the screen text with audio clips, and to add video streaming technology to the screen text is a major advancement. From a pedagogic point of view, on the other hand, the audio and video enrichment is more often than not treated as something parasitic on the screen text. It is even occasionally only decorative in function. This is why the term 'supplement' has been used.

Classroom-teacher-model design

As alluded to in the section 'Preliminary Remarks' (pp. 37–39), this design entails an asynchronous broadcast of a teacher talking to an imagined class (in fact she is talking to a video camera in a studio!), as illustrated in Figure 3.4 (the institution and the presenter have been disguised); see p. 44.

Multimedia-rich design

In this design, the printed-textbook version is significantly enriched with still images, audio and video clips, hypertext links, and so on. It should be noted that the printed-textbook version still serves as the basis on which multimedia materials are hyperlinked and made mouse-sensitive. Figure 3.5 (p. 44) shows an example of this type of design.

Learning-process-model design

Unlike the previous five designs, this design is not based on a traditional printed textbook. The units and their contents reflect a learning process through which a default learner, together with his or her study mates, undertakes planned study. Activities and specific learning tasks are constructed to reflect real-life situations. Figure 3.6 (p. 45) shows this type of design.

Figure 3.4 Classroom-teacher-model Design

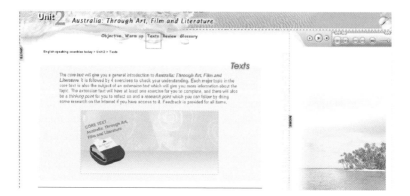

Figure 3.5 Multimedia-rich Design

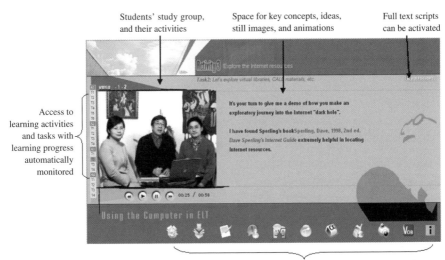

Students' study group,
and their activities

Space for key concepts, ideas,
still images, and animations

Full text scripts
can be activated

Access to
learning activities
and tasks with
learning progress
automatically
monitored

Access tools for synchronous and asynchronous
online activities are integrated

Figure 3.6 Learning-process-model Design

Having overviewed these six types of network-based courseware design, I next examine them from two major perspectives: policy and pedagogy.

Analysis from a Policy Perspective

Preliminary remarks

From a policy perspective, we need to keep in mind not only those factors discussed by Shearer (2003):

1. the goals and missions of the learning organization;
2. the costs that must be recovered;
3. the costs of delivery;
4. the political environment at the time for the learning organization;
5. the faculty compensation;
6. the market competition;

We will also need to bear in mind the ways online education has been perceived by various education authorities. In a recent paper (Gu 2005b), I discuss seven major problems in China's current online education practice, three of which are highly relevant here. First, there is a widespread practice of equating students' learning via online courseware with online education. This constitutes what I propose to call *the fallacy of equating learning behaviour with an educational system.*[2] Second, there is an equally widespread practice of transferring traditional printed textbooks verbatim to the Web through a digitalization process only. This constitutes the fallacy of equating online learning with classroom learning. Third, using a computer for self-study, and receiving automatic feedback and answers, creates a false impression of autonomous study. This is the *fallacy of reducing autonomous learning to support-less solitary study.*

Bearing in mind Shearer's (2003) six factors and the three fallacies, let us examine the six designs, not one by one, but in three groups.

The Printed-textbook-transfer, audio-supplement, and video-supplement

Of the three designs, the printed-textbook-transfer is the cheapest and the quickest way of getting a course published on the Web. The production of audio clips nowadays has become fairly straightforward and inexpensive. The production of video clips, in contrast, is labour-intensive and costly. For some universities, the adoption of a particular design is determined largely by cost considerations. For instance, a university I knew made a budget of 3,000 RMB[3] available per courseware. This amount was hardly enough for the simplest digitalization of a 300-page printed textbook. In other universities, however, the adoption of a particular design is less determined by the cost than by the misconceptions of the enterprise (i.e. they are victims of the three fallacies). For instance, one university made available a budget of over 200,000 RMB for a particular piece of courseware. By Chinese standards, this amount is quite reasonable for good quality courseware production, even with rich multimedia input. I was invited to evaluate the final product, and I had little doubt that the money had been spent unwisely. The courseware designers clearly lacked expertise and adequate research.

Classroom-teacher-model and multimedia-rich designs

These two designs involve rich multimedia input and are obviously more costly to implement than the previous three. The pay-off for the extra cost lies in the fact that the amount of screen text reading is considerably reduced, and is replaced by watching and listening, which are far more comfortable than reading text on screen. The classroom-teacher-model, as explained in the section, 'Classroom-teacher-model Design' (p. 43), involves videotaping a real-life teacher talking to a video camera. This can be quite a challenging task for the staff. In the instance shown, no auto-cue device was used. The teacher had to look at the camera from time to time and thereby run the risk of losing track of her lines. It is quite easy to fall into the trap of re-recording a particular bit again and again, which can be very frustrating. Shearer's (2003) 'faculty compensation' becomes relevant here.

The classroom-teacher-model and the multimedia-rich designs can be integrated; for example, one of the tutorial programmes produced by Beiwai Online has done this. Some of the tasks of the real-life classroom teacher are modeled by animation, and video clips are used to contextualize the tasks or as a way of presenting content. This integrated design is much more costly to produce, but the final product is far livelier and more varied than a talking head talking all the time!

Learning-process-model design

This design is innovative and is the most expensive to produce. It requires a complicated integration of real-life presentations, animations, video clips, and tools for synchronous and asynchronous Web-based activities. It stretches technology to its limit. This design, of which I am a chief player, has created considerable tension between business-minded stakeholders and educationalists. As will be shown later, this design is pedagogically superior to the other five designs, as judged by Mayer's (2001) seven principles. However, it depends on economy of scale to recover its production costs. In the current situation in China, where the reputation of e-learning has been seriously damaged by some bad practices, it will take several years for the economy of scale to happen. In other words, there is a tension between a quality product which aims at long-term sustainability and a quick-profit product which is eventually suicidal.

Analysis from a Pedagogic Perspective

Approaches to pedagogic evaluation

The evaluation of both pre-network CALL and network-based CALL is generally made according to pedagogy rather than to policy, as we did in the section above, 'Analysis from a Policy Perspective' (pp. 45–47). It is worth noticing from the start that reactions by the general public to both types of CALL are frequently off-the-cuff or on the basis of a few limited attempts at using the technology, or even following small talk in social contexts. Odell (1986) and Windeatt (1986) are among the early attempts to evaluate CALL academically. Odell (1986: 61) "looks at an experimental model for CALL software evaluation, using a database to store the resulting information". Windeatt, in contrast, adopts a fieldwork approach by observing learners using CALL materials. Chapelle (2001) spends a considerable amount of space on evaluation issues. She argues that, since there are so many variables involved, an evaluation of CALL applications cannot be categorical. In other words, it cannot simply be a black or white matter. "Instead, an evaluation has to result in an argument indicating in what ways a particular CALL task is appropriate for particular learners at a given time . . . The idea of evaluation as a context-specific argument rather than a categorical judgement, of course, makes evaluation a complex issue, which needs to be addressed by all CALL users" (Chapelle 2001: 53). Five general principles of evaluation can be formulated from her work:

1. evaluation of CALL is a situation-specific argument;
2. CALL should be evaluated through two perspectives: judgmental analysis of software and planned tasks, and empirical analysis of learners' performance;

3. criteria for CALL task quality should come from theory and research on instructed second language acquisition;
4. criteria should be applied in view of the purpose of the task;
5. language learning potential should be the central criterion in evaluation of CALL.

Proposals for evaluating Web pages and website design are abundant, as a keyword search using Google.com will quickly show. However, Web page and website designs are only one part of Web-based CALL programmes, and there are few evaluation schemes currently available for Web-based CALL per se. In essence, Web-based CALL can be regarded as a Web-based extension of the former PC-based CALL (see the quote from Chapelle on p. 40). We can start with the safe assumption that the scheme for evaluating PC-based CALL should be equally applicable to Web-based CALL but supplemented by some extra features that are specific to the Internet medium. It is worth noting that Mayer's cognitive theory of multimedia learning and its derivative principles do not constitute an evaluation scheme as such, but they are fundamental for the development of an evaluation scheme.

Drawing insights from system ecology, I outline in several papers (Gu 2005a, 2005b, 2005c) an ecological model for evaluating e-learning programmes. An e-learner lives and studies in a triple-component eco-environment: (1) physical eco-environment, (2) academic eco-environment, and (3) administrative eco-environment. Each of the three sub-eco-environments consists of its own sub-sub eco-environments. Take the academic eco-environment for example. Its sub-eco-environment comprises (1) platform eco-environment, (2) courseware eco-environment, and (3) tutorial eco-environment.[4] In educational terms, an environment both frames and enables the learner's perceptions and behaviour (cf. Gibson's theory of affordances, see Gibson 1986). Through his or her perceptions of the environment, the learner is engaged in both adaptive learning and active learning. The two types of learning require the expenditure of the learner's limited cognitive resources, so an ideal e-learning environment will be where an optimal level of expenditure of the limited learning resources results in maximal learning.

In this ecological model, learning is given a very broad coverage. It includes (1) formal and informal learning, (2) implicit and explicit learning, and (3) inside-class and outside-class learning. This is particularly appropriate, given the fact that the e-learners considered in this paper are adults who have full-time jobs and may or may not have a family to look after.

In what follows, I use the ecological model, in conjunction with Mayer's seven principles, to evaluate pedagogically the six types of design.

Printed-textbook-transfer, audio- and video-supplement designs

As we know, printed textbooks are traditionally used in a classroom, a human teacher mediating between the textbook and the learner. Figure 3.7 (p. 49) shows a well-equipped classroom learning eco-environment.

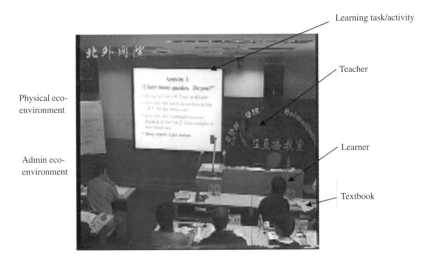

Figure 3.7   Teacher-led, Printed-textbook-based Classroom Learning Eco-Environment

From the learner's perspective, the learning eco-environment consists of (1) the physical eco-environment, e.g. chairs, tables, and equipment; (2) the academic eco-environment, e.g. the teacher, the printed textbook, classmates, teaching methodology, and learning activities/tasks; (3) the administrative eco-environment, e.g. the timetable, equipment maintenance, and the power supply. The learner's eco-environment and his or her learning process can be graphically reconstructed, as shown in Figure 3.8.

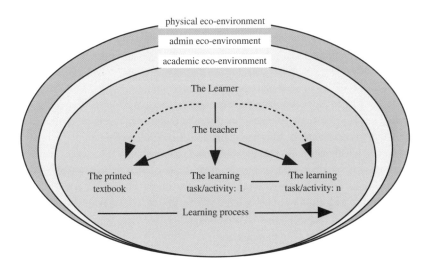

Figure 3.8   Reconstruction of the Learner's Eco-Environment and Learning Process

Now let us consider what happens when the printed textbook is transferred digitally. First, the learning eco-environment changes quite drastically: (1) the physical eco-environment changes from a well-equipped classroom to a home environment with or without a private study room; (2) the academic eco-environment changes from teacher-mediated instruction to independent self-study; (3) the administrative eco-environment changes from zero administration to full administration for the learners, e.g. technicians take care of the maintenance of equipment in the classroom, while at home the students have to maintain their own desktops either by themselves or by seeking help.

As mentioned above, the eco-environment is evaluated in terms of framing and enabling functions. Table 3.1 (p. 51) demonstrates how this is implemented. In the existing literature, the enabling functions of home and Web-based eco-environments are frequently listed, while their framing functions are ignored. The designers/developers tend to see only the enabling side, while students have to cope with the framing effects. As a result, the former feel disappointed or even bewildered, and wonder why their 'fantastic product' is not duly appreciated by the learners. Let us take the flexibility of the timetable as an example. It is almost universally assumed that flexibility of the timetable is one of the advantages that the Web-based learning environment has over the traditional campus learning environment. What has been overlooked, however, is that the fixed timetable of the latter has an enabling function; that is, students are enabled to enjoy a dedicated period of time without interruptions by others or by themselves. As we all know, an interrupted learning period is less effective than a continuous one.

Another advantage often attributed to a Web-based learning environment is self-management of the learning process. In the Chinese traditional campus environment, students rely on their teachers to manage their learning progress. All they need do is simply to attend the scheduled classes, and the course progress will take care of itself. This is not the case with Web-based learners, who do not have to attend any fixed classes. In other words, they are enabled to have the power to manage their own learning progress. We have failed to see, however, that such management sets an extra demand on the learner's limited cognitive resources. For those learners who have commitments to their jobs, families, friends, and social life, the learning progress management can be extremely demanding and costly.

The transfer of a printed, paper-based textbook to a Web-based hypertext enables learners to access it without the need for physical paper, which can be quite heavy and burdensome to carry around. Moreover, the audio and video clips supplemented by the hypertext add an advantage, in that the traditional cassette and VHS players are no longer required. Having said this, we must not forget that a paper-based book enables the reader to read it without switching anything on, except for a light when it is dark.

Everything else being equal, if we endorse Mayer's (2001) cognitive theory of multimedia learning, we can conclude that the audio- and video-supplemented design is definitely superior to that of hypertexts only.

Table 3.1

Comparison of the Classroom and Home Eco-Environments

| | Classroom Eco-Environment | | Home Eco-Environment | |
	Framing	Enabling	Framing	Enabling
Physical	Being there on the spot	Use of equipment	Sharing space with family members	Use of home equipment
	Fixed timetable	Non-interference from other commitments	Open to other commitments	Flexible timetable
	According to the teacher's schema	Let the teacher manage the learning process	Extra demands on the limited cognitive resources	Self-management of the learning process
Academic	Teacher-controlled turn-taking	F2F interaction with the teacher and classmates	No F2F interaction with the teacher or classmates	Asynchronous and indirect interaction
		Enjoy the teacher's interpretation of the textbook		Downloading and uploading of files
		Enjoy the teacher's extra input Instant help		Instant answer key or feedback
Administrative	No tampering with facilities	Free use of equipment	Subject to power failure	
			Subject to lost hyperlinks	
			Subject to interruptions by family members or telephone calls	

Classroom-teacher-model design

This design enables learners to watch their real-life teacher talking to them, very much as they do in the traditional campus classroom. Interviews with learners about this type of design show a general consensus that it is definitely preferred to the plain hypertext design (i.e. the first type of design discussed above). Human interaction, even though it is one way and indirect, has advantages in its own right. The 'presence' of a human teacher creates a sense of closeness, care and intimacy that counterbalances the effects of solitude and isolation, which are so typically experienced by distance learners. From this point of view, a talking head, which is often condemned, is not educationally unwelcome, from the student perspective.

What we should be on guard against, however, is the practice of videotaping a real-life teacher's performance and publishing it without making any adjustments to enable learners to interact, asynchronously and using a keyboard, with the courseware content. This practice is seen in the training packages I have reviewed. (Note that I do not wish to name them here, for confidentiality reasons.)

Multimedia-rich design

In theory, this design has all the advantages of the previously reviewed designs yet without any of their weaknesses. In practice, however, the final product often falls short of this ideal. The main problem comes from the shortage of expertise in instructional design, multimedia production and the integration of the two. As a result, if we use Mayer's (2001) seven principles as benchmarks to evaluate the product, defects quickly emerge. In my review, I have found that the animations are often more suitable for entertainment than for the enhancement of learning. Similarly, the video clips are often well made, and hence costly, but pedagogically they are not made full use of, due to a lack of expertise in instructional design and learning theory.

Learning-process-model design

This design contrasts sharply with the classroom-teacher-model design discussed above. The latter design, like all the other types of design so far analysed, constructs its content primarily on the basis of knowledge structure, which is typically divided into chunks (i.e. units or chapters) for the teacher to teach and the learners to learn. The actual teaching process, or the actual learning process, is peripheral to the overall design schema. The learning-process-model design, on the other hand, as its name indicates, builds on a projected default learner who undertakes a goal-directed process of learning. The stages of this process become the units or chapters. The activities/tasks the default learner is engaged in become the content of the courseware. The users of the courseware become the cyber-mates of the default learner, who study together in a cyber-community. The default learner organizes classes and public lectures by inviting professors and guest lecturers. Forum debates, reading groups, workshops, brainstorming sessions, etc., are also part of the default learner's learning process. The progress the default learner makes is used as auto-normal benchmarks for real-life learners to assess their own progress. This feature is very affect-friendly. As we know, uncertainty about progress is a concern felt by nearly all distance learners, and it often causes anxiety and loss of confidence. The fact that the client learners are prompted with the message that they are making progress ahead of the default learner removes uncertainty and greatly enhances their confidence.

The learning-process-model design is in essence a design simulating real-life learning activities. There are three essential components: (1) the analysis of real-life learners' learning activities, (2) the construction of a default learner's learning activities on the basis of the first, and (3) the client learner's interactive activities with the constructed default learner. In the present case, real-life learning activities are not exclusively those taking place in a traditional classroom. Rather, they are clusters of learning activities taking place at home, in the workplace, at tutorial centres, or even on a train or on an aeroplane. The three components are shown graphically in Figure 3.9.

Learning Process Modelling and Course Structure

It is recommended that learners' learning process be the object we attempt to model. The material development thus becomes a creative process of constructing such learning experience from the perspective of a learner, who is projected by the developers as the default learner.

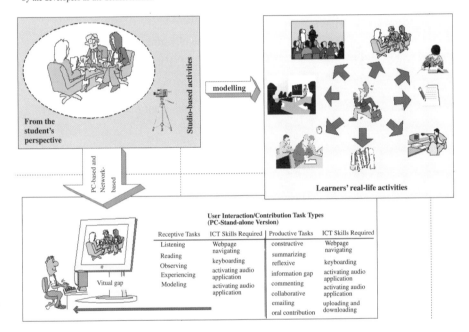

Figure 3.9   The Triple Components of the Learning-process-model Design

The final Web-based courseware design is shown graphically in Figure 3.10 (p. 54). This design is based on the four principles identified by Gu, Hall, McGrath, and Sinclair (2005: 27):

1.   The principle of multimedia presentation and multimodal interaction. Multimedia presentation means that the materials should include (1) e-texts, (2) images, (3) audio recordings, and (4) video recordings. Multimodal interaction means that the user should be able to interact with the PC or online users (other students or tutors) via keyboarding, voice, and video capture, which can be saved on a local drive or uploaded onto a remote server for synchronous or asynchronous access.

2. The principle of maximizing experience-sharing. The multimedia presentation and multimodal interaction should enable the possibility of experience-sharing, which means that learners can share their learning processes or experiences among themselves. The pedagogical advantages of experience-sharing hardly need emphasizing. It is particularly useful for modelling and establishing new practices.

3. The principle of maximizing active participation and engagement. One of the weaknesses often found in CALL and online programmes is that all the users have to do is simply sit and read the screen, or sit and watch. This weakness is partially due to the affordance limitations of accessibility of the Internet, and partially due to poor design. The maximization of active participation and engagement is the hallmark of an optimal use of ICT, which calls for a great deal of interaction between ELT and ICT experts.

4. The principle of maximizing user-friendliness. ICT manuals are notoriously difficult to understand and hence are off-putting. Our past experiences have shown that user-friendliness is greatly improved if everything — the content, the presentation methods, the online publication and the user manuals — is designed from the perspective of the user rather than of the developer.

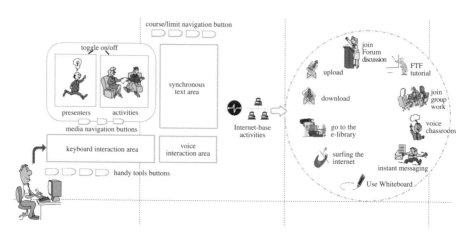

Figure 3.10 Graphic Presentation of the Learning-process-model Courseware developed in the *eChina-UK* Project

At the time of finalizing this chapter, the courseware development has been successfully completed. Both Web-based and DVD-based versions will soon be made available, and a sample of the courseware will be available for viewing on this website: http://www.beiwaionline.com. Readers interested in getting to know more about the courseware can also consult the printed textbook accompanying the courseware (see Gu, Hall and Hall 2006).

Overall Assessment

This pedagogic assessment of the six types of design can only be indicative; a fully developed assessment would require a major report. To conclude, I would like to point out one defect that occurs in all six types. As studies of learning have shown, mental internalization of what is being learnt is crucial for long-term retention. In the traditional campus classroom eco-environment, a one-hour lecture or interactive lesson can be treated as initial learning, which needs internalizing for long-term retention. The initial learning uses working memory, while internalization involves transfer from working memory to short-term memory and then to long-term memory. Some students report that effective teaching leaves them with a 'deeper impression' than Web-based learning. One of my PhD students once told me that he preferred printed books to e-books because the paper-based books helped him recall better. Whether or not habituation with the traditional learning eco-environment plays some role here is a research issue for another occasion. What is certain to me is that none of the Web-based CALL under the six types of design I have reviewed takes learners' mental internalization of what is being learned into serious consideration, or even considers it at all. Web pages are made glaring and eye-catching, and are often overloaded with information (a violation of Mayer's [2001] fourth Coherence Principle). Activities and tasks are designed as a one-go business. What has been retained after a busy session of clicking, surfing, dragging, etc. can be quite disappointing. Learners' limited cognitive resources are not utilized in a cost-effective way.

Conclusion

My critical reflections on the six types of Web-based courseware design have been more negative than positive. The negative reflections do not mean that we cannot learn from them; on the contrary, we learn more from negative reflections than positive ones. The lesson I have drawn from carrying out this review is that a holistic approach to Web-based courseware design, i.e. what I call an ecological approach, holds the key to successful design. Among all the factors, in both policy and pedagogy, designers must give priority, I suggest, to the learners' learning process, to learning process management, and to conservation of learners' cognitive resources. In China, and perhaps elsewhere in the world, designers have been overwhelmingly biased either towards technology or towards the teaching process. The concept of learner autonomy or learner-centredness has remained a bandwagon slogan and has not yet been translated into courseware development practice.

4

Designing an Innovative Online Course in Language Teaching Methodology for Middle School Teachers of English in China: Encouraging Learner and Teacher Autonomy

Ian McGrath, Barbara Sinclair and Chen Zehang

Introduction

Currently, some 470,000 teachers are involved in the teaching of English at junior middle school level (students aged 12–15) in China, many of whom possess only a two- or three-year diploma in teaching, rather than a specialist qualification (e.g. a first degree, BA) in English. The Chinese Ministry of Education (MoE) has recently stated that by 2010 all junior middle-school teachers should have at least a first degree.[1] However, until recently, the only option for those wishing to upgrade their qualifications to degree level has been to take correspondence courses, attend night schools or study at a Radio and Television University. Since most of these courses have fixed class timetables, e-learning programmes which offer flexibility and almost unlimited resources are becoming a real alternative.

The e-learning materials developed by the University of Nottingham (UoN) and Beijing Normal University (BNU),[2] as part of the *eChina-UK Programme*, were designed to form part of a 'top-up' or 'upgrading' programme leading to a BA. Since diploma level courses do not include a subject-specific methodology component, a module dealing with methodology for the teaching of English was seen as a key element of this programme. For target participants, this programme thus represents not only an extension of their formal education[3] but also an opportunity for vocationally related professional development.

The distinction made in the next section of the paper between learner autonomy and teacher autonomy therefore has particular salience in relation to the teachers targeted by this project. As (part-time) participants in an award-bearing in-service programme, and one which is effectively compulsory, their status is that of learners; moreover, since many were experiencing online learning for the first time, that status would doubtless feel real, both cognitively and affectively. Yet in the world in which they work, their status is that of teacher.

This distinction between learner and teacher is, of course, somewhat artificial. After all, most teachers accept the need to go on learning as part of their professional responsibility and would be likely to see any learning which finds expression in the classroom or in teaching-related activity, whatever its origin, as being relevant to their role as teachers. From this perspective, the experience of being an online learner may, in itself, help teachers to empathize with the anxieties that learners may feel when faced with new modes of learning. We therefore see participants *continuously* shifting roles between learner and teacher in response to specific stimuli, and as they themselves see fit.

In designing materials to support the professional development of such teachers, we had in mind a number of pedagogical principles. These included relevance, personalization, interactivity and the development of learner and teacher autonomy. Our focus in this chapter is on the last two of these principles. The following section presents the rationale for a focus on autonomy and reviews the literature on autonomy (principally learner autonomy) from both Western and Chinese perspectives. The section 'Theory and Practice: Online Learning and the Development of Autonomy' (pp. 64–71) shows how this principle was implemented, with reference to a number of extracts from the materials; and 'Piloting the Materials' (pp. 71–76) reports on participants' responses during the piloting of the materials.

The Rationale for a Focus on Autonomy

One of the most striking features of recent educational curriculum development in many countries is the growing emphasis on 'lifelong learning'. In school curricula, we now see a greater focus on the need to help learners develop the skills and knowledge to learn independently, so that they may continue to learn and develop throughout their lives; in other words, to develop a measure of learner autonomy. In the fast-paced societies in which many of us now live, it cannot be guaranteed that what we learn during a period of formal education will continue to be useful to us as we move through our lives. Technology is constantly being updated and redeveloped, and we need to keep up with the changes in the ways we work and think. In particular, it is in governments' interests to have a workforce of people with up-to-date knowledge and expertise in order to compete successfully in the global market. In addition to these more pragmatic reasons for helping learners to develop the ability to learn independently, there are important philosophical arguments for enabling members of society to have a measure of control over their own development and actions.

The notion of learner autonomy is not, of course, new. A concern with the nature of learning and the role of autonomy is well established in the literature; it is possible to find reference to human autonomy from the earliest of writings. For example, Confucius (551–479 BC), the Chinese philosopher, has provided us with one of the most succinct, and familiar, definitions of autonomy with regard to the responsibilities of the teacher: "If you give a man a fish, you feed him for a day. If you teach a man to fish, you feed him for a lifetime." However, much of the literature currently cited in the field has emanated from the West. Indeed, learner autonomy has more recently been criticized as being a Western concept, based on Western ideology and an obsession with the individual (Pennycook 1997). The study of learner autonomy in language learning is not, then, a simple matter and requires careful interpretation of the particular cultural, social, political and educational context involved.

In this section of the chapter, we first consider a current conception of learner autonomy, derived largely from the West, which the project team felt was appropriate as a starting point for the project. We then consider how learner autonomy is conceptualized in Chinese cultures.

Influences from the West

A number of theoretical and research influences, emanating principally from the West and exerted more or less simultaneously during the last two to three decades, have contributed to current understandings of 'autonomy' in language learning. They include a more widespread concern with the rights of the individual within society; the development of an educational philosophy which has emphasized learners' rights and freedom to learn (Rogers 1969; Freire 1972); and research into cognitive psychology, particularly into learning style (Kolb 1976; Pask 1976; Berry 1979; Willing 1988).

Other influences on the development of autonomy in language learning are related more specifically to language learning and teaching, and include the development of a charter of 'language learners' rights' in Brazil (Gomes de Matos 1986) and the application of humanistic approaches to language teaching, largely based on the therapeutic work of Rogers and popularized in the United States by Moskowitz (1978) and in the UK by Rinvolucri (1984) and others.

An enormous influence on language teaching in recent years has been the emergence of communicative approaches, in which the learner is accepted as an individual with real communicative needs and personal meanings to express (Littlewood 1981; Pattison 1987; Nunan 1988). As in other fields, learner-centred approaches to teaching in general have become something of an expectation in ELT (English language teaching), particularly in the West (see, for example, Nunan 1988; Tudor 1993). However, in China, too, the new curriculum for English in schools (国家英语课程标准[National Curriculum for English] 2001) now emphasizes a more learner-centred, communicative approach to teaching the language.

Although the expansion of learner-centredness towards greater learner responsibility and the promotion of autonomy in language learning are becoming more familiar concepts in many parts of the world, differing interpretations of autonomy within political and cultural environments mean that this concept is explored in a range of different ways.

'Learner Autonomy': Definition and Misconceptions

'Learner autonomy' is a notoriously difficult and slippery term to define, since there are a number of different conceptions of it based on differing philosophical points of view.

Our starting point for conceptualizing learner autonomy for this project is the so-called 'Bergen definition' offered by Dam, which is perhaps the most commonly cited and widely accepted definition in the literature at present:

> Learner autonomy is characterized by a readiness to take charge of one's own learning in the service of one's needs and purposes. This entails a capacity and willingness to act independently and in co-operation with others, as a socially responsible person. (Dam 1995: 1)

■ Capacity

The Bergen definition seems most relevant because it contains a number of important points. Firstly, it recognizes that autonomy is a construct of capacity (as originally suggested by Holec in 1981). In other words, learner autonomy consists of the *ability* to make informed decisions about one's own learning. Being able to do so requires a good deal of specific knowledge about four major areas: one's self as a learner, the learning context, the subject matter to be learnt and learning processes. This may be termed metacognitive knowledge, or knowledge about learning (Flavell 1987). It also involves *conscious* awareness of this knowledge and *conscious* reflection on learning (Ellis and Sinclair 1989; Wenden 1991; Dickinson 1992). In other words, the term 'learner autonomy' relates to capacity rather than actual action, informing one's self, rather than actually carrying out the learning.

> Autonomy is thus a term describing a potential capacity to act in a given situation — in our case — learning, and not the actual behaviour of an individual in that situation. (Holec 1981: 3)

The conceptualization of autonomy as a capacity is important here, as it enables us to differentiate between 'knowledge' and 'action', and to dispense with the misunderstanding that 'autonomy' relates only to freedom of action (rather than capacity or ability) and is something which can be fully attained in our social communities. Teachers, quite understandably, worry that such 'freedom of action' is untenable in a classroom and would lead to chaos and educational failure. In a wider context, others might be concerned that such 'autonomy' would produce anarchy and the breakdown of society as we know it. In so-called collectivist societies, such as China (Hofstede 2001), autonomy of this kind may be seen as anti-social and undesirable. However, conceptualized as a 'capacity' or a conscious and reflected upon body of knowledge, 'learner autonomy' can be seen as an essential component of an individual's ability to take greater responsibility for his or her own learning and, thus, engage in lifelong learning. For example, without a conscious awareness of strategy use in language learning, developed through reflection and experimentation, learners will not be able to transfer learning know-how to other learning situations (Wenden 1987), or to 'transcend' the classroom (Little 1996: 204). We address the issue of 'autonomous action', or what we term 'independent learning', later in this chapter.

■ Co-operative learning

Also included in the Bergen definition of autonomy is the notion of co-operative learning. This reflects the acknowledgement by researchers and practitioners in the field of the importance of sociocultural theory (or Social Development Theory), in that learner autonomy does not only relate to the individual learning in isolation. Sociocultural theory states that human behaviours cannot be understood by focusing on the individual. In other words, human behaviour needs to be examined within the prevailing political, cultural, and historical contexts (Renshaw 1992). The social basis of learning is highlighted through the use of interactive processes, such as reciprocal teaching, collaborative learning and the 'scaffolding' of learning (Bandura 1977; Vygotsky 1978; Lave and Wenger 1990; Renshaw 1992; Mercer 1995).

One of the most common misconceptions about autonomy is that it is concerned with the person only as an individual rather than as a social being. The importance placed on social learning by our conceptualization of learner autonomy reflects a current resurgence of interest in the work of Vygotsky in children's learning, and its relevance to learning in general. The major theme of his theoretical framework is that social interaction plays a fundamental role in the development of cognition. Little extends this view to the development of learner autonomy:

> I make the Vygotskian assumption that the development of a capacity for reflection and analysis, central to the development of learner autonomy, depends on the development and internalization of a capacity to participate fully and critically in social interactions. (Little 1996: 211)

Interaction is, thus, necessary, but it might take place indirectly with others through learning materials, such as books, computer-based activities and those presented in other media. In the case of the materials developed for this project, participants have the opportunity to interact directly with each other and their tutors through synchronous and asynchronous bulletin boards, and indirectly with others (course authors, experts in the field) through text, video and audio materials presented on computer, as well as through tasks designed to promote reflection on experience, learning matter and learning processes.

■ Autonomy and social responsibility

The Bergen definition also recognizes the social dimension of autonomy. It is clear that we live in a world where what we do affects the lives of others, and where we are constrained in our actions by social mores, politics, laws, conscience and consideration for others in our social groups. As 'socially responsible' members of society, it could be argued that we need to be responsible for ourselves and our interactions with others in order to coexist harmoniously and appropriately, i.e. be fully functioning, interdependent human beings. However, such social responsibility does not entail the total sublimation of an individual's needs and desires. Rather, it assumes that a person who has a good knowledge of self and context is able to understand whether actions are appropriate or not, both in relation to him or herself and in relation to others' needs and desires. In the learning context, a socially responsible learner is one who has a good knowledge of self as learner, the learning context, the subject matter to be learnt, and learning processes, so that he or she can take responsibility for his or her own learning, negotiate roles within the learning community, share and discuss ideas and opinions without feeling embarrassed, and with respect for others' views. In other words, there is a cyclical, reciprocal relationship between independent action and co-operative action. By taking responsibility and contributing to the learning community, the learner also has the opportunity to learn from others and to develop a greater capacity for autonomy. Thus, in this project, the development and sustaining of a learning community among the e-learning participants was seen as a crucial means of developing autonomy.

■   **Willingness and independent action**

The Bergen definition of learner autonomy includes the notion of 'willingness'. Clearly, learners will not act independently unless they have developed a positive attitude towards taking greater responsibility for themselves, and have the motivation to do so. Those who do have both a measure of capacity and motivation will take action and attempt to take some control over their learning to become more independent in their learning. However, such motivation or willingness is not always present. Even a learner who has developed a high capacity for autonomy may not always feel like acting independently. The willingness to take independent action in learning fluctuates in a learner according to a range of variables, such as how tired he or she feels at the time, environmental conditions, state of mind and of health, whether the subject matter is appealing, whether the task looks too daunting, and so on.

It is important to distinguish between capacity or ability (autonomy) and action (independent learning), because capacity cannot be observed, residing, as it does, in the learner's head. This has implications for assessment, since we are able to assess only the product of learning, not the hidden psychological processes involved.

To summarize, the concept of learner autonomy described here requires the building up of a body of knowledge about learning, including learner factors, contextual factors, the subject matter itself and learning processes, to form a basic capacity for informed decision-making about learning on which effective independent action depends. It has both an individual and a social dimension, recognizing that individual learners are different from each other, but that interacting with others can provide greater potential for development. Finally, it acknowledges that willingness to take responsibility for one's own learning is needed in order to exercise independent learning, and, thus, the need to nurture motivation is crucial.

Teacher autonomy

A great deal has been written about learner autonomy in the last few decades, but less on the related concept of 'teacher autonomy'. Teacher autonomy has been defined as "teachers' control over their own teaching" (Smith 2000: 9). Little describes teachers with autonomy as:

> having a strong sense of personal responsibility for their teaching, exercising via continuous reflection and analysis the highest possible degree of affective and cognitive control of the teaching process, and exploring the freedom that this confers. (Little 1995: 179)

McGrath (2000) has added to this definition of teacher autonomy the notion of 'self-directed professional development', which may include the teacher acting as researcher and as a reflective practitioner. It is this aspect of teacher autonomy that is of particular importance to these materials.

The Chinese cultural perspective on autonomy

As mentioned, most recent accounts of learner autonomy in the literature emanate from the West. However, many centuries ago, Chinese scholars clearly supported the notion of learner responsibility. Confucius has already been mentioned. According to Hsu, who has researched the concept and practice of learner autonomy in the Chinese heritage culture of Taiwan, "Confucius encouraged conscious and constructive thinking in learning and despised aimless elaboration" (Hsu 2005: 23). Hsu further describes the ideal learner, from a Confucian point of view, as one who is active in seeking new knowledge and "employing constructive dialogue in class" (2005: 23), which he considers reflects the principles of learner autonomy. Another Chinese scholar, Chu Hsi (1130–1200), who followed Confucian philosophy, wrote:

> If you are in doubt, think it out by yourself. Do not depend on others for explanations. Suppose there is no one you could ask. Should you stop learning? If you get rid of the habit of being dependent on others, you will make advancement in your study. (Chiang 1963, cited by Pierson 1996: 56)

Hsu (2005), however, suggests that the more traditional Chinese views of autonomy, and their emphasis on critical thinking and constructive discussion, have given way to a more pragmatic approach. This is largely due to the importance through the ages (from the Sui Dynasty, 541–618, until 1911) of the Imperial Examinations which were taken by men in order to gain employment in the Imperial Civil Service and, thus, to gain status in society and prestige for their family. These examinations emphasized the rote memorization of ancient texts (Hsu 2005) and required a great deal of dedication, hard work and self-discipline. Thus, although there is a long tradition of self-directed study in China, learner autonomy has become associated with the concepts of effort, strict self-discipline and willpower.

In 2004, Wang conducted a national survey on tertiary-level Web-based English education in China. Her aims were to investigate the systems of learner and tutor support, and data were collected from institutional decision makers, tutors, and learners from eight participating institutions. Wang found that 91.4 percent of the tutors perceived the students' greatest problem as 'lacking qualities for autonomous learners'. Furthermore, 88.6 percent of the tutors agreed that the students lacked 'English language learning strategies'. Interestingly, data from the learners showed that their biggest obstacle to successful learning was their 'heavy workload' (54.6 percent). However, 34.7 percent said they lacked 'autonomous learning strategies', and 34.3 percent claimed they did not know how to use 'resources effectively'. She also found that technical support was not viewed by the students as very important (presumably, they felt they were familiar enough with the new technologies). This important research provided the project team with useful insights.

Findings from the needs analysis

The project team's own preliminary needs analysis also uncovered some interesting views from Chinese teachers and teacher trainers which seem to support Hsu's views to some extent.

Interviews were conducted with 11 Chinese tertiary teachers of English, 15 middle school teachers of English, and 5 Chinese teacher trainers (some of whom were interviewed up to three times). All of the interviews were audio- and/or video-recorded, and permission was granted by the interviewees to include relevant parts of the transcripts and recordings in the materials to be developed, as well as to use the findings for research dissemination. The transcripts were analysed and themes categorized using the proprietary software NVivo.

These in-depth interviews, and other information collected during project visits to Beijing, provided interesting insights into current beliefs about and attitudes towards learner and teacher autonomy in the target population of potential course participants. A strongly emerging theme was that learner autonomy is characteristically linked with the current enthusiasm for and growth in new technologies for learning in China: "Students are getting more independent because there are more resources for learning — not just the teacher" (university professor, Beijing). Support by teachers for autonomy consisted mainly of providing opportunities out of class for students to practise self-direction, particularly with the new technology, rather than implementing explicit learner training and reflection on learning processes in class. There was much talk of self-discipline and effort, and the need for learners to review their materials and prepare for lessons without having to be told to do so. Motivation and self-drive were considered to be essential components of autonomy.

Theory to Practice: Online Learning and the Development of Autonomy

As noted in the introduction to this chapter, the needs of the target group, junior middle-school teachers of English with no previous formal training in how to teach English, argued for a high priority to be given to the development of materials for a module on the methodology of English language teaching. This section discusses and illustrates some of the pedagogic decisions which influenced the design of this module, with particular reference to the development of learner (and teacher) autonomy.

The aims of the methodology module were to:

- enable participants to develop greater knowledge, understanding and experience of alternative ways of organizing English teaching and learning, particularly with regard to learner-centred methodologies and the use of new technologies;
- help participants develop their own capacity for independent learning and self-directed professional development;
- enable participants to develop greater confidence and independence as teachers.

In view of the different conceptions of autonomy prevailing in China and the West, discussed in 'the Rationale for a Focus on Autonomy' (pp. 58–64), the term 'autonomous' does not appear explicitly in these aims. It will be evident, nevertheless, that the overall goal was to enable participants to develop the knowledge and confidence to function independently as both learners (in this case, as language learners and learners about technology) and as language teachers. As Sinclair has argued, management of others, and facilitation of autonomy in others, may be dependent on the capacity to manage one's own professional development:

> [it is] only through experiencing some degree of control over his/her professional development that teachers may be better able to take informed and principled decisions about managing their own teaching context and, in turn, helping their own learners develop a measure of autonomy. (Sinclair forthcoming, a)

Preparation for autonomy and independence

In designing the materials, we took account of the need for:

- psychological preparation
- methodological preparation
- practice in self-direction.
  (Dickinson and Carver 1980)

Psychological preparation acknowledges that learners who have never had much opportunity to take responsibility for their own learning may find the concept of doing so unfamiliar and difficult to accept. Research (Sinclair forthcoming, b) has found that Chinese teachers of English (on a master's course at UoN) do not, for example, 'trust' their own ideas and opinions about issues in pedagogy, and that they feel happier having an 'expert' to tell them the 'correct' view. Such preparation therefore requires time and a gradual introduction. Learners need to know that learner autonomy and independence are part of the aims of the course, and they need to have an understanding of what these are and why they are important. Learner initiative needs to be encouraged through specially designed tasks and valued by peers, tutors and assessors. Without such psychological preparation, learners may find it difficult to develop the motivation or willingness to take on more responsibility for their own learning.

Methodological preparation refers to helping learners understand what they are doing and why. In particular, the aims of activities that require learners to undertake unfamiliar kinds of tasks, such as discussion of questions with no 'right' answers, need to be made explicit.

Finally, an important part of learning to take more responsibility for one's own learning is actually having opportunities to do so. Research has shown (Ellis and Sinclair 1989) that it is not useful to expect learners who have been used to depending completely on a teacher for expert input, direction and assessment, to suddenly take control of their own learning. It can be a difficult and overwhelming task for anybody, at any age (see also Cotterall 1995; Chan 2001; McGrath 2001). One way to do this in teaching is to provide learners with choices so that they can practise making informed decisions about their learning. This might involve, for example, learners deciding who to work with in pairs or groups, selecting tasks to do from a range available, deciding on a topic for assessment, and so on.

We now offer some examples of the means by which we attempted to realize these principles.

The Participant as Strategic Learner

One source of anxiety for most students is the knowledge that sooner or later their performance will be assessed. As the following extracts from a pre-unit quiz on the new curriculum demonstrate, formative assessment of some elements of a course, at least, can be carried out by participants themselves.

As the question at the top of the screen indicates (see Figure 4.1, p. 67), the quiz allows participants to assess how much of the content to be covered they already know. It also alerts them to what the designers feel are the key points in the material, and encourages them to make decisions about what to spend most time on (i.e. exercise their metacognitive strategies).

Automated feedback, though individualized, is limited to indicating whether an answer is correct. A summative report (see Figure 4.2, p. 67) includes a percentage score for each subsection of the quiz. This is intended to encourage self-motivated and focused further study.

The post-unit quiz, which recycles many of the questions, then allows participants to assess their own progress. Both quizzes can be accessed at http://www.echinauk.org/cases/nottingham/curriculum.php/.

Participants are also encouraged to engage with the material by formulating their own questions about the topics to be covered and using the materials as sources of information. As Figure 4.3 (p. 68) shows, they can also follow their own preferences as to a route through the materials.

A similar approach was adopted for the provision of readings, which were included in a Study Guide. Since these were conceived as supplementary, no tasks were designed to accompany them. An instruction was given on the relevant screen saying simply: "If you wish to know more about this topic, go to page X in your Study Guide. You'll find more readings there."

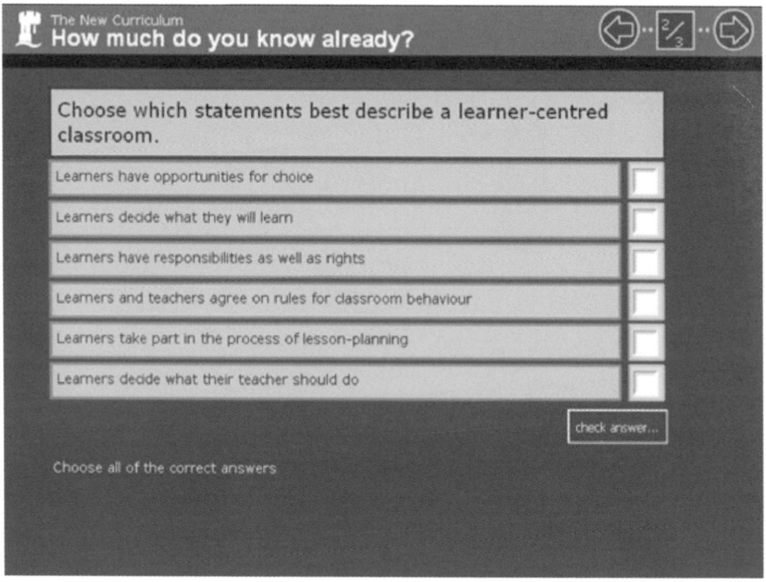

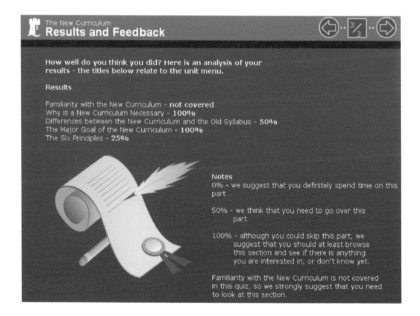

Figure 4.1 Extract from a Pre-Unit Quiz

Figure 4.2 Extract from Feedback on a Pre-Unit Quiz

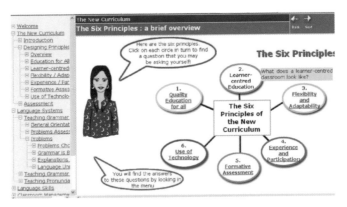

Figure 4.3 Extract from the New Curriculum Unit

The participant as self-directed teacher

The next example is taken from a unit on teaching grammar. In the earlier part of this unit, participants are encouraged to think about — and rank — their problems in teaching (English) grammar (this activity can be accessed at http://www.echinauk.org/cases/ nottingham/gramor/Presentation_Frames/BNU_Moodle_Mockup.htm/). They are then offered a set of ideas and resources for dealing with these problems and asked to try out and report on their experience with one of these.

One of the tasks involves participants in the following steps:

- deciding on a grammar topic which poses problems for their learners;
- finding websites that provide information on this topic;
- creating a worksheet based on the information/examples in the websites;
- making notes on what happened (optional);
- sharing their experiences with classmates and adding their thoughts on other ways of using websites for language teaching.

In short, the task encourages participants to take action to solve their own problems, but it does this in a series of carefully graded steps, and it provides support (for example, by suggesting suitable websites and, subsequently, through a dialogue with other members of the learning community). Here, and in Figure 4.5 (p. 70), autonomy is presented not as isolated self-sufficiency but as independent action which makes intelligent use of available resources — and these will include other people.

Finding one's own voice as a learner and teacher

■   The role of the 'Workspace'

One feature of the infrastructure designed by the UoN team which has attracted much attention during the development phase is the facility to store an individual participant's interactions with his or her computer on a database. We have called this the individual *Workspace*. The *Workspace* can be thought of as a file repository: it is where a participant stores everything he or she chooses to keep. It contains separate spaces for notetaking (Notebook), for communication (the Tea House for socializing and personal exchange; the Bulletin Board for posting of tutor announcements and learner products; the Discussion Group for professional exchange, normally on topics set by the tutor), and for directed reflection (Reflective Journal). Participants can access items whenever they wish, modify them if they are so inclined, copy them into another file, or send them to someone else.

| BA English Home | Workspace | Glossary | Library | Discussion Groups | |
| Methodology | Notebook | Bibliography | | Bulletin Board | Tea House |

Figure 4.4   Component Features of the University of Nottingham's *Workspace*

From a broader and slightly different perspective, the *Workspace* is also the record kept of individual participants' work by the database that lies behind the system. While this database enables tutors to keep track of participants' progress — a feature of other data-based systems — it also opens up the possibility of a personalized learning experience. When an individual logs on, the system remembers him or her, the route through the materials the individual has taken, the choices made in relation to automated tasks, his or her contributions to the Bulletin Board and Discussion Groups, where the individual has reached, and so on; in short, the individual's personal interactions with the technology. Further discussion and illustration of the *Workspace* can be found at: http://www.echinauk. org/tools/workspace/workspace.php/ and at http://www.echinauk.org/cases/nottingham/ workspace.php/.

Several of the features just mentioned are of particular relevance for the development of autonomy.

1. The 'personalized memory' offered by the *Workspace* facilitates — and may therefore encourage participants to exercise — such key metacognitive functions as reviewing their work, reflecting on their progress and setting further goals.

2. The distinction within the *Workspace* between the Notebook and the Reflective Journal is not merely an organizational convenience; it also gives explicit form to the expectation that learners and teachers who are serious about what they are doing will engage in reflection on a conscious and regular basis, which may involve reviewing their Notebook entries and the records of their contributions to Discussion Groups, for example.

3. The Bulletin Board allows all participants to make a concrete contribution to the group: to offer ideas or resources which others can use or adapt.

4. On the face of it, the Discussion Group is simply an outlet for individual views, and a stimulus to refining or modifying these; however, it also constitutes a form of (positive) pressure on participants to think through and formulate their own standpoint

in relation to a particular issue. In theory, autonomy might be demonstrated by deliberate non-involvement or by 'lurking'; in this module, however, participants are told that contributions to Discussion Groups will be assessed, but *they can choose which Discussion Group(s) they wish to be assessed on.*

In combination, the Bulletin Board and Discussion Group — like the Tea Room — can also be seen as meeting-places. If used (and the frequency and nature of their use will depend in part on the demands of the course), these can play a vital role in encouraging participants to feel that they belong to, have a voice in, and are valued in a professional community. The next example from the materials shows how this might be achieved.

The screen reproduced in Figure 4.5 comes at the end of a sequence of activities designed to extend participants' understanding of learner-centred teaching (available at http://www.echinauk.org/cases/nottingham/CurrAug05/learnobj.swf). Resources used include a video-recording of an English lesson taught by a Chinese middle school teacher and comments on this lesson by one of the materials developers.[4] What is important from the autonomy perspective, however, is that participants are asked to respond in writing to a series of questions about the lesson before they hear the views of the outside 'expert'.

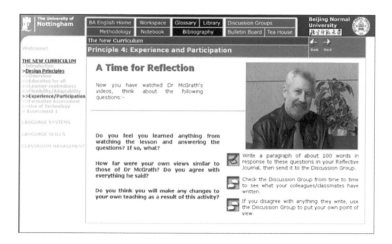

Figure 4.5   Extract from the New Curriculum Unit

As can be seen from the screenshot in Figure 4.5, participants are then encouraged to:

- reflect on their own learning;
- critically evaluate the views of the expert;
- consider the implications for their own teaching;
- discuss the lesson (and their responses to the other questions) with their classmates.

Carefully structured tasks such as these not only support the development of confidence in making and voicing independent judgments and provide for learning from others but also, we would suggest, are a stimulus to autonomous *action*. The expectation that participants will state publicly, through the Discussion Group, what changes they plan to make in their own teaching in effect raises the status of what would otherwise be simply private reflections to something akin to a commitment.

Piloting the Materials

The materials were piloted in Beijing over five weeks during March and April 2005. Twelve participants, all secondary school English teachers, volunteered to complete five weeks of online learning using the materials on the New National Curriculum for English and Teaching Grammar (from which the extracts above have been taken). Table 4.1 offers brief details of the participants:

Table 4.1
Details of Participants

School type	Junior middle	10
	Vocational	2
Gender	Female	11
	Male	1
Experience (years)	6+	8
	3–5	3
	1–2	1

Although the pilot involved at least four hours of work per week in addition to their normal full-time teaching and their part-time study at night schools, all 12 participants completed the piloting, engaging with the chat room and discussion forum as well as the materials.

Induction

A half-day face-to-face induction was conducted before the pilot began. The purpose was to introduce the materials to the participants, provide a basic introduction to the technology and the interactive tools, and collect information relevant to research and evaluation processes. As part of this latter process, participants were asked to give written answers to the following questions:

1. How autonomous (independent) would you say you are as a teacher?
2. How autonomous (independent) would you say you are as a learner of English?
3. How autonomous are your learners?
4. Do you see teacher/learner autonomy as a good thing?

In responding to these questions, four participants offered their own definitions of autonomy, namely:

I think autonomy means when people have to deal with a problem or complete a task, they can have their own ideas and are able to do it in their own way without being restricted or interrupted too much. (P1)

I think autonomy means you have to take the initiatives to some extent in everything. (P2)

I think autonomy means to do things actively, initiatively and from the bottom of one's heart. (P3)

I believe autonomy means one can be in control of something freely. (P4)

What emerges from these definitions is that these teachers relate autonomy to concepts of freedom from external control (P1, P4) and self-directed initiative-taking (P2, P3). (See the discussion of teacher autonomy in 'The Rationale for a Focus on Autonomy, pp. 58–64.) However, in their teaching practice, none of them claim to be autonomous. They have no right to decide the textbooks, the teaching schedule or the language points to be taught. The national examination restricts the latter, and institutions normally impose textbooks and teaching schedules. However, some do mention that they have some freedom in choosing teaching methods and in designing their lessons to suit their own students' needs. One participant also acknowledged that, though she was not a very self-driven person, "the responsibility of being a teacher" drove her to learn continuously.

In contrast, as learners of English, all but one considered themselves to be quite autonomous. They said, for instance: "I can decide how I learn, what to learn, when to learn"; "I am quite a good student. I can finish my work in time"; "I can learn most of the new words and grammar by myself. I was very active in learning and asking others for help in many courses"; and "I can choose to learn at my own time and my own speed and decide on how much and how well I should learn". The exception was a participant who did not feel very confident about learning independently and believed this was caused by the model of learning which she had experienced while at school.

As far as the autonomy of their own students is concerned, the teachers seemed to be dissatisfied. They expected students to preview, review, and do exercises after class, but only a few would do so. Some noted that many of their students were forced by their parents or teachers to learn.

As to whether teacher/learner autonomy is a good thing, opinions varied. Four respondents thought it was a good thing, four favoured some but not too much, and two did not see autonomy as desirable. The most positive saw autonomy as the key to achievement and interest in learning. Those who had doubts believed that too much autonomy would result in chaotic classrooms and make the national standard hard to achieve, while conceding that a certain amount of autonomy would make both teachers and learners active and enthusiastic about what they are doing.

Participants' responses to the materials

As we have seen, the pilot materials were intended to encourage autonomy in participants as learners and teachers. The illustrations in 'Theory to Practice' (pp. 67–71) focus on:

- the participant as strategic learner;
- the participant as self-directed teacher;
- finding one's own voice as a learner and teacher.

How did participants respond to such autonomy-oriented activities? The following findings are based on observation of and interviews with the participants.

Teachers as online learners

■   *The quizzes* (Figures 4.1 and 4.2)

It is perhaps important to emphasize that performance on the pre- and post-unit quizzes does not contribute to formal assessment. This might be seen as a possible weakness and that, as a result, participants would not take them seriously. To judge by participant responses to the pilot, this is not the case. In the materials originally devised, automated feedback on the post-unit quiz was also relatively minimal. However, piloting indicated that participants would have liked to know why particular answers were correct or incorrect and be given a reference to the relevant section of the materials so that they could review this. As this feedback illustrates, they were thus demonstrating just the kinds of self-directed behaviour the materials were designed to encourage.

■   *Choice* (Figures 4.1 and 4.3)

Several participants mentioned that they liked the idea of choice:

> *I normally browse first and pick up the things that interest me and learn these first. Sometimes I would browse first and learn in details.* (P5)

> *I like to be given choices. I can learn what I'm interested first so that I feel very free.* (P6)

However, some found it hard to cope because there was too much choice.

> *I think this course gives us too much freedom and too much space. I feel that I can't grasp too much in my hand. I want to have something solid, something that is practical and effective to my teaching.* (P4)

Others resolved this dilemma by first studying all the materials in the order they were presented, because they were concerned not to miss any information. However, they would then go through it a second time more selectively.

I won't select things to learn for the first time because I don't want to miss anything. I'll probably choose things to look at from the second time. (P4)

Several participants mentioned that they are very passive in learning and need some pressure from outside to push them to learn.

I'm a very passive person. I need pressure to force me to learn. I'm accustomed to being forced to learn. (P6)

I want to be guided by experts. I can try things out and I have my own thoughts but I do need them to offer me feedback so that I feel relieved. I'm not an active person who takes initiatives to do things if not asked to. (P7)

This was true of their approach to the supplementary readings in the Study Guide. As some participants admitted, they did not read these materials because they were not required to do so:

I didn't read them because I thought they were not required. I think if the course writers want us to read these, they need to create a small task. Even a simple question like 'What do you think of this?' will give us the need to read. (P5)

Some of these answers appear to contradict participants' characterizations of themselves (in their responses to the questionnaire) as autonomous learners. Some at least still seemed to consider learning a task set by others and were unwilling to extend the limits of their learning beyond what was required.

Teachers as practitioners

Although the five weeks of the pilot were too short for clear evidence of teacher autonomy to be visible, there was some evidence of quite striking effects on participants' thinking. The experience clearly made the teachers think about what they were learning. One of the participants said: *"unlike traditional teaching, I can't stop thinking about it because it's not a 45-minute lesson. I have to think about it all month"* (P6). Other participants realized that learning online made them think harder because they could not choose not to listen as they might in a classroom. As P1 commented:

I feel this is really demanding. It is more complicated than studying in a classroom where you might choose not to listen or think. However, learning online makes people think more and learn to study on your own.

Participants' written reflections also revealed that their beliefs had been challenged by activities which involved them in experimenting with new kinds of activities, recording their lessons and reflecting on the experience.

I've recorded two of my lessons and I feel they were so interesting. Students really communicated in my class! I want to record another one to see whether it's better. (P8)

Some of the ideas introduced in the course material also opened a new window for participants. They began to reflect on their practice and explore ways to make use of new ideas:

When I was learning the unit about grammar, I thought about my own way of teaching. I want to summarize my teaching methods first and try some of the methods introduced here. (P5)

When I finished some of the tasks, I wanted to compare my thoughts with the course writers' and I would copy their explanations if there is any difference. After I learned the example of "the usage of some and any", I asked myself whether I could use similar methods in teaching other words. (P1)

Although not all were convinced, they were obviously prompted to give serious consideration to the new ideas:

I'm a bit worried about using games with my students. Will they focus on the content or the form? They probably will enjoy doing the game but they won't learn as much as I want them to. (P9)

Professor Wang said we shouldn't give spelling check everyday, but I feel insecure if I don't do this everyday. Students also feel they have nothing to learn if you don't give dictation. At least students who are of middle or upper level will recite words after class. Spelling check is actually interrupting the teaching flow of the whole class, but I don't know whether I can really give it up. (P8)

Such critical thinking perhaps signals the beginning of autonomy.

Self-reports suggest that some teachers not only thought more about what they had learned but also started to change what they had been doing in their classrooms. One questioned her past teaching practice and tried something different with her students, which brought about a very positive result:

I reflect on what I did in the past and realized I put too much pressure on students. Neither the students nor I were happy. I recorded my lesson yesterday and I felt that I talked too much. Then I thought about the ways to realize learner-centred classroom. I thought about this in the past but not as shocked as I am now after the course. In the past, I felt as long as students did well in the exam, they should be happy and that was the correct thing for me to do. But now I feel there might be better ways to achieve the same result. Why should I make learning and teaching such a torture? Now I feel I should try to change myself. I didn't leave any homework in the past two weeks and changed my way of motivating them. I praised them for any progress they made and I allowed them to be tested in different content. Those who can't read well can choose to be tested on reading and those who can't write well can choose to be tested on spelling. My students really accept this change and do learn even if there is no homework. I feel very happy for them and for myself. (P6)

In the Chinese context, where students, teachers and parents consider exams and marks the most important thing in life, this is a very creative and brave way to teach. However, the response of her students appears to justify her faith in what she was doing.

Finding a voice

■   *The discussion forum relating to the video-recorded lesson* (**Figure 4.5**)

Messages about the lesson provoked 15 postings in the discussion forum, compared to an average of 3.3 postings on other topics. Analysis of these discussion messages reveals not only that the lesson helped participants to clarify the concept of learner-centredness (one of the intended outcomes) but that they were also prepared to share their comments about the lesson, raise concerns and worries about classroom practice, and offer suggestions. In short, the lesson stimulated reflection on practice and on participants' own practices. Here is just one example:

Table 4.2
Extracts from the Forum

Do you feel you learned anything from watching the lesson and answering the questions?
If so, what?

How far were your own views similar to those of Dr McGrath? Do you agree with everything
he said?

Do you think you will make any changes to your own teaching as a result of this activity?

I really feel I did learn a lot from this part. — 1. To be a natural teacher. 2. To respect and cherish Ss' work. 3. To try to give every student proper opportunities to present himself in class.

I agree with Dr. McGrath totally. What he said made me know more clearly what to do and how to do in the future.

I will make some changes to improve my teaching and encourage my Ss from now.

But recently, a problem is troubling me: I'm trying to take more group work in class. But my Ss sit individually and it's impossible to move the desks and chairs before every class. And don't want to change a place, either. What should I do?

It will be clear from this and other quotations reproduced in this section that the experience of working with the pilot materials, in a safe learning community with an understanding tutor, did produce many of the desired effects. Participants had certainly started to find their own voices. In the longer term, we hope that they will have been encouraged to find their own way.

Conclusion

We have considered how the development of a capacity for autonomy through scaffolded experiences involving choice, self-assessment, progress monitoring, conscious reflection on learning, and opportunities for autonomous decision-making can support online programme participants in acquiring the independent learning skills necessary for success in this increasingly popular mode of learning. The importance of such support cannot be overestimated:

> To create a successful learning experience, it is paramount to develop self-directed learners in the first place. By so doing can web-based education grow into a new educational paradigm rather than a clone of traditional campus-based mode. (Wang 2004: 15)

The materials in this project, as partly described above, support this development in the following ways: they focus on *learner factors* by encouraging participants to explore themselves as learners on the programme, e.g. their past learning experiences, beliefs about and attitudes towards learning, their learning preferences, personalities, and affective and physiological needs as learners. They focus on *contextual factors* by encouraging the participants to explore their learning contexts and the constraints that hinder the promotion of learner-centred methodology, autonomy and the use of ICT, e.g. student attitudes and preferences, large classes, examinations, time constraints, and they consider appropriate ways of dealing with these. The materials focus participants on *language teaching* by encouraging them to explore the theory and practice of learner-centred language teaching methodologies, the promotion of greater learner autonomy, and the use of new technologies in language learning and teaching. Finally, they focus participants on the *processes of learning* by encouraging them to reflect critically on their learning and teaching, develop awareness of suitable learning and professional development strategies (e.g. metacognitive, cognitive and socio-affective strategies; O'Malley and Chamot 1990), experiment with new ideas and practices and evaluate these.

The field of e-learning is continually and rapidly evolving, and it is clear that projects such as those funded by the HEFCE (Higher Education Funding Council for England) for *eChina-UK* are only stepping stones to the future. We suggest that further research and development work is required, focusing on online methods and technological tools to support successful independent study. In particular, longitudinal studies following the experiences of learners and tutors, as well as the effects on their personal and professional development, would be useful. As the teaching profession becomes more familiar with the requirements and constraints of developing e-learning programmes, there is a growing need for the development of new, evidence-based courses for the training of e-tutors and, indeed, for e-learning course developers on how to encourage and support the necessary learning skills for independence and lifelong learning.

5

A Socio-Emotional Approach to Building Communities of Learners Online

Carol Hall, Eric Hall and Lindsay Cooper

Introduction

It has long been recognized that English language teaching in China is teacher-centred, textbook-based and examination-orientated, with an emphasis on the teaching of grammar and vocabulary at the expense of language skills and communicative competence. Recently however, two events in particular demonstrated the urgency with which the Chinese Ministry of Education (MoE) would need to introduce policies which would require teachers to shift the emphasis from the grammar-translation method to pedagogical approaches aimed to develop the communicative competencies of listening and speaking. These two events are the entry of China into the World Trade Organization in 2001 and the announcement that Beijing would host the Olympic Games in 2008.

The requirement to supply large numbers of confident, fluent English language speakers to business communities nationwide necessitated an urgent and wholesale reform of the national curriculum for language education from primary to tertiary. The MoE's New Curriculum for the teaching of English language (see Spencer-Oatey, this volume, pp. 4–5), with its emphasis on communicative competence, demands that teachers re-engineer the way they design and deliver language classes, and the incorporation of ICT as a learning resource is seen as integral to the process. In order to deliver the reform agenda, teachers are required to undergo extensive in-service training, which demands of them no less than a seismic shift in the way that they conceptualize and carry out their role. It is also recognized that Web-based courses of study will be needed to augment the opportunities for traditional forms of face-to-face (F2F) in-service training, given the sweeping nature of the reforms and the enormity of the task which lies ahead. For the profession, adopting a learner-centred approach to language teaching will mean undergoing a *psychological* as well as a pedagogical transformation process. Development of the MA eELT (e-English language teaching) was in part a project designed to produce examples of Web-based advanced teacher training materials which are capable of delivering on the professional transformation agenda for teachers at the tertiary level. The Personal Development for Professional Purposes element within the master's programme was designed to specifically address the *psychological* and *emotional* demands that role transformation will make on teachers.

But exactly who were our target learners, and what conclusions might we draw from knowing more about their social and emotional needs as well as their professional needs in a period of fast-paced educational reform? Demographic data suggested that the typical learner profile for a teacher wishing to undertake a Web-based course of advanced professional study, such as the MA eELT, would be a mid-career, female language tutor at tertiary level with a family and limited time to devote to study but with a strong desire for career advancement (Gu, Hall, Sinclair and McGrath 2005). A study (Chen 2006) carried out with a group of Chinese secondary school English language teachers, evaluating online learning materials at undergraduate level, provided a helpful reminder that, since

> teachers are the target learners of web-based teacher education, there is a need to understand their culture and thoughts so that suitable e-learning materials can be designed and delivered successfully. (Chen 2006: 1)

In addition, Chen's study revealed that what these learners said they wanted from Web-based study was:

- a clear relevance to their own context;
- the capacity to facilitate learner autonomy and reflection;
- the opportunity to learn by *sharing*.

This same study revealed that both language teachers and their online tutors felt that ice-breaking and self-introduction tasks were needed in addition to the teaching of subject-specific material when working online. Such affective tasks would have the potential to shorten the psychological if not the physical distance between people and foster a community where shared learning could take place. Salmon (2005) notes that distance is not merely a geographical construct (distance in place and isolation from other learners) but a psychological one (distance in thoughts, feelings and aloneness). McConnell (2006) argues that learning in itself is a social process and therefore learning communities have the potential to foster both co-operative and collaborative forms of learning. Sclater and Bolander (2004) agree and point out that 'community' by itself does not guarantee production of co-operative or collaborative behaviours in members and thus cannot be taken for granted in learning design. McConnell underscores this point when he argues that e-learning designers and tutors are challenged to see their students in "the light of the post modern self", who "do not want to become isolated but are interested in social relations and interactivity" (McConnell 2006: 2).

We argue that building communities of learners online requires course developers in their production of materials, design of tasks and creation of the technological infrastructure, to aim consciously to reduce emotional distance and promote interactivity, social cohesion, co-operation and collaboration between peers and tutors. Thurston, in a study of 31 master's students supported in their course of study by a virtual learning environment, reached a similar conclusion:

> Considering how to develop a sense of community and connectedness between students could therefore be a critical design feature that is vital to the success of online learning opportunities. (Thurston 2005: 366)

Findings from his study also indicated that students who actively engaged in online learning opportunities reported a heightened sense of connectedness in relation to the wider learning community.

> Findings from the research indicated that carefully structured VLEs [Virtual Learning Environments] can provide the potential for students, educators and communities to be fully connected without the limitations imposed by spatial and temporal barriers. (Thurston 2005: 367)

The Nottingham-BFSU (University of Nottingham and Beijing Foreign Studies University) design team set out to create a learning environment which facilitated the systematic development of community through promoting learner intimacy via carefully structured tasks and experiential, interactive online exercises relevant to the personal and professional context of the learner, and which promoted managed levels of self-disclosure. Research undertaken by McPherson and Nunes (2004) graphically describes the lessons they learned after constructing the shell of a virtual social space (VSS) which failed to appreciate the need to carefully choreograph the community-building process. In McPherson and Nunes's study, 34 adult learners on a master's programme had revealed to them the importance of a social support network. Specifically, they mentioned that such a network should provide:

- support directly related to course tasks;
- confirmation of their own understanding through discussion with others;
- reassurance at critical points in the course;
- sharing of similar experiences and anxieties;
- a sense of connection with each other.

To facilitate the development of these social networks, the authors created a VSS for students, intending to re-create some of the amenities that might be available on campus; for example, notice boards with contact information, advice points, course news and committee minutes, contact with alumni and so on. Surprisingly, despite the evidence from their survey showing that learners really valued the sense of belonging to a learning community, the VSS failed. The authors cite a number of reasons for this failure. However, what does not seem to have occurred to them is that a paucity of social or self-presentational skills specific to online interaction might have been one of them,

> It was clear that respondents visited on a few occasions, but either weren't sure what to do next, got no response or feedback from messages posted, or never saw activity that convinced them others were making use of this space. (McPherson and Nunes 2004: 318)

Interestingly, a potent image used by one of their own respondents summed up the need for socio-emotional learning to be an explicit feature of online learning communities:

> the VSS as a social space is akin to sitting alone in a bar with no atmosphere drinking diet tango and, just before you leave, jot a cryptic message to say that you have been there on a post it note and stick it on the fruit machine — a bit sad really. (McPherson and Nunes 2004: 319)

Community Building Online

When people meet for the first time F2F, the impressions they form of each other are profound and long lasting. The two constructs which we unconsciously employ to judge others are along the 'warm–cold' dimension (Asch 1946) and 'like me–not like me' dimension (Kelly 1955). The cues to make these judgements are predominantly non-verbal, in the form of gestures, eye contact, physical attractiveness, gender, age, ethnicity, paralinguistic features and so on. These filter systems, though notoriously inefficient and inaccurate, are difficult to change. It seems that, once we have made our mind up about a person, no matter what he or she does differently or how hard the person tries to change our perception, we still cling to first impressions. This can be due to what has been called Uncertainty Reduction Theory (Berger 1987); that is, human beings above all dislike conditions of uncertainty and unpredictability in relationships. Speedy initial interpersonal appraisals give us the illusion of the certainty we crave, and help to reduce feelings of anxiety and cue us in to habitual behavioural patterns based on the conclusions we draw about the other person. However, two characteristics of high emotional intelligence are empathy and social adaptability (Goleman 1996), so it seems that some of us are more flexible when it comes to a readiness to cognitively restructure our perceptions of others in the light of new information or conflicting evidence. We believe that the ability to suspend initial judgements and to be prepared to rethink or revise our appraisals of learners' competence is a prerequisite for professional educators.

However, it seems likely that an individual's appraisal mechanism can be slowed or even controlled to some extent by the context within which the person is introduced to strangers for the first time. Taking account of the uncertainty reduction factor in the design of F2F or online learning environments is therefore crucial to the development of resilient and lasting interpersonal bonds. In other words, the mismanagement of the introductory or formation phase of an online community can result in a sense of isolation, weak social affiliation and a reluctance to disclose views or opinions which might lead to hostile or critical reactions from others. Data reveal high student dropout rates from online education courses in China, and this might be an indication of the extent to which affective factors such as social networks and friendship groups have been ignored in the materials and technological design processes.

We know, however, that we ignore these psychological variables at our peril. As Wallace points out:

> Much of the early research on socio-emotional expression online, the kind that leads to impressions of a person's warmth or coldness, showed that we all seem cooler, more task orientated and more irascible than we might in person. (Wallace 1999: 18)

If indeed this is the case, as Wallace claims, then course designers need to adopt techniques which improve the likelihood of warm first encounters. We also know that social behaviour is promoted through self-disclosure, verbal interaction and sharing personal information such as family histories. In other words, materials designers need consciously to create a learning environment which reduces uncertainty and promotes increased levels of self-disclosure, if they are to build community successfully. The elements of building communities of learners online have been summarized by Rovai (2002) as spirit, trust, interaction and learning. He recognizes the importance of socio-emotional interactions in promoting self-disclosure, building trust and thus enhancing learners' sense of community. He defines spirit as cohesion and bonding that produces feelings of friendship, and he sees it as essential to the development of an environment that promotes both intellectual challenge and emotional nurturing. Rovai identifies trust as a second element that engenders candour in social exchanges so the members of the community are more likely to identify gaps in their learning, in the expectation of a supportive response from others.

Altman and Taylor's (1973) social penetration theory argues that people are like onions, in so far as interpersonal trust and bonding increase over time, as levels of disclosure move from superficial to intimate. Social-emotional interactions such as self-disclosure are generally reciprocal, and so contribute to social exchange and friendship creation (Jourard 1971). Web-based community builders need to respect and harness this interactional layering process when designing activities which require the sharing of personal information. Tasks which require high levels of disclosure in the form of personal information, academic judgement or critical reflection, too early in a course of study, are likely to engender anxiety and uncertainty in the learner. Designers need to stage tasks according to the perceived level of learner disclosure they require.

Initial Planning and Design Process of the PDPP (Phase 1)

The Personal Development for Professional Purposes (PDPP) course design team were conscious of the need to develop the social and support-giving skills of learners as well as providing the technical infrastructure for social exchanges (a house, after all, is not a home). The PDPP course sat within the MA eELT as part of a foundation module and in sum had two educational aims:

- to create resilient affiliative and emotional bonds between learners and between learners and tutors in an online environment and to enable the participants to be capable of reproducing these conditions with their own learners in either F2F or Web-based environments;
- to develop the emotional intelligence of English language teachers in order to support their personal and professional development and confidence in delivering the new curriculum in English language teaching.

The innovatory feature of the course is that it was designed to develop community spirit, promote interpersonal communication and develop relationship skills simultaneously. Using Hall's (2003) emotional development curriculum as a model, the team set out to develop these innovatory features using an experiential, interactive, task-based approach. It was intended that the PDPP course would satisfy the personal needs of learners to engage in shared learning and knowledge creation within a community of practice and that it would meet the professional development challenge created by the national reform of the language curriculum.

The course development process began with the team articulating a set of shared educational goals on a series of informal, team-building 'away-days'. These team development events produced the following work schedule for the collaborative project:

- first, establish if there was a set of epistemological values and beliefs that the Sino-UK partners shared in relation to personal and professional learning;
- then, translate these shared values and beliefs into actionable theories related to individual and group psychosocial development, pedagogical and educational practice and technological innovation;
- apply these theories to the development of Web-based educational materials;
- design a research model which was capable of generating formative and summative feedback to each phase of the design process;
- provide accounts of learning in relation to intercultural collaboration in a multidisciplinary team.

From these often passionate and enthusiastic discussions, what emerged was a core educational value summed up by the phrase, 'whole person development'. This value became embodied in the aims and objectives of the MA eELT programme:

> It is our conviction that it takes all-round qualities for a trainee to be successful in the study of the programme and in their future duties as ICT-competent teachers of English in the Internet era. (Gu, Hall, Sinclair and McGrath 2005: 26)

Whole person development was a construct informed by the work of the positive psychology movement (Seligman 2003; Linley and Joseph 2004) and conceptually incorporated the intellectual, emotional and spiritual dimensions to personal and professional growth. While recognizing that terms such as 'whole person development', 'fully-functioning individual' (Rogers 1961) or 'self-actualizing person' (Maslow 1954) were culturally saturated, the Sino-UK team found that philosophically we appeared to be in fundamental agreement over what this approach to learning and teaching represented. However, it was in the interpretation and design of what are commonly called 'learner- or student-centred' online learning tasks (Salmon 2005) that divergences of view would later emerge. These were not always as might be anticipated on cultural grounds but rather educational, stylistic or 'taste' differences.

Factors in Materials and Task Design for PDPP

As we have argued previously, the development of an online community conducive to emotional and academic learning cannot be taken for granted. Electronically mediated communication on the whole is devoid of the normal range of non-verbal and paralinguistic features which characterize F2F social intercourse. As a result of the absence of real-time cues such as smiles, nods, frowns, winks, hand gestures and so on, electronic exchanges can take on very different meanings for both originator and recipient. The accurate reading of feelings and emotions in authentic online communication becomes fraught with difficulty; hence the early development in Internet chat rooms of emoticons. People generally want to communicate feelings in order to be more fully understood. This is intriguing when put together with the findings of Kruger et al. (2005) that actually people *believe* they are able to communicate more effectively via an electronic medium than they actually can. This overconfidence, they argue, is borne out of egocentrism and an inability to take on board the perspective of the receiver of the message. Perspective taking, seeing the situation *as if* you were the other person, is a dimension of empathy, itself a key element of emotional intelligence (McCrae 2000), and it would seem likely that the higher the level of empathic understanding, the lower the level of egocentrism, which is why the PDPP course emphasized the development of empathy in the emotional skills development curriculum.

Structure of the Personal Development for Professional Purposes Course (Phase 2)

Using the conceptual framework drawn from psychosocial theory discussed previously, the PDPP course was designed around four units of study, namely:

- Unit 1 Understanding Yourself
- Unit 2 Personal Relationship Skills
- Unit 3 Learning to Support Students and Colleagues
- Unit 4 Setting and Achieving Life Goals

Taken as a whole, the course of study focuses on intra- and interpersonal development, counselling, empathic and helping skills and goal setting. Tasks are designed with the English language teacher in mind but are in themselves sufficiently generic to be adapted for use with other groups of learners. At the outset, learners are provided with a rationale for introducing personal development as a way not only of building an online community but also of developing their emotional intelligence to support their personal and professional relationships on- and offline.

From a pedagogical perspective, the course was designed as a series of linked experiential and task-based exercises (Beard and Wilson 2002) which challenge the learners to reflect on themselves and how they relate to others. Experiential learning refers to learning that derives from authentic experience rather than learning vicariously through lectures or texts. This learning can emerge from real-life experience or from experiences structured by a course designer or facilitator, as in the two exercises we describe below. Once completed, the initial task provides the experience which the learners are encouraged to reflect upon and consider in relation to modifying or adapting future behaviour. Having undergone the reflective and goal-setting elements, they then repeat the process in what Kolb (1984) describes as the experiential learning cycle. Other experiential methodologies included the use of fantasy, imagery, relaxation, goal-setting, real-life problem-solving, and paired and co-operative group work.

Some critics might argue that developing intra- and interpersonal intelligence can only be achieved in a F2F learning environment. The challenge for the design team was how to adapt the experiential approach to a Web-based environment, as experiential learning in human relations involves the experience and communication of feelings which are not readily or easily communicated via technology.

Here we provide two examples from Unit 1, Understanding Yourself, to illustrate how the design team set about facilitating the process. Both tasks invite learners to engage with each other at an emotional level and lead to mutual but managed self-disclosure. The first example, 'Choose a Panda', is a classic warm-up exercise or ice-breaker (Lewis and Allen 2005) and is the very first interactive task of Unit 1. Following a short, informal video welcome message from the course team, it provides a means for the learning group to make initial contact with each other in a light-hearted and playful manner. The 'Choose a Panda' task allows them to share some of their initial feelings related to embarking on an online course and this unit in particular, and promotes at an early induction stage, a sense of group-belonging and community. The second example, 'The Self-disclosure Card Game', also taken from Unit 1, asks learners to consider their patterns of self-disclosure at a deeper level, although still within the context of a game. The game environment provides the learner with the emotional security that he or she cannot lose face, as this is 'play' rather than academic 'work' (Liu and Littlewood 1997). The 'Choose a Panda' example can be viewed on the eChina-UK website: http://www.echinauk.org/cases/nottingham/pandas.php/.

The tasks themselves were designed to create maximum visual impact, using strong colours, cartoon-type characters and stylized images in keeping with popular Chinese culture; for example, kites, pandas, mythological figures, and so on. This was intended to create cognitive dissonance in the learner and turn on the head stereotypes of academic environments as being serious and stuffy. The aim was to create a task which actively intrigued and involved the learner from the outset. An additional element was to make the visual presentation of the exercises 'funky', meeting the criteria set by the 74 e-learners surveyed by Lambe (2002), for the *Straits Times* newspaper in Singapore. When asked about the immediate visual impact of the 'Choose a Panda' exercise, one of the female trial volunteers commented:

> *I just think pandas are very cute, so when I saw the pandas gambolling on the tree, I just thought, 'Oh how nice', and I wanted to actually take part. I wanted to get my hands on the exercise.*

A male participant noted that the cartoon-like style of the images seemed off-putting: "I thought it was maybe an exercise for younger aged school levels", yet it still managed to capture his interest:

> *. . . and I'm there talking about it being for school children and I'm saying I found it entertaining, so that might worry me a little bit, but it was . . . it was good.*

Experiential Learning Task: Example 1, Choose a Panda

The 'Choose a Panda' ice-breaker presents learners with a screen displaying a stylized tree with 24 playful-looking pandas in different positions on and around it, from waving cheerily to looking decidedly precarious. Each panda has a number in order to be able to identify its exact position on the tree (see Figure 5.1).

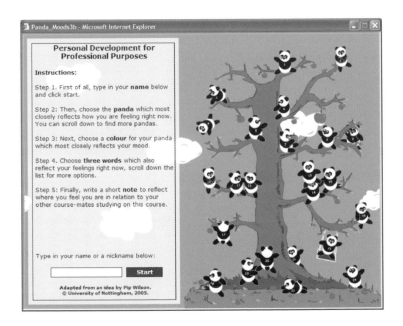

Figure 5.1 Screenshot from 'Choose a panda' Task

The first instruction is to choose the panda which best represents the learner's feelings at the forming or induction stage of the course (Salmon 2005). The choice of panda is a conscious projection of each learner's own state-of-mind as he or she begins the unit and will lead to sharing of this information informally with fellow 'pandas'. Next, learners are asked to use the brush provided and colour in their chosen panda with a colour selected from a palette, the colour representing their mood at that particular time. The next stage is to choose three words from an emotional vocabulary menu which best represents their mood in words. A final mouse click reveals a postcard with their chosen panda as a stamp, and learners are asked to compose a brief message explaining their choice of panda using three words from the vocabulary menu. For example,

Hi there fellow pandas,

I chose the panda waving from the middle branch because I feel in a good mood at the moment. I'm happy to be on the course but a bit anxious about the assignment. Look forward to hearing from you all soon. PS I chose the colour red because I feel energetic (at the moment!).

Best wishes, Ye Ming.

The card is posted to the student *Workspace* (Joyes 2006; Joyes this volume) where it is possible to view everyone else's choices, begin conversations and develop a sense of the mood of the group. Throughout, we emphasize that learners are in control of the degree of personal disclosure. This makes it a self-managed process, in which the individual can reflect on the intra- and interpersonal impact of his or her disclosures in a safe environment.

Evaluation of the 'Choose a Panda' Exercise

A trial run of the Web-based exercise was carried out with a group of six volunteer graduates, from a range of cultural backgrounds (including Chinese), mixed gender, and in age similar to the target group. Following the trial run, an evaluation was undertaken to determine if the objectives of the exercise were being met, namely to:

- introduce learners to experiential learning online using easy-to-follow instructions, high-impact images and informal, stimulating tasks;
- provide an opportunity to reflect on personal feelings related to joining the course;
- encourage sharing these feelings with other learners (self-disclosure);
- bring the group together as a social unit, reducing feelings of uncertainty at the induction or forming stage of the group's life;
- improve learners' use of an emotional vocabulary and increasing the likelihood of presenting the self in a warm, open manner to others in the community (emotional development).

One hour, individual semi-structured interviews were conducted with five volunteers following the trial run. The interview probed the extent to which the design objectives that we outlined above had been met. There was evidence that volunteers were reflecting on their own experiences and were willing to share this with other members of their group. All commented positively on the design element, in particular the design of the pandas. One participant reported that the slowly moving clouds in the background had a calming, relaxing effect. As reported above, one respondent felt the design was rather 'young' but later found that he was intrigued by it, despite his reservations.

Three commented that the exercise encouraged a reflection on feelings that they would not normally engage in, indicating that new learning was taking place, particularly in relation to how they felt in the forming stage of relationships.

> *I learned it's one of those sort of reflexive moments when you think a bit more about how you're feeling at the moment and why.*

Four out of five reported that it was helpful to have three choices from the emotions menu, as they experienced a mixture of feelings while trying out the exercise. There was some initial reservation about sending their postcards, because they were unsure who would be reading them, but interestingly, they were all curious to read about the cards from others.

> *I'm reluctant to share these things. It's just that you don't know who else has access then I think a certain caution comes in.*

And,

> *I think it's very good to write a postcard and then I can see other people's postcards and know what they think and feel.*

The task seemed to go beyond mere self-disclosure, as the volunteers appeared to gain fresh insights into their feelings and their ability to share this insight with others. The hesitancy about sharing their experience appears to be offset by a burning curiosity to learn about other people's experience and reactions.

Experiential Learning Task: Example 2, The Self-disclosure Card Game

We have emphasized the importance of appropriate self-disclosure for the development of online learning communities and how this process needs to be carefully choreographed by course designers. 'The Self-disclosure Card Game' challenges learners to consider patterns of self-disclosure in their ongoing relationships and to reflect upon the inhibitions or boundaries they experience in relation to sharing this information with others. It shares the overall objectives of the Panda exercise but takes the particular issue of self-disclosure to a deeper level by inviting learners to identify which aspects of their lives they are willing to share, and with whom.

Initially, the learner is presented with playing cards against a green baize background, featuring silhouettes of real-life characters, such as father, mother, partner and so on. Along the bottom of the screen, there is a deck of cards, each card containing a topic such as, 'What makes me angry' or 'My health' (see Figure 5.2, p. 90).

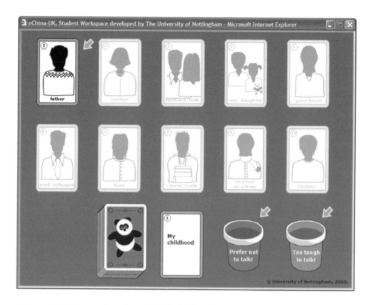

Figure 5.2   Screenshot from the 'Self-disclosure Card Game'

The learner is asked to consider each topic card in turn and decide whether he or she would be able to talk freely about it to each of the characters displayed. If the learner decides to talk freely about the topic, he or she drags and drops the topic card onto the character; if not, the learner drops it into one of two discard bins, either, 'Prefer not to talk' or 'Too tough to talk'. Finally, a screen will provide a visual summary of all the learner's choices. The learner is asked to reflect on the patterns of disclosure the collated data throws up and invited to discuss aspects of his or her learning with other members of the community. The response to the invitation gives the learner a further opportunity to become more aware of the parameters of his or her willingness to self-disclose in general and at the same time, the willingness to self-disclose within the community at that moment. However, the learner is not required to disclose (unless he or she chooses to do so) material directly related to the topics or the characters.

No theoretical explanations are offered in the preamble to the exercise, and in fact learners are encouraged to develop their own 'self-theory' through personal interpretation and analysis of data presented by the table of results. They develop self-theory in relation to their own reported behaviour patterns and consider their appropriateness. This is one approach to what has been described above as experiential learning (Beard and Wilson 2002). For many of us, this level of self-awareness and insight is available only if actively prompted. It is not an area of our lives which we often reflect upon, and for the learner, the collated data screen, provides a rare opportunity to receive feedback in a safe, controlled environment, reducing learner uncertainty.

Evaluation of 'The Self-disclosure Card Game'

A trial run of 'The Self-disclosure Card Game' was conducted with a group of six volunteer graduates, who had not participated in the 'Choose a Panda' evaluation process but whose profiles matched the first group. These volunteers were asked to complete the card game online and then each was interviewed to elicit his or her responses in relation to the objectives previously outlined.

All six found the instructions clear and easy to follow, and five reported that presentation of the task 'grabbed' their interest. Three reported total involvement in the task, while one found it neither interesting nor boring. The volunteers were asked about their emotional reaction to the completed task, and four reported initial feelings of anxiety, sadness and even apprehension about the possibility of changing their behaviour in the light of what they had learned about themselves. Superficially, these may appear to be negative reactions but in our view reflect a new understanding of the need for change generated by the exercise. Several volunteers were surprised by the limited communication they had with their parents, and this in particular was a source of sadness, though they were glad of the opportunity to reflect on these issues:

> *it brought to light a lot of things that I would think are probably hidden, like for example my relationship with my parents.*

And,

> *Well, I think it made me think . . . should I be more open to my parents? I think I should. I've been looking for the opportunity to be more open to them, so probably now that it's in my face, you know, I'll probably need to do that.*

None felt embarrassed by taking part in the exercise, even when asked directly about this. Five volunteers provided examples of new learning as a result of completing the exercise, the sixth reporting that it merely told her what she already knew. For three of the volunteers, the learning was regarded as important and they expressed this with feeling.

> *I felt bad at certain times when I was saying I couldn't discuss this with certain people, especially people that are close to me.*

None expressed concern about sharing their responses to the task with an online group. Three of them would positively welcome it. There were reservations expressed about sharing F2F, but this was still not regarded as particularly difficult. One spontaneously referred positively to the privacy afforded by working onscreen. Interestingly, there was a minimal preference overall for sharing thoughts and feelings online rather than F2F.

> *I think I find it easy and comfortable to have online discussions. This is because I am not looking at the person and the element of shyness is not there. I can sometimes be a shy person and don't always like looking at people in the eye when talking. So this medium removes those barriers.*

Two of the volunteers suggested that there should be a third discard bin, but for different reasons. One would have liked a category, 'Would have loved to talk to them, but they would not be interested', and the second, 'It depends on the situation'. This implies that the individuals were so involved in the task that they identified patterns of their own self-disclosure that were masked by the exercise and wanted to volunteer ways of improving the task design.

Discussion

Both experiential tasks engaged the attention of the volunteers who found them fun to do. The instructions were easy to follow and the design element strong.

> *I think the pandas had a big impact on me . . . I was definitely interested in taking part.*

The exercises tapped into real feelings and emotions that were immediately relevant to the volunteers and revealed emotional and behavioural patterns that they had not previously been aware of, until they viewed the summary data onscreen. In spite of initial hesitation, the majority were not only happy but eager to share personal findings with other group members, and several were keen to see other people's responses. These reports, although limited in number, indicate the extent to which the tasks triggered community building through a direct connection with socio-emotional learning and a reduction in the uncertainty factor through promotion of managed levels of learner disclosure.

> *I just wrote it according to the feeling I had at the moment . . . and I think it's very good to write a postcard and then I can see other people's postcard and know what they think and feel.*

Both tasks generated self-awareness by providing a rich source of both intra- and interpersonal learning.

> *If someone were to ask me how I was feeling, I may not have expressed it the way I did here because I was reacting to what I could see . . . (the task) gave me the opportunity to come out and express my views using the visual things that were there.*

A noteworthy feature was that both volunteer groups responded to the tasks in similar ways. No one reported that the tasks felt inappropriate to their personal or professional context. Experiential tasks are sometimes criticized for lacking cultural sensitivity, but no evidence of this was reported in the cross-cultural groups of volunteers, which confirms previous research and professional academic experience of working with cross-cultural groups experientially (See, Hall and Hall 1998).

Conclusion

The small-scale evaluations reported here form part of work-in-progress and the tasks discussed are just two out of many which make up the four units of study on the PDPP course. Further research with target learners needs to be undertaken to determine questions related to the extent to which experiential learning in human relations online can develop emotionally intelligent behaviour which is transferable to the F2F situation. However, initial responses to the tasks reported here indicate that individuals are willing to engage in experiential exercises online which involve significant degrees of personal learning and have the potential to contribute in positive ways to the socio-emotional development of a learning community.

CUTE:
A Flexible Approach to the Integration of Online and Face-to-Face Support for Language Learning

Debra Marsh, Eric Brewster, Nicola Cavaleri and Anny King

Introduction

The *CUTE* (**C**hinese **U**niversity **T**eacher Training in **E**nglish) Project is one of the component projects of the *eChina-UK Programme*. In its initial phase, which is known as *CUTE 1* and is reported here, the project involved staff at the University of Cambridge (UoC) and Tsinghua University working collaboratively to design, develop and deliver two integrated English for Academic Purposes (EAP) course modules that combine online learning support materials with face-to-face (F2F) interaction.

The aim of the *CUTE* Project is to develop a course which will enable Chinese teachers to teach their specialist subjects in English and to participate effectively in academic exchange. The project responds directly to a Chinese Ministry of Education (MoE) proposal, issued in 2001, that university lecturers should teach a proportion of their classes in English (see Spencer-Oatey, this volume, pp. 4–5 for more details). *CUTE* thus aims to develop an integrated online/F2F EAP course in order that Chinese university teachers may communicate more effectively and appropriately in English, teach specific subjects in English, and write and present papers in English at international conferences and colloquia.

This chapter discusses the initial pilot phase of the *CUTE* Project, which explored an integrated online/F2F approach to language learning. This approach was founded on the fundamental principle of learner support and built upon the principle of the integration of online and F2F language support developed by the Language Centre at the UoC and implemented since 2000 through their Cambridge University Language Programme (CULP).[1]

e-Learning, Online Learning and Language Learning

Despite the millions of dollars that have been spent [. . .] we have [. . .] failed to deliver on many of the earlier promises of e-learning. [. . .] teachers have been drawn to assurances of increased quality of learning, while students have eagerly anticipated the opportunities for just-in-time, just-for-me, just-enough, learning. Unfortunately, evidence that these promises have been realised is thin on the ground. (Alexander 2004)

Many today would agree with Alexander that the early e-learning initiatives of the 1990s resulted in varying degrees of success. Indeed, it is recognized that the early days of e-learning, with some notable exceptions, have left a legacy of unfulfilled promises in which a number of expansive claims were made but which, by the turn of the century, had simply not lived up to expectations. What, then, went wrong? In an attempt to find answers as to why early e-learning initiatives appear to have failed to live up to expectations, a number of key issues have been identified (Mitchell 2003; BECTA 2004). These issues serve as important lessons learned for anyone embarking on the latest e-learning initiatives.

Firstly, the early e-learning initiatives were predominantly technology led. Persuasive arguments by vendors and computer experts alike for the widespread installation of learning management systems (LMS)[2] appeared to suggest that the technology provided the backbone of e-learning. However, e-learning initiatives today tend increasingly to be led by the learning professionals themselves, with a clear view that we do not necessarily need the complexities of an LMS to support our learners learning online and that instead we should be exploring the appropriate use of the technology in response to learning and learner needs (Achacoso 2003).

Secondly, early e-learning content was primarily focused on off-the-shelf, externally sourced generic resources which did not necessarily take into account individual and group learner needs. Much was made of the promises of reusable content which would be learner, context and even pedagogically neutral. This view has now evolved, and today we are seeing moves towards more tailored development, relevant to individual learner needs and the learning context (CIEL Project 2000; Conole and Dyke this volume).

Thirdly, e-learning technology has been considered a 'cost-saving' way of eliminating the tutor. This view is increasingly losing value and the tutor's role is today considered essential, to create, support and implement e-learning. The self-paced, 'do-it-yourself' approach for learners, with minimal support from either online tutors or other learners, did little to motivate the early online learner. Today, it is widely recognized that successful e-learning needs proactive support from tutors and greatly benefits from collaborative support from other learners. Second language acquisition (SLA) research has shown that appropriate support from the tutor can undeniably make a significant contribution to the language learning process (Larsen-Freeman and Long 1991: 6), and a recent study (Lamping 2004) suggests that many learners find learning a language on their own hard to sustain over time because of the isolation of the learning experience and difficulties maintaining motivation.

In short, too much attention was paid to the 'e' in e-learning (in other words, the technology), at the expense of what really lies at the very heart of it all, the learner and the learning process. As a result, and quite justifiably, e-learning has been heavily criticized for an overemphasis on technological development for materials delivery and information management, rather than focusing on the "learner and enabling students and other users to develop more independence in learning and to share resources" (HEFCE 2005: 4).

Language learners are no strangers to the use of technology, as computers were applied in the language learning process some 50 years ago in the early days of CALL (Computer Assisted Language Learning) (cf. Gu, this volume, pp. 39–41, 47–48). On the face of it, today's technology appears to provide the solution that was much sought after in the early years of CALL, namely, the need for interaction and interpersonal support for effective language learning. Many are now exploring the potential of the online medium to develop communicative competence, including the following: Colburn (1998), who explores the use of role-play over IRC (Internet Relay Chat) with non-native speakers of English; Lapadat (2002), who examines the effectiveness of asynchronous written interaction for language learning; Lee (2004), who details a study in which network collaboration between native Spanish speakers with American learners of Spanish is used; and Warschauer (2004), who explores the use of the Internet for English language learning.

It is generally accepted that the online environment, as with any other medium, tool or technology, has the potential to enhance the process of learning, if, and only if, it is used appropriately. In language learning, we also need to factor in the very complexity of the language learning process itself.

> L2 [Second language] learning is itself perhaps the most challenging subject [. . .] because of the multiple dimensions that are incorporated into the construct of communicative language ability, which is arguably the goal for many language learners. (Chapelle 2004: 13)

Language learning is a unique skill because it involves the communication of thoughts and feelings through "a set of sounds and written symbols used by the people of a particular country or region for talking or writing".[3] Technology cannot, and indeed probably will not for some time to come, replicate the human-to-human social interaction which is fundamental to learning a language for communication.

Today, calls to 'bridge the gap' between pedagogy and technology (Conole 2003; Maor 2004) focus our attention on the need to go back to the fundamentals of the learning process and recognize that the 'e' of e-learning is but one facet in a multidimensional process. As language educators, we need to identify the role that the online medium can effectively play in the language learning process and as a result identify its most appropriate use. An understanding of learner needs, the learning context and an appropriate use of the technology for the task at hand, are key fundamentals to effective e-learning and, as a logical consequence, to effective online language learning. In short, the use of technology to support language learning should be 'integrative' (Warschauer 2000) or as more recently termed by Bax (2003) 'integrated'. As outlined by Bax (2003: 26–7), an integrated approach starts with an analysis of learner needs and learning context before decisions about technology are considered.

CUTE: An Integrated Approach

As explained above, the *CUTE* pilot project was grounded in the principles established through the UoC Language Centre's experience of running integrated online/F2F language learning courses at basic and intermediate levels. These CULP courses, which have been running since 2000, offer two hours of F2F contact time per week, which is supplemented with one hour of online learning support material, developed in-house, that integrates with the classroom teaching.

The CULP integrated approach emphasizes learner support (McLoughlin 2002). This entails analysing learner needs and identifying the appropriate use of technology to support language learning. The focus is on ensuring that the strengths of each medium are maximized rather than attempting to replicate what happens in the classroom. In CULP, the online environment is primarily used for input (through authentic video/audio-based presentation of language, visualization, animation) to train receptive skills (listening and reading). It provides practice in the receptive skills and preparatory support or 'rehearsal' for real-life interaction. The decoding and deconstruction (analysis) of language happens online at a time selected by the learner and at a pace chosen by the individual.

The F2F classroom environment is used mainly for output (via role-play, simulation, and discussion-type activities) relevant to learners' interests and needs. These activities encourage the development of the productive skills (speaking and writing). Through active participation in the F2F environment, the learners benefit from immediate contact with and support from their tutors and peers, which provides them with the opportunity for authentic communication. In other words, the interaction allows them to negotiate meaning and construct a joint discourse (co-text), which helps them 'externalize' their knowledge (the language inside) and create their own texts (Hymes 1974).

The CULP approach to integrating online and F2F support provided the *CUTE* Project team with a key guiding principle, namely learner support, and a model on which to develop an integrated course appropriate to the Chinese university teachers' needs and learning context.

CUTE: The Learner Needs Analysis

The starting point for the *CUTE* Project was an analysis of learner needs. The needs analysis focused on three key areas: language needs, professional development needs, and views and attitudes towards online learning.

The learner needs analysis was conducted between September 2003 and January 2004 with 25 teachers from a range of different schools and departments at Tsinghua University. Most of the trainees were associate professors and most had completed their PhD degrees. Their teaching experience ranged from 1 to 30 years. None of them were language specialists; they were specialists in their own fields. They were all required to teach their specialist subject in English. The *CUTE* Project was voluntary and, as such, there was no official attendance requirement.

Each of the 25 trainees took a reading and a listening comprehension test and wrote a personal profile of his or her academic background, experience in learning English, and personal goals for the course. In September 2003, a team of Cambridge EAP tutors visited Tsinghua University and conducted 15-minute interviews with each of the Chinese teachers.

These interviews served as a useful means by which a more thorough and detailed profile for each teacher could be established.

Language needs

An analysis of the listening and reading tests and the oral performances in the interview sessions indicated there was a range of abilities within the group. The speaking levels ranged from 4 to 6.5 on the IELTS scale.[4] The Chinese teachers' listening test scores ranged from 4/40 to 19/40, and their reading test scores from 10/40 to 31/40 (representing a range of approximately 1 to 4.5 for listening and 2 to 4.5 for reading on the IELTS scale).

Equally, there was a range of ability in writing skills, particularly in the organization and structuring of ideas. It was clear that many of the trainees had had very little guidance in how to structure academic writing in English. Interestingly, despite their differing levels of proficiency in English, the Chinese teachers demonstrated very similar structural weaknesses, which allowed for some common ground in the syllabus in terms of grammatical guidance. However, more flexibility and a wider range of proficiencies needed to be catered for in writing, listening and reading skills.

Professional development needs

Unsurprisingly, given the requirements of the Chinese MoE, extrinsic rather than intrinsic motivation figured predominantly in the reasons they gave as to why they were taking part in the *CUTE* course.

All the teachers stated their main motivation for doing the *CUTE* course was to improve their English language skills for academic exchange and bilingual teaching. In order of priority, they identified the following language needs: to express themselves fluently in order to give lectures and presentations at international conferences; to write more effectively in order to increase their chances for international exposure through publications; to become more effective classroom teachers; to improve their listening skills in order to listen to lectures, media, and informal conversations. In addition to language needs, the teachers expressed their need to develop their teaching techniques and cross-cultural awareness. The needs analysis also revealed the teachers' need for reassurance that the knowledge and skills gained from the project would be directly applicable to their own teaching practice and as a result be of direct benefit to their learners.

Views and attitudes

The interviews revealed that very few of the teachers had had experience of using computers in language learning. What little experience they had had was limited to the training received in their required study of English — usually confined to reading texts and searching for words in the Chinese/English online dictionary — and to the occasional use of CD-ROM language training software. Interactive, Web-based support for language learning was unknown to the teachers. This information was important for planning the early F2F phase of the course, because it would clearly be important to support the teachers in their practical use of the computer and in independent learning.

The *CUTE* Course Content and Structure[5]

The needs analysis provided a target learner group profile upon which decisions about course structure and content could be made. In addition, the CULP experience of integrating online and F2F support informed the subsequent decisions as to which language skills were best served by the online and which by F2F support. In other words, the learner and the learning context were the starting point for the course design, followed by considerations of appropriateness of the medium for providing effective support for this target group of learners.

The ensuing *CUTE* pilot consisted of a three-month EAP course which integrated online learning support material (75 percent of the course) and F2F classroom interaction (25 percent of the course). It was structured in three stages. Each stage had a specific purpose, and each had a role to play in support of the learning process (see Table 6.1).

Table 6.1
The Structure of the Pilot Course

Stage	Number of Weeks	Mode of Delivery	Aims/Purpose
1	2 weeks	Face-to-face	• Language skills development • Learning to learn online • Integration of F2F and online
2	9 weeks	Online	• Independent learning with online support material • Tutor/peer support via a forum • Progress monitoring
3	1 week	Face-to-face	Evaluation of Progress

The 75:25 split between the two mediums represents more online, independent learning and less F2F classroom support than in the CULP courses. The F2F element for the *CUTE* pilot took place at the beginning and end of the course rather than, as with CULP, at regular weekly intervals. This difference was largely a matter of logistics, given the distance between the Chinese trainees and the Cambridge team, but was also recognition of the fact that all the trainees had full-time jobs and required periods of flexible learning at their own time and pace.

Stage 1: Face-to-face

The first stage of the three-month EAP course was conducted over a two-week F2F period in July 2004 at Tsinghua University. This stage was facilitated by native English speaker tutors from the UoC.

The primary focus of this stage was the development of those language skills best supported by F2F. This phase therefore focused on output, i.e. the productive skills of speaking and writing, appropriate use of language in context, and pronunciation practice. This stage also provided a basis upon which the Chinese trainees could further develop their language competence through the online support material. Integrating the online and F2F components of the course was therefore a key aim throughout this part of the course.

Awareness-raising of cultural issues in giving academic presentations, and the skills required to write academic papers, were also a key focus of this first phase. Studies, such as González, Chen and Sanchez (2001: 439), indicate that " . . . in order to achieve higher developmental levels in EFL [English as a foreign language] learning, students need to understand conceptual uses of language within a particular cultural way of thinking". It was felt that such conceptual understanding was best served by the F2F environment, which allowed for immediate feedback, open discussion and clarity of explanation and that this could then be followed up independently online.

The third key component of this stage was preparing the Chinese trainees to learn online. Learning to learn online is more than simply learning how to click on the buttons of onscreen navigation and learning tools. Learning online makes particular demands on learning in terms of independence, cyclical ways of learning, critical reflection, peer support and interaction, and time management skills. The two-week F2F stage provided important support for trainees unfamiliar with learning online, in particular independent learning and self-assessment. Much of the classroom interaction took place in small groups and was learner led, in order to prepare them to take responsibility for their own learning.

Stage 2: Independent learning

Following the two-week F2F course, the Cambridge team returned to the UK and the Chinese teachers embarked on nine weeks of independent learning, supported by the online material and facilitated by the Cambridge tutors via an online forum.

The online learning support material consisted of two modules, a Lecture Module and a Research Module, and focused on providing input (primarily through authentic video/audio-based presentation of language) to practise receptive skills (listening and reading). The purpose of the online learning support material was to build upon, and further develop, the language and skills focus of Stage 1. More specifically, it aimed to support the Chinese trainees in their preparation of a presentation to be given 'live' during the final stage of the course, in front of the Cambridge team and their Chinese peers. In addition, many of the Chinese trainees wished to submit academic papers to international conferences at the end of the course, and so the online material also aimed to support them in this task.

The Lecture Module consisted of four units, with three field-specific lectures (in earth sciences, computer technology and engineering) that corresponded closely to the different subjects of the Chinese teachers' fields, and one lecture to cater for interdisciplinary learners. Each unit within the Lecture Module focused on the skills of listening to lectures and giving presentations, and the lecture input formed the basis for addressing specific functional language and grammatical points related to the purpose of each lecture. A teaching skills section in the Lecture Module aimed at providing tips, and points for reflection, concerning presentation skills. The Research Module was designed to raise trainees' awareness of the steps involved in academic writing, and provided a step-by-step process approach to academic paper writing. This module also focused on the language, conventions and styles particular to writing abstracts for research papers and project proposals.

The online content for the *CUTE* course was designed on the principle of guided yet flexible paths through the input and activities, in order to respond to individual needs, language level and learning style. Flexible entry points allowed the more independent learner to choose his or her own language path (see Figure 6.1). For those learners who required some guidance, a suggested more linear path through comprehension and language manipulation activities towards a final production activity was available. Moreover, the modular design allowed for an individual approach to the tasks. The accessibility of the content online allowed the Chinese trainees to work at their own pace through the units.

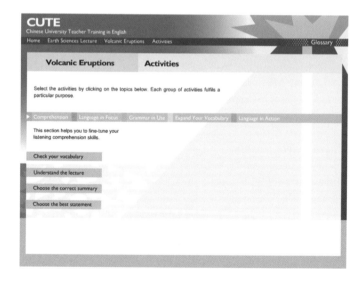

Figure 6.1   Flexible Entry Points in *CUTE 1*

Support for understanding was provided throughout the modules in the form of Activities, Key Functions, a Grammar section, a Transcript, Cultural Notes and a Glossary (see Figure 6.2).

Figure 6.2 Various Types of Support for Learning in *CUTE 1*

The activities in turn were supported by a range of techno-pedagogic help functions, in the form of tips and hints (for further details, see Zähner's discussion, this volume, of scaffolding and the Lifebuoy, pp. 136–138 and Figure 8.2), automated feedback, and model answers. These tools were designed to help the Chinese teachers make their own choices about what aspects of the key language they wished to practise, which tools they wished to use for assistance, and which activities were suited to their individual learning styles and interests.

The online forum

The purpose of the online forum in the *CUTE* pilot course was to provide continued tutor and peer support to the Chinese teachers during the independent online learning stage. It was not envisaged for this pilot that the forum would provide a focus for language development or language support. Instead, after preliminary guidance from the Cambridge tutors, the Chinese teachers were expected to take on responsibility for initiating and continuing discussions, as and when appropriate and required. The discussions were thus peer facilitated rather than tutor facilitated, in an attempt to encourage peer to peer support.

Stage 3: Face-to-face

The final week of the *CUTE 1* course was conducted F2F in Tsinghua and focused on assessing the Chinese teachers' oral presentation skills. The presentations were field specific and represented a wide range of subject areas. Each presentation was 15 to 20 minutes long, and was followed by 5 to 10 minutes of questions.

Nineteen teachers gave presentations; an additional two teachers were excused for medical reasons or because of personal circumstances. Thus, a total of 21 out of 25 trainees followed at least two-thirds of the entire *CUTE* programme.

Outcomes

The trainees had volunteered for the course and were not language specialists themselves. Their motivation for participating in the course was quite specific, namely to be able to teach their specialist subjects in English and to participate effectively in academic exchange. Thus, the final assessment of the course needed to reflect these specific learner needs. As a result, the trainees were asked to give a final presentation in their own specialist subject and to provide at least a draft version of a paper intended for publication.

Speaking skills: The presentations

The Cambridge tutors used an oral assessment marking sheet to record their comments on the performance of each Chinese teacher. Additional evaluators from the *CUTE* Project took turns in attending the presentations and used the same evaluation pro-forma. All the Chinese teachers were rated as performing from 3 (average) to 2 (above average) or 1 (well above average) on a five-point scale. The comments of the Cambridge team and additional evaluators were consistent with each other. Those who had participated most consistently in both the F2F and online components of the course demonstrated especially marked improvement, both in English language and in teaching/presentation skills.

Writing skills: The academic paper

The original intention had been for the Chinese teachers to submit a draft paper intended for publication. Given time limitations, this was not enforced, at the request of the Chinese teachers themselves. However, they were all, by the end of the course, in the process of preparing papers or presentations for international conferences and/or preparing lessons in English for bilingual teaching in order to immediately put into practice what they had learned during the *CUTE* pilot course. Over 50 percent of the trainees submitted their papers within six months of completion of the course, and all were accepted for publication.

Focus group feedback

The *CUTE* pilot course was evaluated by end-of-course questionnaires and focus group interviews, and was evaluated positively. The majority of the teachers reported that they felt more confident and better prepared to teach in English, present at international conferences and write for publication.

Without exception, the F2F component was reported as key to the success of the course. The trainees unanimously reported on the usefulness of the F2F component and were convinced that they would not have achieved so much had all the learning been online. They identified the following as key advantages of the F2F environment, namely opportunities provided for:

- speaking practice;
- correction of language and pronunciation;
- individual feedback and identification of strengths and weaknesses;
- meeting and practising authentic language in context;
- demonstrations of and practice in teaching methodology;
- explanations and practice of writing conventions, in particular the structure of academic writing in English.

The teachers felt the F2F to be a vital component, not only for language development but also significantly for preparing them for learning online. Without this support, their experience of the online learning would have been significantly different. Ideally, all trainees would have liked more F2F interaction; however, they did recognize the limitations in time and resource for such a provision.

The teachers reported that they found the video input the most interesting and useful part of the online course content. They found it particularly informative watching people's styles of presentation, their facial expressions and gestures, and the language and manner in which they talked about scientific topics. The identification of key functions was also found to be very useful, and for most, the grammar and vocabulary sections provided important support in their understanding of how the language is used in context.

The forum was the part of the pilot course in which the teachers engaged the least actively. Although generally the Chinese teachers did view the forum as a useful support tool, only one-third of them posted messages. The majority of these postings fell into one of the following three categories.

1. Requests for Language Explanations

    In Prof. Collins' Lecture, there is a sentence like: What I'd like to do is first of all describe the differences between . . . and . . . Why he use 'describe' here? I think 'to describe' or 'describing' is correct.

    What can I say politely when I have completely different ideas with the presenter in a lecture? Can anyone give me some (not only one) examples? Thanks in advance.

2. Requests for Technical Support

    I don't know if it is because my computer doesn't work, or the webpage can not be accessed these days.

3.   Requests for Peer Review of Writing

> *Dear colleagues, the following is a one-page abstract which my group is going to submit to a conference. If you would like, could you please review it and give your comments. I really appreciate your kind help. Thank you in advance.*

It would appear that, for the other two-thirds of the Chinese teachers, the usefulness of the forum lay in browsing the postings by their colleagues and the Cambridge tutors rather than actively engaging in discussion themselves. Input by the Cambridge tutors constituted over 50 percent of the postings in the forum, and of the total messages posted by the Cambridge tutors, more than half were in response to requests for language explanations. The Cambridge team did make several attempts to generate more structured online discussion and to explore grammar and vocabulary difficulties, but these were not followed through by the teachers themselves.

This would suggest that the support role identified for the forum at the beginning of the course was perceived as important by those teachers who sought help via the forum. However, the pursuit of general, online discussion was not necessarily perceived as vital to their immediate needs.

There were a number of reasons that can be attributed to the lack of activity in the forum. It is important to recognize that the Chinese teachers were not used to contributing openly to online forums. Such contributions may well have been perceived as potentially face threatening, in case they made a mistake in their English. In fact, one teacher did report that she would have been more likely to contribute to the discussions had she been able to do so anonymously.

The use of the forum to support learners is well documented in the e-learning literature and its use in language learning has shown a number of benefits. Chappelle (2004a: 12) suggests that "Learners can gain some L2 practice in online communication that may be valuable for performance in other contexts", e.g., in building and maintaining co-operative learning communities. Moreover, some studies (e.g. Gerbic 2005) indicate that the integration of computer-mediated communication can increase Chinese learner participation in group discussion because, unlike the immediate F2F context, asynchronous online gives time for reflection and more careful composition of responses. This is certainly an area for further consideration and research, and is to being explored in the follow-up phase of the *CUTE* Project.

Conclusion

This chapter opened with a review of a number of key issues which led to some disappointment in the early implementation of e-learning. The issues identified were attributed to the overemphasis on the technology at the expense of learning, on content-led development rather than a focus on learner needs, and on cost-saving and elimination of the tutor.

This pilot phase of the *CUTE* Project endeavoured to learn from the lessons of the past, and focused on the learning process, the learner, the appropriate use of technology to support language learning, and the key role played by the tutor. The rationale for integrating online with F2F learning was primarily based on the requirements specific to the characteristics of language and language learning processes, which require social interaction and authentic practice of the target language. The project did not attempt to establish a single model for the integration of F2F and online learning. Instead, it aimed to build on the key principle of learner support to produce an integrated course relevant to the learning needs of Chinese university teachers. The rationale for determining which skills are best developed online and which are best developed F2F remained essentially the same as with CULP; however, the implementation and focus of the online and F2F support differed, as it was determined in response to learner needs and context.

In line with Garrett (1991: 75), the *CUTE* team were keen to establish that the use of the computer does not constitute a method, but rather it is a "medium in which a variety of methods, approaches, and pedagogical philosophies may be implemented". In other words, the effectiveness of online language learning does not reside in the medium itself but in how it is used. Further research and development into this 'how' is ongoing with the next phase of the *CUTE* Project, currently in progress.

7

A Generic Framework for the Training of e-Learning Tutors

Gordon Joyes and Wang Tong

Introduction

This chapter presents a generic framework for the training of e-learning tutors. The need for such a framework emerged during the tertiary-level *eELT* Project of the *eChina-UK Programme*, in which the School of Education, University of Nottingham (UoN), UK, formed a collaborative partnership with Beiwai Online of Beijing Foreign Studies University (BFSU), Beijing, China. The *eELT* Project involved the development of exemplar online materials for a master's degree programme in English Language Teaching (MA eELT) which would be delivered wholly online (for more details, see the Case Study section of the *eChina-UK Programme* website: http://www.echinauk.org/). This ambitious development, with its wholly online mode of delivery, raised important questions about the nature of the support needed from e-learning tutors. Key issues included:

- What should be the curriculum for online tutor training within this context?
- What pedagogic model should be chosen?
- How should the programme be designed?
- Would it be possible to design a tutor training programme that would be applicable to a wide range of subject and cultural contexts?

The scope of the *eELT* Project precluded addressing these issues in detail, yet effective tutor training is vital for the successful delivery of online courses. So, a follow-up project, the *e-Educator* Project, was funded by the Higher Education Funding Council for England (HEFCE) and the respective institutions, in order to address these issues, and is currently in progress. This chapter discusses this *e-Educator* Project. The aim of the project is to develop effective training materials designed to enhance the quality of e-learning tutor support and thereby to enhance the student learning experience.

Our challenge has been to develop a tutor training curriculum that is of use to both the UoN and Beiwai Online, and yet also be applicable to a variety of other contexts. The

UK and Chinese partners needed to develop materials that could be of practical use in training tutors for the online programmes they offer, as they needed a return for the investment made. Beiwai Online needed to develop tutor training materials for use with the MA eELT, and the UoN needed tutor training materials for a range of tertiary-level online courses. We were also aware that there is a need for such materials in the higher education (HE) sectors as a whole, both in Britain and China, and so we wanted to develop a framework that would be of relevance to the sector as a whole. Kukulska-Hulme and Shield (2004) argue that there are subject specific pedagogies that apply to the online learning of languages, and so our challenge has been to ensure that the tutor training materials we develop can allow for these subject differences across online courses.

We argue that a new approach to tutor training is needed, in which tutors are not just trained to use the new learning tools/technologies of a given platform, or how to handle the tasks/activities within the course materials, but rather are provided with the conceptual tools to analyse such tools and materials for themselves. We propose that Activity Theory (Engeström 1987) offers a useful conceptual framework for facilitating such an approach.

In this chapter, we start by considering the training needs that classroom teachers have when they want/need to become e-learning tutors. Next we examine the current models for e-learning tutor training and their respective weaknesses, after which we present our generic framework. It consists of a curriculum framework, combined with a tool designed to support tutors in analysing online learning activities, so that tutors can provide appropriate support for learners. The resulting e-Educator module, which is designed for use across the HE sector in Britain, China and elsewhere, is described and exemplified.

e-Learning Tutor Training: Tutors' Needs

Working with new pedagogies and new tools for learning

Online learning in China, as elsewhere, is moving to flexible learning models (Taylor 2001) that provide a personalized and more student-centred learning experience. These are incorporating a wide range of media, all of which have to be managed in order to support learning. Transitions to these new approaches are inevitably difficult for the academic tutors supporting learning online, in that they are expected to work with new media which allow online asynchronous and synchronous communications, online feedback, online group work and so on, and yet such tutors are often recruited because of their traditional academic experience.

It is difficult to make generalizations about the pedagogy involved in online higher education courses, as these tend to be influenced by subject discipline (Joyes 2006a) and institutional cultures. Online courses often tend to reflect the variety of teaching and learning approaches that are used in face-to-face (F2F) modes (Oliver and Herrington 2001). For example, tertiary courses that are designed for continuing professional training tend to relate theory to practice and to encourage reflection and the sharing and co-construction of ideas. Therefore, the online versions of these courses tend to be complex, and characterized by activities that involve a mixture of self-study, personal reflection and collaborative working, and may incorporate a problem- solving/enquiry element (Joyes and Fritze 2006).

Increasingly, new online tools are being developed to support learning. For example, the *eChina-UK* Project materials developed by the UoN use an online student *Workspace* (Joyes 2006b; Joyes this volume, pp. 147–152) which has a range of functionality to support reflection, peer review, and formative and summative assessment. The use of authoring tools such as blogs for personal reflection and sharing of perspectives and wikis for collaborative working is now widespread in academic and social contexts on the Internet (Godwin-Jones 2003). Importantly, online tutors need to understand that e-learning can usefully encourage learner autonomy (Laurillard 1993) and that the learning tools that they may use, such as *Workspace* or *Elgg* (Campbell et al. 2005), were specifically designed to achieve this. Experience of using these tools is important if tutors are to understand how to support learners' use of them online. This argues for tutor training which has an online experiential element. As the next two sections explain, working with new pedagogies and new tools for learning are significant challenges for Chinese tutors, as indeed they are for many 'traditional' tutors worldwide.

Chinese students' and tutors' current perceptions of e-learning

In association with our *eChina-UK* project, we carried out research with 261 respondents from eight institutions in China offering online English degree courses with e-learning elements (Wang 2004). We found that students would have preferred to have been following traditional F2F courses if they had been given the choice. The reality in China at present is that only a small percentage of those wanting to, and often needing to, study for undergraduate and postgraduate qualifications are able to do so, because of the limited number of higher education places available. Places are highly competitive, and so those with lower qualifications only gain entry onto the less popular distance learning courses. In terms of preference, online learning in China is a third choice, behind the campus-based study mode and the second choice of studying F2F at a distance in a regional study centre supported by an off-campus tutor.

Our research also found that the students prefer to use printed textbooks (and VCD materials, if available), rather than experience any of the online components. This may have been due to the fact that, in these programmes, the e-learning elements were only a supplement to the F2F tutorials for the majority of institutes in China. The move to mainly or wholly online courses in English education, in which the e-learning elements are compulsory, is only just beginning in China, and the *eChina-UK* projects (which are reported in this book and on the *eChina-UK* website, http://www.echinauk.org/) have been instrumental in developing this approach. It should be noted that this move has been a practical one: the high bandwidth needed for multimedia approaches to online learning has become more commonly used in China, and this reduces the need to produce the VCD materials. In addition, monitoring of tutor performance is made easier if all their interactions with students are online: quality assurance is a central issue in distance delivery learning programmes.

So what are the views of the tutors supporting online learning? Research into the views of 35 of the tutors who were supporting the students (sampled in the research reported above) revealed that over half (57.1 percent) felt that Web-based education was unsuitable for producing graduates in English. It also found that the tutors:

- are less ICT (information and communication technology) confident and competent than many of their students;
- have almost no experience of online learning themselves;
- are insecure about their role and their abilities as online tutors.

However, on a more optimistic note, a primary reason for these tutors to become involved with an e-learning course was their perception that this was an important part of their continuing professional development. They felt that e-learning was the future and they wanted to be part of this. They also wanted to enhance their research capability (71. 4 percent) and to experiment with new teaching methods (68.6 percent).

Developing learner autonomy in Chinese students

Chan (2001) argues that constructivist approaches to learning have not traditionally been nurtured or valued in the Chinese educational context, and that Chinese tertiary students need time to adapt to Western expectations that they develop competence in self-directed study and critical thinking, that they construct and apply knowledge rather than 'digest' it, and that they become reflexive in their learning, developing a level of criticality. Research by Wang (2004) found that higher education tutors and students reported learner autonomy to be problematic; notably, 91.4 percent of tutors and 34.7 percent of students felt that the expectation for learner autonomy was a major stumbling block for online learning. However, there is evidence that Chinese learners can work effectively in an environment which encourages the development of autonomy (Watkins et al. 2001; Joyes and Chen 2006; McGrath et al. this volume, pp. 57–77). But tutors need to be aware of the demands that the pedagogic approach makes on the students and the problems this may present for them. So, in addition to developing an appreciation of the versatility of the tools for learning and how to support students in their use, tutors will need to develop an understanding of how to support students in the transition to these new ways of working in higher education.

Current e-Learning Tutor Training Models and Approaches

A literature review carried out within our *eChina-UK e-Educator* Project revealed that there are few empirically based models for e-learning tutor training, apart from the models proposed by Salmon (2000) and Lewis and Allan (2005). Both these models for e-learning tutor training guide students through stages or phases identified as being important in the learning process. The following discussion critically analyses these two models and compares them to current practice in China, and then proposes an alternative approach suited to a wider range of contexts.

The computer-mediated communication model for e-Learning tutor training

Salmon's (2000) computer-meditated communication (CMC) model focuses on the skills needed to support online discussions with groups of students. In the model, the students move from being dependent to being independent or autonomous learners within the online discussions. The model identifies five stages through which the student is supported, moving from being wholly reliant on the tutor and where they are not engaged in contributing to knowledge construction, to a stage in which:

> participants become responsible for their own learning . . . [they exhibit skills of] critical thinking and the ability to challenge the 'givens'. . . [they may] become guides to newcomers . . . [and may] wish to start conferences of their own and ask the designated e-moderators to withdraw. (Salmon 2001: 35)

This notion is a useful one to consider. Salmon is not suggesting that students come to their studies incapable of criticality or never having been autonomous (though some experience difficulty with this). She argues that, until students move through the transition from F2F to online study, in this case becoming familiar with a computer-mediated conferencing system, they will be unable to work effectively in their online studies. The role of the tutor, therefore, is to support this transition to what may be new ways of working for some, and to what will be a new context for learning for all: all students will be working with new materials, and will most likely be working with new colleagues and tutors, and with new learning tools.

However, the application of this stage-wise approach to e-moderating needs to be engaged with in reflexive and critical ways. Lisewski and Joyce, for example, question "whether the five-stage model offers general transferability of educational practice across widely differing teaching and learning contexts" (Lisewski and Joyce 2003: 60).

Even more importantly in the current context is the fact that online learning is likely to engage the student in a much wider range of activities than just CMC, and so a much more comprehensive model for e-learning tutor training is needed.

The virtual community life cycle model for e-learning tutor training

An alternative model is Lewis and Allen's (2005) virtual community life cycle model. This model focuses on problem-solving in organizations, and ways in which virtual learning communities can support collaborative approaches to solving problems and to facilitating learning. The model shares some similarities with the CMC model, but it identifies 'induction' and 'incubation' stages. During induction, the tutor facilitates interaction between group members, through introduction and icebreaker activities, the latter being something they "both have felt reluctant to use . . . online" (Lewis and Allan 2005: 66). An online 'incubation' stage follows, which involves interaction and small group working. The distinction between these stages may be in part due to the fact that induction has been conducted F2F, whereas incubation is an online stage. This is then followed by stages of improving performance and of implementing practice which "involves transferring learning from the community to the work situation" (Lewis and Allan 2005: 105).

This situated learning aspect is a key feature of this model and, interestingly, is an important feature in the training of classroom teachers, the focus of our earlier *eELT* Project. However, this focus makes it difficult to consider how this model could be applied generically for the training of e-learning tutors, given the wide variety of pedagogic contexts mentioned earlier and given that the application of learning to work-based practice is not common to all e-learning. Nevertheless, as in the Salmon model, the approach emphasizes the key role of the e-learning tutor in actively facilitating the development of the online community to support learning and both models provide a range of activities that can be applied in a wide range of contexts.

e-Learning tutor training in China

e-Learning tutor training in China typically provides support for the specific learning and teaching activities of a given course. This has been the approach taken at Beiwai Online for their current programmes, and, like many such training programmes in China, it involves F2F residential training in orienting the tutor to the nature of the course and the tutor's roles within it. At Beiwai Online there is also an online experiential component to the training, which involves an exploration of the materials, including an experience of using a discussion forum.

The focus of the training is on the orientation of the tutor to the types of activities in which the students will be engaged. For example, one tutor training activity involves the tutor in planning a F2F tutorial, and another involves how to assess student assignments. These approaches present models of effective practice, which the tutors then follow as part of a course assignment on which they receive feedback. However, the move to compulsory online learning necessitates a more radical approach to the tutor training curriculum.

An activity theory approach

The UoN-BFSU materials developed for the MA eELT (and for which the trainee tutors will be acting as e-learning tutors) self-consciously set out to include a wide range of self-study, co-operative and collaborative activities, which provide opportunities for students to develop as reflexive and autonomous learners using a wide range of learning tools. This experiential context for learning is 'new' for both the student and the tutor and thus demands a focus within the tutor training curriculum on supporting this new range of pedagogic elements.

Each activity has its own specific demands. Each student and tutor will bring to the activity their own set of expectations and skills, and these will need to be considered if the outcome of the activity is to be successful in terms of meeting the course expectations. The expectations of the students, who desire a relevant, rewarding, motivating and social experience (Joyes and Chen 2006), will also need to be met. Our dilemma as designers of the tutor training curriculum is that a focus on specific activities which use specific learning tools means that the training programme may not be flexible enough for use on other courses offered by different providers and in different subject areas.

Our solution is to define the curriculum in broad areas and to use Activity Theory (Engeström 1987) to help provide a conceptual tool for analysis of the online activities. We focus on supporting the tutors in using this conceptual tool, although we also provide examples of supporting activities that might be used with the students. This approach thus supports the tutors in developing a deep understanding of the context for learning in which they and their students are involved, and of how to support their students effectively within this context. The next section explains this in greater detail.

Developing the Generic Framework

A skills-based curriculum

The development phase of the framework was characterized by desk-based literature searches of the e-learning tutor training literature, evaluation studies of online learning, and research into the online experiences of the students and tutors. This revealed huge arrays of abilities or skills considered necessary for effective tutoring, including session or activity planning, questioning, organization of self and others, monitoring, supporting individual and group working, providing feedback. None of these are particularly unique to online tutoring, but the online context requires the tutors to consider carefully the new context in which they are applying these skills.

The UoN-BFSU development team focused on eliciting the superordinate constructs or pedagogic themes intrinsic to an experiential online delivery mode. It is our contention that, in order to ensure the *e-Educator* training programme is a generic one, the curriculum needs to be organized into groupings of skills and abilities that are likely to be applied in a wide range of online contexts. These contexts may involve individualized learning or group-based collaborative learning, and may be based on transmission or social constructivist pedagogies. To this end, the following set of core abilities or skills for supporting students can be usefully identified within four domains:

- pedagogic aspects: expectations in relation to ways of working;
- cognitive aspects: the intellectual aspects of learning;
- community aspects: the social, co-operative and collaborative aspects of learning (these have limited emphasis in some formal and informal e-learning contexts);
- feedback: diagnostic, formative and summative assessment.

The precise nature of the abilities that are required within each of these domains will depend upon the nature of the course, i.e. the subject content, the level, the pedagogic approach adopted etc. For example, the notion of community may be restricted to that of the institution, the tutor and the student, or it might extend to a community of learners working collaboratively (Joyes and Fritze 2006; McConnell 2000; Redfern et al. 2002).

However, what is missing from this analysis are the qualities possessed by the effective personal tutor, someone who has an empathy for the individual, who acts as advisor or counsellor (Goodyear et al. 2001) and who is able to develop trust and respect (Duggleby et al. 2002) through engaging with the students at a 'personal' and lived-experience level. This fifth set of abilities or skills may be meta-level ones, in that all the other levels of support will be filtered through this level of personal engagement. Figure 7.1 provides one means of representing the relationship between these domains.

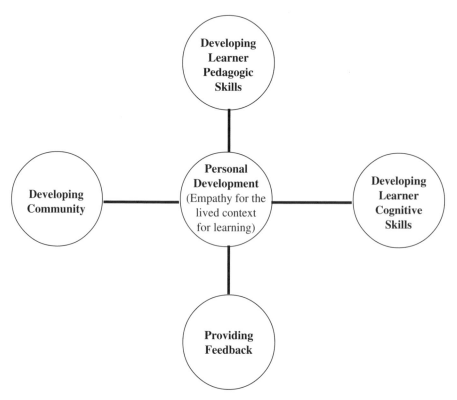

Figure 7.1 A Development Model for an *e-Educator* Training Curriculum: The Five Domains

A Development Approach

The conceptual framework for the development approach was provided by Activity Theory (Leont'ev 1978; Vygotsky 1978). Activity Theory is increasingly being applied to aspects of technology-supported learning because of its emphasis on the mediation of tools and of social factors on human activity. It has been used in the study of Human-Computer Interactions (Nardi 1996), in research into online collaborative behaviour and distributed learning (Andreassen 2000; Russell 2002), and for supporting the e-learning design process (Jonassen and Rohrer-Murphy 1999).

Activity Theory argues that, when people engage in goal-directed behaviour, several elements are involved. Engeström (1987) calls this an activity system, and Figure 7.2 is a visual representation of such a system (see also Motteram et al. this volume). An activity is composed fundamentally of a subject (a person or a group engaged in the activity) and an object (the objective of the activity). The activity is mediated by a tool or instrument, which can be material and/or psychological (such as ways of thinking and language). e-Learning tools might be an online discussion forum, an online notebook, or the study approaches that support effective learning.

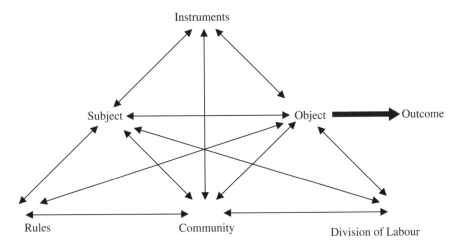

Figure 7.2 Model of a Human Activity System (Adapted from Engeström 1987)

Let us consider the model applied to online learning and the work activity of an online tutor within a course in higher education. The object of this work is to support the student engaged with a particular activity. The outcomes include the intended ones for the students, such as ownership of the learning process and successful activity completion, i.e. development of knowledge, understanding, and skills development. Unintended outcomes, such as possible dissatisfaction, non-engagement, and tutor-dependence behaviour, can have a negative impact on learning, so need to be avoided. The instruments may include communication tools such as e-mail and discussion fora, which may be used to support the development of understanding and encourage engagement. Other instruments may be diagnostic and pedagogic-related concepts and methods enabling the tutor to develop an empathy for, and an understanding of, the student within the wider context for learning in which they are working. The community consists of the tutor and their group, but may include other tutors and staff at the institution. The division of labour determines the roles taken on by the students and the tutor; some of these will be determined by the institution, but some will be additionally negotiated within the learning context. Finally, the rules regulate the use of time, the online behaviours that are acceptable, the measurement of outcomes, and the criteria for rewards (or awards).

The precise nature of each of these activity components will depend upon the context for learning. A change in any one or more of the components results in a disequilibrium that necessitates an adjustment within the learning context (see also Motteram et al. this volume). For example, a new activity may require collaboration and so may need new rules in relation to division of labour, an adjustment in terms of community expectations, and the specification of possible new roles. Additionally, in any formal course of study, the relationships between the activities will also be important. For example, one activity may rely on skills or content acquired in another.

The component elements of an activity system have been used by the UoN-BFSU team to form the basis of a conceptual tool that tutors can use to analyse each of the elements associated with a learning activity. We have named this conceptual tool the *Learning Activity Analysis Tool* (LAAT) and, as shown in Table 7.1 (p. 119), it provides a series of questions specific to each component of Engeström's (1987) Activity System, and offers a means of operationalizing it.

The LAAT, which is a key feature of the *e-Educator* training programme, provides a framework for the tutor to review the learning activity system and so mediate the designed learning experience for the online learners. The LAAT provides the means of matching the designed learning activity to the current context for learning, as well as the means by which the trainee tutors are supported in reflecting upon and researching their own practice.

The Structure of the Module

As mentioned, we needed the *e-Educator* training module not only to be suitable for training tutors for the MA eELT at Beiwai Online but also to be structured in such a way that it could be used for e-learning tutor training for any HE course in China or elsewhere. The UoN had a range of contexts in which the module was needed; for example, there was an emerging need for online tutor training for postdoctoral students who are to support its graduate school online research training programme (with more experienced lecturers acting as chair tutors), and there was a need within an online tutor training course for new lecturers. These various contexts were used to explore the development of the module structure and materials. The module that has emerged contains a set of learning activities and has a duration of 10 to 14 weeks. The structure is shown in Table 7.2 (p. 120).

Unit 1, the induction, provides an introduction to the module, to its structure, the intended learning outcomes, and the pedagogy. It also provides an introduction to online working, including the community within which the tutors will be working. A key element of the induction is the introduction to the use of an online reflective journal to record

Table 7.1
The Learning Activity Analysis Tool (LAAT)
(Adapted from the 8-step model of Mwanza 2001, 2002)

Activity Component	Support Issues
Activity of Interest	• Is the nature of the activity clearly stated? • Is it clear how this is related to other activities? • How and when should the tutor check whether the learners have interpreted this correctly?
Objective	• Do the objectives need clarifying, and how might this be achieved?
Subjects	• Who are the learners? • What are their backgrounds? • How ready are they? • Do they currently have the skills/knowledge needed to carry out the activity?
Tools (mental or physical)	• Do the learners need support in selecting and using the tools that might be useful to use?
Rules & Regulations	• What are the cultural norms involved? • Is the activity compulsory or optional? • Is the nature of the task something the learners would expect to carry out as part of their studies? • How can difficulties due to any conflict in expectations be overcome?
Division of Labour	• Is there a need to support the learners in understanding and carrying out their expected roles?
Community	• What is the nature of the learning environment? • What are the learners' expectations in relation to community? • How can their roles be supported?
Outcome	• How will learners know if they have achieved the outcome? • How can feedback be provided to support the achievement of the outcome? • Is the assessment of the outcome aligned with the nature of the task?

reflections in relation to their own experiences of working online within this module, and of the roles of the tutor and the student(s) in the activities.

This is followed by Unit 2, which provides an experiential orientation to online learning, in which the tutors undertake online activities that require them to work in self-study and co-operative modes using a wide range of online tools. There will be examples of online learning activities from the five domains of the *e-Educator* curriculum, and these will provide the context for the tutors to consider their roles in relation to each of these five domains. At present, Unit 2 is populated by examples of learning materials

Table 7.2

The Structure of the Generic e-Learning Tutor Training Module

Unit	Title	Brief Description	Mode	Duration
1	Induction	Trainee tutors are introduced to the module and its structure, and to ways of working, including the learning tools.	Face-to-face and/or online	1 week
2	Experiential orientation	Trainee tutors study online activities, to explore new approaches to learning and to familiarize themselves with the nature of the course on which they will be supporting students. The LAAT begins to be used to develop a discourse around effective practice.	Online: supported self-study and co-operative learning	2 to 3 weeks
3	Personal Development Planning	Trainee tutors complete an online self-assessment, in order to reflect upon their learning needs in relation to the 5 areas of the curriculum to be offered in Unit 4.	Face-to-face and/or online	1 to 2 weeks
4	Personalized experiential training	Trainee tutors study online using the LAAT and other training activities to explore ways of supporting their online students within the types of activities in which they will be engaged.	Online: supported self study and co-operative learning	4 to 6 weeks
5	Assessment	Trainee tutors complete a portfolio of current understandings of the nature of support for online learning and set targets for future professional development.	Face-to-face and/or online	2 to 3 weeks

from the MA eELT modules for the Beiwai Online training course, but the intention is for the generic module to provide a range of examples of e-learning materials from different subject disciplines. This unit will also need to be populated with compulsory activities from the course for which the tutors are being trained. The curriculum also introduces examples of effective practice that can be used to support the transitions to and between these online activities.

During this unit, the tutors will need to assess the suitability of the activities for any particular context and, in order to achieve this, they will be introduced to the LAAT. They will apply the LAAT systematically to at least three different types of online activity, analysing them in some detail, and, as a result of their analyses, they may find that student support needs to be modified. The tutors will continue to update their reflective journals. The intention is that the tutors' analyses and reflections are discussed as a conclusion to this unit and as a link to Unit 3.

The module recognizes the need for those in training to make choices about the nature of the programme they should engage with, and so Unit 3 focuses on personal development planning. The experiential approach of Unit 2 enables the trainee tutors to make informed choices about the areas of the curriculum on which they need to focus. The use of the LAAT, and the discussion around it, will provide a sound basis for the personal development planning undertaken in Unit 3. The aim is to provide an online self-analysis tool, covering the five aspect curriculum, to aid this process. This tool is currently being developed.

Unit 4 then provides the online personalized experiential training. For the co-operative parts of this unit, there is a need for a group of at least three trainee tutors to study them together, with the support of an experienced tutor. (In fact, this is also important for the experiential orientation of Unit 2.) However, some of the unit is designed for supported self-study. Within Unit 4, the LAAT is again used as a key tool for supporting tutors in their analysis of the online activities.

The tutor's reflections and discussions around these activity analyses forms the evidence base for the completion of a summary portfolio of current understandings of the nature of support for online learning. It will be supported by peer review, and presented for the module assessment in Unit 5. An important feature of this is the further reflection of personal development needs, as well as the setting of targets to achieve these.

It is envisaged that a trainee tutor will *not* be able to complete the module as an isolated learner. A solitary learning experience is a key contributor to non-completion of online courses, and we believe it is important for trainee tutors to experience the benefits and challenges of group-working online. For this reason, some activities in Units 2 and 4 will need to be studied co-operatively, and the peer review in Unit 5 is seen as an important feature of the learning process. We envisage that this work can be carried out in small groups of 3 or 4; where larger groups are to be involved, the recommendation is that these small groups work within whole groups of no more than 20. These recommendations draw on the experience of effective group working within the project institutions and some evidence from the literature (Goodyear 2001; Brook and Oliver 2004).

An example of an e-learning tutor training task

The following example is taken from Unit 4 of the *e-Educator* training module and comes from the cognitive aspects domain of the curriculum. The cognitive aspects domain within the module covers four areas: information literacy, criticality, enquiry, and task management. The following introductory task on criticality engages the trainee tutors in a discourse around the nature of a group reading task. This task has been set within one of the introductory units within the MA eELT materials, and is presented as an e-learning example in Unit 2 of the *e-Educator* module.

The nature of the group reading task, which is presented as a series of video clips of a small reading group together with the transcripts, is as follows. An experienced student is seen working with two students, and the group reading task is explained by this experienced student who acts as the chairperson. This task involves the students each reading a book chapter and providing a written report on this, which they read to each other. The experienced student then sets the same group reading task to the online learners who are viewing the online video presentations. The intention of the original learning design was to model good practice in effective reading at master's level, but it raises a number of issues in relation to what is effective reading, as well as how one might carry out this task with students online. It is perhaps useful to consider just five of the LAAT components, but by the very nature of this being part of an activity system, the issues that arise by considering these components are also reflected within the others.

By Unit 4, the trainee tutors will have already carried out an online community-building activity in small groups within the community aspects domain, and will have begun to develop rapport with each other at a social level. It is the same small groups that carry out this group reading analysis task. They complete and share their LAATs with each other (Table 7.3, p. 123), and then engage in a discussion about the nature of the online task and the nature of the support that could be offered to students involved in the reading task. The LAAT has been designed so that, after each of the nine components (subject, object, tool etc.) is completed online, a summary of the implications for student support has then to be provided (Table 7.4, p. 124). When the trainee tutor is satisfied with his or her entry, he or she can then share this with the rest of the small group who can view his or her completed LAAT.

The completed LAATs and the discussion about the learning activity provide a vehicle for the trainee tutors to explore different pedagogic approaches to online tutoring, ranging from teacher-led to student-centred, and provide a means of discussing the nature of effective support within a given learning context. This particular Unit 4 training activity is followed by an exploration of some of the tools that might support criticality, as well as the nature of the feedback that might be given to the course designers in relation to improving the clarity of the reading group task within the MA eELT courseware.

This Unit 4 task could be modified to include the analysis of a different online task that is included in the examples of e-learning materials in Unit 2 of the module. However, it might be felt that the example can provide the basis for a suitable discussion about the nature of reading and reporting, and a consideration of the affordance and constraints of the online communications technologies that can be used to support such tasks.

Table 7.3

The LAAT Applied to a Reading Group Task: Partially Completed

Activity component	Support issues in relation to the reading group task
Objective	**Do the objectives need clarifying and how might this be achieved?**
	The objective is the completion of the reading group task and then the sharing of this within the group. How do the learners know what is meant by 'reading' and 'reporting'? Is the model of practice presented clear enough?
Subjects	**Who are the learners? What are their backgrounds? How ready are they? Do they currently have the skills/knowledge needed to carry out the activity?**
	This is an introductory module in the course, so we might expect to have to clarify what skills might be expected at master's level.
Tools (mental or physical)	**Do the learners need support in selecting and using the tools that might be useful to use?**
	For the sharing of the reports, a bulletin board might be used to share the written reports, an audio file might be shared, and a synchronous audio/text chat or video conference might be used. Each needs to be considered in terms of pedagogy and practicality.
	For developing reading and reporting skills, what tools or guides might be useful to support the learner in knowledge construction? Would a mind map be helpful? Would a critical reading guide be useful? What tools do they use already?
Rules and Regulations	**What are the cultural norms involved? Is the activity compulsory or optional? Is the nature of the task something the learners would expect to carry out as part of their studies? How can difficulties due to any conflict in expectations be overcome?**
	What are the expectations in relation to reading and writing at master's level? This is an introductory unit. Should we be expecting a level of criticality in the reading? Does the model of practice provide any clues? Is this model an appropriate one?
Outcome	**How will learners know if they have achieved the outcome? How can feedback be provided to support the achievement of the outcome? Is the assessment of the outcome aligned with the nature of the task?**
	The outcome seems to be simply the completion and the sharing of the reports. Is this enough? What is the actual learning outcome of the task?

Table 7.4
Example Summary for This Learning Activity Analysis

The reading group task aims to provide a model for developing reading skills: students describe the ideas and concepts in the reading, share them with their peers, and relate them to their own experiences. However, they do not compare them with any other ideas or concepts, which might be expected at this level of study. So is this model adequate at this level for developing reading skills? It could be useful to find out from the students the 'tools' they use to support their reading and reporting, and agree upon what the expectations (objectives) are to be, and how they might know they have achieved them (outcomes). It might be useful, as this group is just forming, for us to hold a synchronous video or audio conference to share our reports and hold a discussion about our findings, as well as our ways of working. I would check out with the students what they think about these alternatives. An alternative approach would be to just let the task run without any support and then discuss the issues that arise afterwards, but this is probably not the best approach with a new set of students who are going to feel insecure about the learning process.

Sample LAAT entry 2006

Conclusions

There are two interesting by-products of the tutor training framework. The first is the exemplars of online learning incorporated into Unit 2 that provide the tutors with an experiential orientation to e-learning. Exemplars of online learning across different subjects are difficult to find, precisely because they form parts of courses that are hidden behind passwords. These experiential materials are different from those within the open courseware initiative started by MIT (Massachusetts Institute of Technology), which can be found at http://ocw.mit.edu/index.html and which now involves large numbers of institutions worldwide. This is because our experiential materials provide examples of complete learning experiences, with explanations of the pedagogy involved. This repository of a wide range of e-learning activities may prove useful for dissemination and debate about the nature of effective e-learning materials and learner support across subject areas.

The second by-product is the completed LAATs and the discussions around these by the trainee tutors. These provide important research data into the pedagogic understandings of trainee tutors. These insights in turn will provide valuable information in relation to tutor training needs which can be used to inform future development of the module.

As we look back, we realize that we would have been unlikely to develop the Activity Theory-based generic e-learning tutor training module without the opportunity presented by the *eChina-UK Programme*. The requirement to collaboratively develop innovative e-learning materials revealed the need to rethink e-learning tutor training, and this presented an opportunity to reflect upon the nature of this process. At the time of writing, this programme is still being developed, but the intention is that the module will be available as a set of materials and tools on the open source platform *Moodle*.

Section 3

Managing the Interplay
between Pedagogy and Technology

The previous section of the book focuses on pedagogic design issues for online courses. In this section, we turn to the interplay between pedagogy and technology, because the design and development of online courseware requires a team approach in which academics work closely with technical staff. In the *eChina-UK Programme*, all projects were convinced that pedagogy should lead the technology, rather than vice versa, but on a practical level, there were numerous issues that needed to be addressed.

Zähner, in Chapter 8, discusses the factors that the *eChina-UK CUTE* Project team needed to consider when deciding what technical platform to use for their project. He explains the rationale for the choices they made in their project, and demonstrates how important it is to consider local contextual factors. In the second half of the chapter, he turns to a related question: where and how the technical development of the online materials should take place. This is a crucial question, which all distributed teams need to face and which the *eChina-UK* project teams each handled in slightly different ways (see the Production Process sections of the Case Studies on the *eChina-UK* website, http://www.echinauk.org/).

In Chapter 9, Joyes addresses another aspect of the interplay between pedagogy and technology — how the potential of new technologies can be exploited to improve the pedagogy of online courseware. He focuses on the issue of personalization in learning, and argues that designers should take advantage of the ways in which a platform can store information in its database. He presents two case studies which illustrate how personalized and motivating a learning experience can become when the affordances of a database are exploited effectively.

The e-learning tools that were developed by the *eChina-UK* teams in order to meet pedagogic needs can be viewed, interacted with, and downloaded free of charge from the *eChina-UK* website: http://www.echinauk.org/. The website also provides further extensive discussion of the pedagogy-technology interface in e-learning.

8

Translating Pedagogy into Technology: Techno-Pedagogic Aspects of a Sino-UK e-Learning Project

Christoph Zähner

Introduction

This chapter uses *eChina-UK's CUTE* Project (see Marsh et al. this volume, pp. 95–107) as a case study to examine some technical and implementation aspects of a collaborative Sino-UK e-learning endeavour. It argues that, prior to considering any technological choices and implementation options, e-learning projects must establish a firm methodological basis and that the technical implementation must be able to support the chosen pedagogical approach. In the case of *CUTE*, a methodology was chosen that focuses on autonomous learning with appropriate learner support, community building, integrated scaffolding and an appropriate blend of face-to-face (F2F) with online elements. This chapter does not attempt to justify the *CUTE* methodology (Brewster et al. 2005; Marsh et al. this volume, pp. 95–107) but instead discusses the technological consequences that follow the initial methodological decisions.

Apart from the methodology chosen, a range of other factors affect both the choice of platform and the other facilities made available to the learner in the e-learning environment. These factors include the availability of existing platforms, the features offered by these platforms, their flexibility and extendibility, the local expertise at the client site, the management structures in place, as well as issues of maintenance, cost and so on. The particular choices adopted by the *CUTE* Project are explained, and alternatives, with their advantages and disadvantages, are discussed. The chapter then focuses on the implementation procedures adopted for *CUTE*. The project used a rapid prototyping methodology based on a modified form of what is known as eXtreme Programming (Beck 2005). This approach relies on a series of user needs analyses, implementation and testing iterations which involve all project participants: end-users, pedagogical staff and technical staff. Advantages and disadvantages of this process are discussed and alternatives sketched out.

Next, the chapter exemplifies how some of the pedagogical requirements, established during the initial methodological groundwork, are realized through specific technical implementations. The discussion concentrates on two aspects of the system:

- scaffolding in the context of language learning;
- providing feedback to the users of the system, both learners and tutors.

This chapter concludes with a brief reflection on how far *CUTE* was able to meet its initial expectations from a technological perspective, and what lessons can be learned from the implementation for the development of future e-learning systems of a similar kind.

Methodology

The starting point for *CUTE* was its task to produce a programme that would help Chinese academics quickly and effectively to increase their competence in the use of academic English, in both written and spoken forms, for classroom lecturing, presenting at conferences, writing academic papers and so on. The programme was to be developed jointly between the Department of Continuing Education at Tsinghua University in China and the Language Centre of the University of Cambridge, and it was intended to have a very substantial e-learning component. After initial discussions, both sides agreed that the programme should be driven by the adopted language learning and teaching methodology and that generic e-learning strategies would have to follow that methodology rather then the other way round. The aim of the project was, in the first instance, to build a small-scale, fully functional prototype and use it in a pilot to verify the suitability of the methodology adopted, before attempting to produce a large-scale implementation of the programme.

Unlike other approaches to e-learning, *CUTE* aimed from the outset at a principled division of labour between F2F and online elements. While some e-learning strategies ultimately aim to provide the learner with the equivalent of one-to-one tuition (SCORM: ADL 2004), this was never the intention of *CUTE*.

The *CUTE* methodology presumes that language learning activities can be divided roughly into two areas: those that require or at least greatly benefit from direct human interaction (e.g. negotiation of meaning, discursive skills) and those that can be practised by the individual learner making use of technological support (e.g. listening comprehension, preparation for speaking). Depending on the availability and level of sophistication of the technological environment, there is of course some overlap between the two areas, but there is a fundamental belief that certain aspects of language learning require direct human-to-human interaction. Language learning (and language use) involves the interplay of a number of cognitive processes, including the construction of meaning through conceptualization and negotiation, the acquisition and internalization of linguistic structures, the acquisition of perceptual skills, and an awareness and sensitivity to socially and culturally conditioned interpersonal exchanges. Some of these cognitive processes can be acquired through individual practice (typically, but not exclusively, perceptual and senso-motoric skills), some require interaction with other people (prototypically the negotiation of meaning), but most processes probably benefit from and require a combination of the two (Vygotsky 1978, 1986).

The language learning model envisaged by *CUTE* entails the combination of F2F learning episodes, mainly in classroom situations involving 20 to 30 learners, and individual online learning episodes of 30 to 60 minutes' duration. The ratio of F2F to online was assumed to be roughly 25:75. In the *CUTE* Project, computer-mediated human communication played only a secondary role (this is likely to change somewhat in the full-scale follow-up project). It was assumed that most of the direct peer and tutor interaction would happen in the classroom and that fora and so on would only play a supplementary role. The F2F part of the programme was to be split into two sessions of two weeks and one week duration, separated by a phase of online activities extending over two months (this arrangement was dictated by administrative constraints; the separation of F2F and online into sequential phases was not considered ideal but was unavoidable in the circumstances).

Given the above outlined methodological assumptions, it was agreed that the online application of *CUTE* would have the following features:

- it would provide between 60 and 80 hours of language learning (advanced academic English);
- it would focus on extensive listening comprehension (based on academic lectures) and appropriate listening strategies;
- it would present the lectures as exemplars of grammatical and pragmatic structures relevant to advanced learners of academic English;
- it would highlight lecturing and teaching strategies;
- it would provide an extensive introduction to the various phases of academic writing (e.g. planning, drafting, revision) for academic papers, research proposals, academic CVs and so on.

Platform and Facilities

Once the scope of the application had been determined by its core task and the methodology adopted, the next step was the choice of an appropriate platform and the tools to build the application. As far as the choice of platform was concerned, four options were considered:

1. using the UK eUniversities (UKeU) platform
2. using an existing platform at Tsinghua University
3. using a third-party platform like *Moodle, WebCT*™ or *Blackboard*™
4. using a generic Web platform (e.g. Apache, MySQL, PHP)

From the programme's sponsors on the British side, there was a strong preference (at the start of the project) for the adoption of a particular UK-based learning management system under development at the time by the UKeU, a body (no longer in existence) which was seen as providing a common national e-learning platform to British higher education institutions. Using such a platform offered a number of attractions: access to a range of features offered by the platform, the integration into a common UK e-learning system and the removal of the responsibility for maintaining the platform from the scope of the project. Weighing against these advantages was a number of potential difficulties. Firstly, the platform was still under development, and it was unclear which feature set could be relied on as being available during the project's lifespan. It was envisaged, for example, that the *CUTE* system would produce and store extensive information about the students' interactions with the learning resources and that this information would be available to the participating tutors. It was not clear, however, if and to what extent the platform would support such a feature. Secondly, having the physical location of the platform in Britain and the end-users all located in China raised a number of technical, political and administrative problems: would the JANET/CERNET link, the link via the two national academic networks, be able to provide the required bandwidth reliably and cost-effectively; would the Chinese university and state authorities be happy for the users to access the system (both from home and from campus) and what restrictions would they impose; how would the user administration be handled between the Chinese project members and a body which was not a direct stakeholder in the project; and how would any problems be resolved that involved the different parties?

The last point was of particular concern, since the project had only a very small window for the actual running of the pilot. There was also some concern about the financial implications of this approach: Chinese universities have to pay for Internet access outside China, and with a multimedia rich application, containing both audio and video, the costs could potentially become quite significant. With only a relatively small number of participants in the pilot the risk could have been contained, but with an anticipated extension to several hundred users later, the issue was potentially a serious one. Thirdly and perhaps most importantly, there was a considerable philosophical discrepancy between the approach to e-learning favoured by UKeU and the project. UKeU was committed to an approach favouring decontextualized, reusable learning objects as exemplified by SCORM (ADL 2004) and similar proposals, while *CUTE's* methodology starts from the point of view that the learning experience ought to be contextualized and integrated, where each learning unit supports and reinforces the learning experience provided by other learning episodes. Of course, for the sake of technical integration, the whole of the *CUTE* application (60 to 80 hours of learning) could have been linked to the UKeU learning management system as one learning object, but it would have been an uneasy partnership.

The risks involved in relying on a third-party platform were illustrated when the UKeU platform was abandoned during the project's lifetime. Had the project relied on the availability of the platform for the delivery of its resources, it would have faced serious difficulties.

A second option was the adoption of a platform available at Tsinghua University. Tsinghua University already had a straightforward Web-based e-learning support platform, developed by the university and undergoing further development at the time. Research into a complete and sophisticated learning management system was also ongoing at the time. Integrating *CUTE* into a local platform promised several advantages: the intended end-users would have easy access to the materials, the materials would sit in an environment familiar to the users, and user administration could be handled locally. However, integrating the application into the local platform was not going to be without its problems. The primary stakeholder on the Tsinghua site was not directly in charge of the platform, and co-ordinating the work required to integrate *CUTE* into the existing platform was not going to be easy in the time frame available.

Moreover, the work effort on the Tsinghua side of the project was mainly focused on a major share of the content development and the organization of and participation in the teaching of the pilot. In the time available, it was difficult to establish if the university had an overarching e-learning strategy, or if there were different strategies and methodologies adopted by different groups and how these translated into actual practice. During the initial discussion between the project partners, a common language had been developed and a shared language learning methodology had been agreed. So if we were to integrate our plans into any local e-learning strategy, ways of achieving this would have had to evolve throughout the project and be subservient to the pedagogical methodology adopted by the project partners.

Although the Tsinghua platform was not adopted for the initial *CUTE* pilot, this option is being seriously considered for the next stage of the project. The next version of *CUTE*, which is to be rolled out across a number of Chinese universities, will be installed on the Tsinghua platform eventually. The application is likely to be developed in Cambridge in a platform-independent manner (but including a SCORM 1.2 compliant version: ADL 2004), and then tested on a Web server at Tsinghua before finally being ported to the Tsinghua platform.

Using a third-party platform was another option. There was considerable reluctance on both sides to use a commercial platform. Neither the Chinese nor the UK side had any great experience in running such a platform, and Tsinghua had a clear preference for their own platform over any commercial product. There was also some doubt if these platforms would offer all the educational features required. *Moodle*, an open-source alternative, would have had the advantage that the project could have adapted the software to its need, but at the time *Moodle* was not considered developed enough to be seen as a serious contender.

So, based on the project partners' roles and their areas of expertise, it was decided to go for the fourth option and to concentrate the development of the application in the UK on a generic Web platform rather then using a learning management system. This, of course, risked complications of accessing and integrating the software on the final delivery platform in China, including a potential risk to the envisaged timetable. To overcome this risk, while at the same time preserving the ability to integrate the application into the local e-learning platform at a later date, it was decided to build the application as a generic Web-based application that could be installed on any Web server and SQL database. The multimedia rich application was to be built using Flash, in order to be accessible across a range of operating systems and browsers. The server end of the application was written in PHP using MySQL as the database. Using a three-tier architecture, a database independent interface was developed to reduce any dependency on specific platforms. For later integration into the Tsinghua platform, only the database specific code in this interface would have to be changed (to interact with their local ORACLE database), and the user administration part of the software would have to be adapted to the Tsinghua system; the rest of the application could remain unchanged (see Figure 8.1, a diagram of the *system architecture* for an overview). This conservative approach allowed us to develop the application completely in Cambridge with minimal technical integration necessary in Tsinghua. It also made it easy to install the system on different servers to serve different environments. This proved very useful just prior to the pilot, when the software could be installed on a temporary system while some administrative issues with the Tsinghua Computing Unit that hosted the final production server were resolved. These decisions did not reflect any mistrust towards the capabilities of the Tsinghua Computing Unit or their willingness to co-operate, but a feeling that, given the very tight schedule with no real possibility of extension, the additional risks involved in having to co-ordinate too many stakeholders would endanger the smooth running of the pilot phase, which was after all the raison d'être of the project.

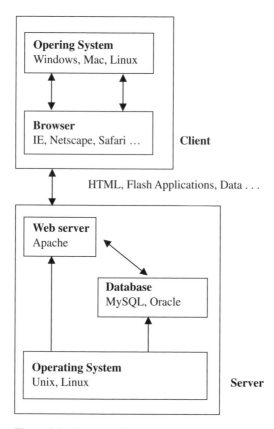

Figure 8.1 System Architecture Adopted

Opting for a generic platform also made it possible to port the application quickly to new environments. The *CUTE* application is now not only installed and run in two separate departments at Tsinghua University, but it is also integrated into the Language Centre Online platform in Cambridge where it supports an English for Academic Purposes programme. The successor to *CUTE 1* is likely to be developed in both a generic Web-based version and a SCORM 1.2-compliant version (ADL 2004) for easy integration in a range of existing and new learning management systems.

Development Process

Having settled on a methodology, a system architecture, an associated platform and a set of tools, the project had to decide where the actual development was to take place. Again, there were a number of different options available to the project. The choices lay along two dimensions. The development could either take place at one location or it could be distributed between Tsinghua and Cambridge; similarly, the development could be carried out by a small and highly integrated group of people or by a large number of people, in which everybody would be implementing a small and well-defined part of the project. The choices along these dimensions were of course not independent of each other. It would be difficult to assemble a large development team in a single location over an extended period, while spreading a small team over different locations was likely to lose some of the expected benefits of working with a small but highly integrated team. Similarly, the development methodology would be affected by these choices. A large team would require a highly structured approach, starting with a careful user needs analysis, followed by a very detailed specification and a very clear delineation of the contributors' various responsibilities. Strong central management would have to ensure that specifications were followed and that the envisaged timetable was strictly adhered to. An approach based on a small group working at a single location suggested a very different methodology, which we describe in more detail below.

The choice of approach ultimately derived from the human resources, expertise and past experience brought to the project by the different partners, and the time and resource context of the project. As mentioned above, the project had a very tight timetable. Following initial discussions, there were no more than nine months between an initial user needs analysis and the start of the pilot; the latter date was determined by circumstances outside the project's control, and failure to meet it would almost certainly have implied a failure to achieve the project's ultimate goal. So, any methodology that was likely to reveal any major problems and shortcomings early on in the development process and allow for early remediation was desirable over one that would provide a workable version only late in the process.

Similarly, the two project partners had no prior history of collaboration and, although general agreement on the pedagogical approach had been reached early in the project, there was a serious risk that misunderstandings and assumptions, that were not shared, could lead to significant problems. Mechanisms needed to be put in place for such issues to emerge as early as possible and to be resolved as speedily as possible. This need favoured both close collaboration, physical and conceptual, and the availability of early versions to provide all participants with a real feel of the direction the project was moving in.

Finally, the time and resources available to the project made it desirable to use a relatively small number of people who would form the core development team working full-time or close to full-time on the project, and to add other specialists to the development process for short but intensive periods. This approach allowed the development to be concentrated in one location and to be carried out over a short but intensive period.

The arrangement finally adopted was thus as follows: after agreeing the pedagogical approach and scoping the intended application at joint meetings in Tsinghua and Cambridge, a small development team was to produce the actual implementation. A content expert from Tsinghua would work with the development team throughout, supported by two to three other colleagues from Tsinghua for shorter periods. Cambridge provided two part-time content developers (half-time), a full-time technical developer and a part-time graphic designer. The short time frame made it highly desirable to use staff with some prior experience in developing e-learning software, to adapt an existing and proven system architecture, and to reuse existing code modules whenever possible. All of these things were readily available in Cambridge. Cambridge also provided the technical project management and the AV expertise required for the multimedia elements of the application (for the recording, editing and processing of audio and video materials). The core team worked closely with the technical and content developers, either sharing an office or working near each other. Regular weekly review meetings allowed problems to emerge early and to be resolved consensually and quickly. This also allowed for the introduction of new features into the specifications at a relatively late stage — if time and resources permitted.

The development itself was broken down into two phases. In the first phase, the content developers familiarized themselves with existing e-learning software, to gain a better understanding of the possibilities and limitations of screen-based, interactive learning software. Subsequently, one of the five content units envisaged for the application was developed rapidly into a fully working version including graphics, navigation and so on. During this phase, the specifications were deliberately kept as flexible as possible so that even fairly fundamental changes and substantial additions requiring a significant amount of re-engineering of the application could be undertaken. This allowed the content developers to let their ideas evolve and to build on the experience that they were gaining with the application. A small but functionally and visually complete version, containing about one-fifth of the final content envisaged, was then taken to Tsinghua for evaluation by the ultimate end-users of the system — the trainees who would eventually use the software.

In the second phase, this version was revised in the light of feedback comments from its evaluation with its end-users. The revised version became the blueprint for the development of the remaining four content units. Although the pattern of regular meetings was maintained during this phase, revisions were limited to specific improvements and small-scale changes, and no substantial re-engineering took place.

In July 2004, the production version of the application was ready for installation in Tsinghua. Two members of the Cambridge team travelled to Tsinghua and installed the software on two different servers. Apart from some administrative difficulties, which were eventually overcome with the help of the Tsinghua project partners, the installation was achieved on time and the software performed as expected during the pilot phase.

The chosen development methodology for the project proved successful. It achieved its major aim of delivering a fully functional application which made it possible to evaluate the underlying pedagogic methodology without being affected by unstable software, missing functionality, and the like. A second beneficial outcome of the development was the expertise gained in the production of multimedia-rich e-learning software, especially by those content developers who had no, or very limited, experience of such software before.

From a slightly wider perspective, the particular approach chosen had its limitations. Concentrating the development process in one location and building heavily on pre-existing work limited the spread of technical expertise and with it the opportunity to adapt and expand the software for use in different locations and under different circumstances. The lack of direct involvement in the development process by technical staff from the eventual 'client' made the local integration of the application just prior to the pilot more difficult. Local technical staff, who were not directly related to the project, had to be relied on to install the software on systems they controlled. They needed to understand the scope of the application and its major technical features and feel confident that its installation would not cause any unexpected problems on their system. Having local staff involved with the actual development of the application would in all likelihood have eased that process. More seriously, any future adaptation of the software for different purposes, for example the addition of other modules, would be hard for the Chinese partners without any local technical expertise and direct experience with the project, despite the close involvement of local content developers in the applications production.

This last issue was less serious in the context of this project since, as a pilot, it was always supposed to lead to a much larger project with an open extensible architecture for further development and adaptation by all project partners. For the second phase of the project, therefore, it is intended that, while we will still rely on a small, highly integrated development team, the actual technical development will involve members from all partners. These partners will then have gained the necessary knowledge and experience to integrate the application into different local contexts (for example, different e-learning platforms) and to adapt and extend the application for local use during and after the project's lifetime. Also, instead of developing a large, monolithic application, albeit over several iterations, which is installed in the target location only at the very final stage of the development process, phase two will see a more modular approach. After the setup of an initial framework all content units (approximately 12 of them are planned) will be separately installed and tested in the final framework immediately after each of them is completed. This will hopefully lead to several benefits: each unit can be evaluated with prospective end-users, both students and tutors, as it becomes available; the modules can be used for the tutor training in advance of the pilot; the technical staff at the hosting site will become much more closely involved in the development process, and this should ease the sustainability and extensibility of these resources in the future. Some of these changes follow from lessons learned during this initial project; others are due to changes in context (e.g. available development time, the need for tutor training, more numerous and diverse users).

Pedagogical and Technical Implementation

At a more detailed, sub-architectural level, the challenge for any e-learning project is to find interesting ways of translating pedagogical ideas into actual software; in other words, trying to let the pedagogy take the lead rather than trying to impose a particular approach to learning simply because the technology most easily supports that approach. As an example, we will look at two particular aspects of the system: the idea of learner support through scaffolding and the idea of user feedback.

Scaffolding

The idea of supporting the individual learner by adapting the learning environment to his or her needs is not new. Research into intelligent tutoring systems has grappled with this problem for a number of years. However, most of this work is focused on modelling the student's progress at a fairly high level of granularity and on creating adaptive environments that provide the student with learning opportunities suited to his or her current state of knowledge and proficiency (SCORM: ADL 2004). This approach has a number of challenging problems, particularly in the field of language learning, where learning consists of a complex interaction of different skills and different sets of knowledge, where progress cannot easily be broken down into a small number of easily monitored discreet steps, and where progress often appears spasmodic and difficult to predict. This makes locating the logic of learning and teaching decisions in the machine a difficult, and perhaps ultimately unnecessary, step. A less ambitious and more realistic approach leaves the high-level learning and teaching decisions to humans, but attempts to provide the learner with guidance and support suited to his or her individual needs. This approach extends in principle from high-level decisions about the overall learning strategy and a particular learning path, to the highly granular level of the individual learning activity.

Looking at traditional learning software, it is often striking how closely individual learning tasks resemble testing activities. Learners are typically presented with multiple-choice type questions and a simple scoring system. Feedback tends to be limited and there is only limited opportunity for scaffolding. Human student-tutor interactions, in contrast, more often resemble collaborative tasks that engage both the student and the tutor, the tutor providing gradual support which allows the student to achieve the intended goal (assuming a Vygoskian model). The student is provided with a challenge which lies just beyond the current level of proficiency but where he or she is able, with the appropriate support, to master the challenge successfully (proximal zone of learning, Wells 1999). This support can take on different shapes and forms: explicit hints, demonstrations, pointing to exemplars, encouraging the student to externalize his or her thinking and to reflect on it, the interposition of immediate steps and practice, and so on. Clearly, not all these elements can be provided by software, nor can there be the level of adaptation typical of the human student-tutor interaction. However, some approximations are possible, and there is still considerable room for innovation and development.

To illustrate, we will give just one example here. In language learning, students are often presented with gap-fill activities. Typically, the student fills the gap and then clicks a button to check the answers. Right and wrong answers are indicated and, occasionally, some feedback is provided in the case of wrong answers. This presents the student with an 'all or nothing situation'. In a similar situation, with a human tutor present, the learner would normally not simply receive the correct answer but a hint or some other form of help to arrive at the desired answer. We have tried to simulate this approach by the introduction of a little icon that the user can drag to various parts of the task to gain some additional help. In our implementation, the icon consists of a little lifebuoy that the user can drag across the screen (see Figure 8.2). At locations where support is available, the icon turns green, and by dropping the lifebuoy at such a location the support can be accessed.

The request for help is entirely under the students' control. So in a gap-fill, dragging the icon to the gap might first reveal some indirect hints that highlight relevant information necessary to find the correct answer. A second attempt might provide a partial answer and a third, final, attempt might give the complete answer, but only for that gap. A general support mechanism is thus available which can provide scaffolding for very specific bits of a task. As the learner progresses through the gap-fill exercises, he or she is likely to meet the same problem several times: by receiving support initially, and then resolving the same problem again but usually with less help, the interaction is likely to produce a much better learning effect than can be achieved by providing a final score and some explanations which the student might or might not understand.

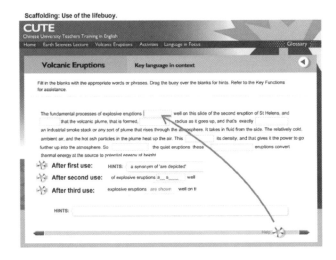

Figure 8.2 Lifebuoy Support in *CUTE 1*

The ultimate aim is to move away from e-learning as something closely resembling testing to a form of activity in which learners within a fairly wide range of abilities and skills can successfully complete the task provided. Proficiency is then not measured primarily by how much of the task was achieved but by how much support was required to achieve the task. This way, the student should rarely leave a task uncompleted or be shown correct answers that he or she does not understand.

Clearly, providing such detailed support is relatively time-consuming and costly, and requires a considerable amount of thought from the content developer, who not only needs to design a task and provide a set of answers but also to reflect on the thought processes the learner might go through and the obstacles he or she is likely to face, and then to think about the appropriate support that can be given. The extra effort by the content developer, however, is likely to lead to a much richer learning experience for the end-user.

User feedback

Feedback on the user's interaction with the system fulfils a dual purpose. First, it provides the tutor with information about the student's progress. The tutor can see which tasks the student has tackled, how intensively the student worked with particular tasks and which areas of study the student appears to have avoided. The intention here is not primarily to assess the student's performance but to provide starting points for the tutor to explore further during his or her direct interaction with the student. A sudden change in the intensity of the student's interaction with the system might signal problems of motivation or understanding; intensive interaction with certain aspects of the system might highlight areas where the student still feels insecure or in need of more practice. Clearly, the ultimate reason for any pattern of interaction can only be established during the direct interaction of tutor and student, but it appears that this kind of feedback allows the online part to be much more closely integrated into the F2F episodes than would otherwise be the case. For *CUTE* specifically, this means that the tutor can see for each activity and section of the online resources when a student accessed them first, how often she or he accessed them and when the most recent access took place. Second, the feedback is important for those who build e-learning systems. Here, the focus is not on the individual learner but on the group of users as a whole. The pattern of distribution of usage across the site gives important clues about which sections of the site might need clarification, modification or extension. While the statistical information offers only a starting point for further investigation, it also provides an important set of objective data to be cross-checked against the more subjective feedback obtained from individual users.

Conclusions

The evaluation of the pilot appeared to confirm that the pedagogical methodology was sound. The major learning objectives appeared to have been achieved and the integration of F2F with independent online working worked reasonably well (see Marsh et al. this volume, pp. 95–107). The system proved to be stable and reliable, and was subsequently used successfully in different environments under different technical and pedagogical conditions. The open architecture makes the integration of the system into new learning environments relatively straightforward, while the modular nature allows for the easy addition of new content modules.

The many different contexts in which Sino-UK projects are set up make it difficult to provide generic advice which is likely to be useful across different projects. However, there are a number of lessons learned, which might be relevant beyond the confines of *CUTE* or the *eChina-UK Programme:*

- the need to build initial rapport
- the importance of appropriate risk management
- the focus on mutually beneficial outcomes.
  (See also Spencer-Oatey and Tang this volume, pp. 159–173)

Particularly in situations in which project partners have no or almost no history of prior collaboration, projects face a large number of initial uncertainties. There is an important period at the start of the project when each side needs to try and understand as much as possible about the background, intentions, working practices, management structures and the institutional and technical context of the other side. One way of tackling this issue is to try and develop a common language at the various levels of interaction: content, technical and managerial. It is useful to identify those areas where critical differences in approach exist and that need to be resolved for the project to succeed, and to distinguish those from areas where progress can be made without necessarily coming to a complete common understanding. The latter approach is particularly useful when third parties are involved, like local university computing services and other service providers, who are not directly involved in the project and who might be less flexible in adjusting their outlook and working practices to suit the project's aims and objectives. The outcome of this process is likely to involve a number of compromises and distinctions between what is essential and what is only desirable. From a technical perspective, it is important to be clear and unequivocal about the tangible outcomes expected, the time and resources available, and the responsibilities for the delivery of specific parts of the project.

Risk management is an important but often overlooked aspect of project management. Given the initial uncertainties but also the vagaries introduced by other stakeholders, like funding bodies, third-party service providers, institutional management and so on, it helps to identify the critical parts of the project early on and to explore alternatives should the initial plan fail. Questions like what happens if the chosen platform ceases to become available, if the promised technical support does not materialize, if the content development falls seriously behind schedule, and so on, need to be played through to ensure that the overall objectives of the project are not put at risk. This, of course, presumes there is agreement between the partners about what is to be seen as a central objective and what is considered a desirable but not necessarily crucial benefit. For each of the critical elements in the project, appropriate fallback positions should be considered and the necessary resources made available. For such risk management to work effectively, it is useful to build into the project's plans a number of early warning systems that indicate if the project is likely to run into difficulties and of management procedures that ensure that remedial action is agreed and implemented promptly. In this sense, a staged delivery of project outcomes is often preferable to an all-or-nothing effort at the end of the project's lifetime. From a technical point of view, the whole process of risk management can be made easier if a deliberate effort is made to reduce complexity and to test early and frequently.

The identification of critical elements in the project is closely linked to our third point. Given the different contexts and cultures of international projects like *CUTE*, one cannot necessarily assume that there is obvious and immediate agreement about what the crucial outcomes of the project are. In Western academic projects, it is often the experience acquired, the new insights gained into process mechanisms, and the extensive research findings about aspects of the project that are seen as just as important as the explicitly specified and tangible outcomes of the openly stated project objectives. For the project to succeed, it is useful to be open about what is a legitimate outcome of the project and to ensure that, as far as possible, these outcomes are achieved. Such outcomes might include the development of an actual, usable product as well as the technical expertise acquired, or the opportunity to generate important data for further research and so on. As projects inevitably change and adapt over time, so do the expected outcomes. This process needs to be well managed by handling it as transparently and fairly as possible.

9

Personalized Online Learning:
Exploiting New Learning Technologies

Gordon Joyes

Introduction

Computer intelligence has been likened to that of a worm, in that computers are able to respond predictably to stimuli but in rather limited ways. Human intelligence, when it comes to exploiting new learning technologies, has been rather worm-like — responding to the technologies that exist rather than demanding more of them. Little is understood, in fact, about the affordances of different learning technologies (Conole and Dyke 2003), in part due to the failure to exploit their potential.

The challenge is to reconceptualize the learner experience, as the context for learning moves from face-to-face (F2F) to online, and to explore the benefits that technologies can bring to this: to ensure it is an attractive and rewarding one. This requires a collaborative approach to design, in that an understanding of the potential of the technologies and of pedagogy is needed. There needs to be a willingness to take an approach to design which allows for a genuine dialogue between technologists and academic writers. What follows is an exploration of some of the affordances offered by new learning technologies, in particular online servers. The context for these developments were the two *eChina-UK e-English Language Teacher* (*eELT*) training projects, which involved the University of Nottingham (UoN) working with Beijing Foreign Studies University (BFSU) and Beijing Normal University (BNU). The need to be sensitive to both the contexts for learning and for design within these projects, together with the drive to produce innovative e-learning, provided a unique opportunity for some rethinking about key factors that would make e-learning an attractive alternative to F2F learning. The chapter begins by exploring the context for online learning by considering the UK and Chinese contexts and what is a shared goal: to ensure e-learning is a rewarding experience for the learner. A key issue is the need to secure higher student retention for online courses (Gibbs 2003), and the personalization agenda in the UK is considered as a means of addressing this. Research findings that explore learner and tutor needs within online ELT contexts for learning in China are also considered.

This is followed by a description of the context for design within the projects. An understanding of the nature of the learning environments in use both in the UK and in China, in particular within these projects, together with the approaches used to develop online materials provide an important background to the origins of the learning materials and tools that have been developed within the projects. One of the learning objects developed, as well as one of the learning tools, the *Workspace*, are then described in relation to the affordances and constraints they offer (Gibson 1979; Greeno 1998), an approach that has proved useful in analysing and evaluating new learning technologies (Kennewell 2001; Laurillard et al. 2000). Affordances are the attributes of the setting which provide potential for action; constraints are the conditions and relationships among attributes which provide structure and guidance for the course of actions.

The e-Learning Context

The Chinese government has made computer literacy a necessary skill for both teachers and learners, in recognition of the increasing importance of new learning technologies and the Internet in learning and teaching. It is also recognized that e-learning has a role to play in meeting the growing demand for higher education (HE) in China and elsewhere, and the Chinese government has approved e-learning pilots within 68 HE institutions in order to meet these needs (see Kang and Song this volume, pp. 11–32). However, there is a deeply embedded perception within China that e-learning is somehow 'third rate' (Gu 2003), below that of campus-based and F2F courses offered by institutions at regional study centres, and is mainly limited to continuing and adult education (Huang and Zhou 2006).

e-Learning in HE has been promoted for a variety of reasons: for playing a key role in providing cost-effective and efficient HE (Daniel 1996); for providing effective collaborative learning environments (Joyes and Fritze 2006; McConnell 2000; Redfern and Naughton 2002); for providing flexibility of access to HE for part-time and work-based learners (O'Donoghue and Singh 2001); for developing competence in using the technologies themselves to support lifelong learning and to contribute to society (DfES 2005a). However, it is important to be sceptical about claims of the value of e-learning, as the quality of research evidence that supports these has been acknowledged as weak in a number of respects (Conole 2003), a key criticism being that many of the current research studies are considered too anecdotal, case-based, and lacking in theoretical underpinning (Mitchell 2000). Recent moves have been to research the student experience of online learning (Timmis et al. 2004), in recognition that experimental approaches that involve comparing F2F learning and e-learning in relation to achievement of learning outcomes misses the point. In fact, such comparative studies have historically shown little evidence of gains (Russell 1999) and are fraught with methodological (and practical) problems. Surely the point is that if the benefits are not transparent to current and potential online learners, then their motivation to learn online is unlikely to improve and the learning process is likely to be ineffective. This is particularly true in China, where the majority of online learners are mature professionals who have busy lives (Huang and Zhou 2006).

Learners quite naturally compare the online experience to a F2F one, and not only can find it different but to be of less value. It can be argued that, if e-learning design is driven by user needs and pedagogy rather than the technology and notions of efficiency gains that can often predominate, then it is more likely to provide a quality learning experience, one which is attractive to the learners.

This notion formed the basis of the *eELT* training projects, which aimed to collaboratively develop exemplar innovative e-learning. The *eELT* secondary training project involved collaboration with BNU and set out to develop exemplar materials for secondary school teachers of English wishing to upgrade their foundation teaching qualifications to degree level. The *eELT* tertiary training project involved collaboration with Beiwai Online at BFSU and aimed to create exemplar online materials for Year One modules of a master's degree in eELT to be offered to tertiary teachers of English in China.

Designing for Learning

> The search for effective pedagogy is of key importance since the need to excite learners'
> interests, retain them on courses and enable their progression is vital to institutions and
> practitioners as well as to the learners themselves. (HEFCE 2004: 21)

The learning context is critical to whether learning technologies are successful (Laurillard 1994), and an understanding of the learning context needs to influence the design. Developing this understanding is complex, and within the projects there were differing perspectives in relation to whose views should be accommodated. Should the needs of the learners be sought and influence the design, or should the institutional expectations of learner behaviours predominate? Learners' perceptions will be based on current and past experiences, and they are likely to be unaware of the need for particular requirements for learning within a new course, especially at a higher level. For example, the need to develop a more autonomous approach to learning is not likely to be something learners are likely to identify as being important, yet this may be something an HE institution will require. Knowledge of learners' perceived needs and preferences are, however, important to know, as this provides an indication of the challenges the learners will face in their transition to their new learning experience. Moreover, there is research evidence that lecturers are not good at predicting learners' perceptions of their needs (Spratt 1999), so these do need to be sought.

Influences on the pedagogic design include those due to subject culture (which in this case was that of the English language teacher trainers) and the chosen mode of delivery, in this case electronic. The influence of perceptions of e-learning pedagogy by those involved in the pedagogic design, i.e. the perceptions of the academic writers and the learning technologists, needed to be carefully managed for innovation to emerge, because there was a need for the pedagogic designers to be creative rather than to be restricted by notions of what the technologies allowed. The projects needed to explore fully this context for learning in order to determine the pedagogic approach.

The context for learning

At the start of the projects in 2003, our Chinese partners used online courseware to supplement F2F working at regional learning support centres. Beiwai Online in fact provided CD-ROM-based multimedia as well as text-based versions of their course. BNU's distance materials tended to be videos of campus-based lectures which could be accessed at regional learning support centres. In addition, online synchronous tutorials were offered at these centres. Research carried out by Beiwai Online, covering eight providers of English language education Web-based degree programmes, found that the Internet-based courseware was rarely used by the students and that print-based materials were most widely used (Cao 2004). This may have been in part due to the fact that the online materials offered nothing of added value to the print and CD-based materials and in part due to the unreliability of Internet connections at the time. Access to, and reliability of, broadband was expected to increase dramatically across China during the life of the project, and both BNU and Beiwai Online were considering offering wholly online courses — work at learning support centres would then be an optional activity or might not even be offered. These decisions would in part depend upon the results of the evaluation of the pilot materials, which were to be delivered wholly online. One important reason for moving to a wholly online approach was the need to assure quality of support by tutors at the regional centres, which was found to be variable (Wang 2004) and difficult to monitor.

The Beiwai Online research revealed that the learner and institutional preference was for the simple transfer of campus-based pedagogy to the online, despite the fact that,

> when the primary media between the learners and the courses becomes the Internet or a computer instead of a teacher, and when the resources can be delivered and retrieved synchronously or asynchronously in spite of time and space, web based learning and teaching is by no means the same as on campus. (Cao 2004: 27)

This same research found that of the 261 distance learners sampled, 71 percent preferred a print-based delivery mode and only 14 percent would choose online learning as a preferred mode. This provides a real measure of the challenge for the course designers in deciding upon the guiding pedagogic principles: the ways these were supported needed to be carefully considered. Consideration of the findings of this Beiwai Online research, as well as interviews with potential students for the course materials being developed, revealed that learners wanted the theory they learnt to be related to classroom practice. This need for relevance is recognized as an important motivational factor in designing for learning (Keller 1983). Learners also wanted instant and frequent feedback on their learning.

The academic writers focused on learner autonomy as a guiding pedagogic principle (see McGrath et al. this volume, pp. 57–77), as this is something that appears central to the English language education culture both in China and in the UK. Interestingly, the Beiwai Online research found that the majority of learners (65.3 percent) did not feel that they lacked the ability to work autonomously; however, the majority of tutors (91.4 percent) felt that students lacked this ability, and this was perceived to be the prime obstacle for supporting learning online by institutional managers (Wang 2004). Autonomy was defined in projects as being

> characterized by a readiness to take charge of one's own learning in the service of one's needs and purposes. This entails a capacity and willingness to act independently and in co-operation with others, as a socially responsible person. (Dam 1995: 1)

This recognizes that learner autonomy does not relate only to the individual studying in isolation, but that learning occurs in a social context which requires scaffolding and involves reciprocal teaching and collaborative learning. Importantly, this involves a conscious reflection on learning. A key issue in the design was the need to provide support for learners to practise and develop the capacity to be autonomous, which would involve reflection on learning and interaction with peers.

In summary, the following pedagogic principles emerged from the analysis of the context for learning: course materials were to be relevant, provide effective feedback, encourage the development of autonomy, and support the sharing of ideas and practice. However, beyond this, the materials needed to be attractive to the learners, and this led to designing for visual appeal and ensuring learners had a personal and engaging experience — one in which the technology was seen by the learners to enhance their learning, not merely duplicating campus-based courses or acting as an online textbook (see Gu this volume). Technologies existed that could achieve all of this, and the projects needed to consider the context for design in order to explore ways of meeting these pedagogic requirements.

The context for design

There were significant differences in the contexts for design between the UoN and its Chinese partners, BNU and Beiwai Online. These differences broadly related to the nature of the online learning platforms and the approaches to designing online materials. Interestingly, the UoN typifies the UK approach to e-learning design and delivery, and BNU and Beiwai Online equally typify the Chinese approach.

The UoN uses a commercial online learning platform, *WebCT*™, to deliver online courses. This platform, though expensive, is popular in North America and the UK, as it requires little central maintenance and support. Academics in schools initiate new courses and will often develop new courses in *WebCT*™ within their schools, with little or no central support. This approach is made possible because *WebCT*™ has a relatively easy to learn course designer interface which requires no specialist programming knowledge, not even a knowledge of html, and allows the creation of a course that can include a wide range of resources, including interactive assessments and online discussions. The creation of animations, interactive multimedia, video streaming and so on, are not supported by the *WebCT*™ designer interface, and so these need additional specialist support which is provided by a central information services learning team of learning technologists and programmers.

The Chinese partners did not use commercial platforms, in part because they were too expensive, but also because they wanted to integrate additional tools such as multipoint Web conferencing and video streaming, and this was not possible with commercial platforms. Both Chinese institutions therefore had custom-built platforms that incorporated student login, course announcements and discussion groups, just like *WebCT*™, as well as the additional video streaming functionality. These platforms were built around a database which at the time used the open source MySQL software but more recently has changed to the commercial ORACLE database. This approach gave the institutions control over the customization and integration of the bespoke functionality they required. This mindset of accepting that pedagogy should determine the functionality of the platform, which could be adapted, became important within the projects: it meant that e-learning innovation within the projects could exploit this opportunity. The issue was agreeing upon what those functionalities should be and how this could be resourced, not about how we should work within and around the functionality of a commercial platform that cannot be adapted.

It was agreed within the *eChina-UK Programme* as a whole that each Chinese institution could use its own platform, and this then led to some difficult discussions about the platform on which the pilot materials could be developed and evaluated. In essence, both Chinese partners were in the process of developing new platforms and so were unwilling to resource the adaptation of their existing ones. Eventually, the open source platform *Moodle* became the platform of choice, in that this had the required core functionality of login, administration, announcements, discussion forums, and could accept a wide range of file formats for resources such as Microsoft Word™, html, pdf, swf. It also had Chinese language functionality, but as the medium for instruction for the materials within the projects was to be English, this functionality was not used. *Moodle* was developed in Australia but has a global community of users and has recently been adopted by a number of UK HE institutions such as the University of Bath and the Open University, the largest distance provider in the UK. It uses a MySQL database, and all of the code that supports the functionality can be adapted under a GNU general public license. This is an open source license guaranteeing freedom to share and change the free software. An additional advantage of using *Moodle* was that any new functionality that was developed within the project could be offered to the wider community under an open source license and had the potential to be developed as a component module (tool) within *Moodle*. This provided potential added value to the project.

Interestingly, the Chinese platforms did not have a designer interface, and this reflected their model for course development. At BNU and BFSU, a central unit led the whole development process, from identifying suitable courses and creating the materials, to organizing their delivery and training the tutors to support this. Academics were invited to be writers, and the usual practice was for the learning technologists to take the written materials and interpret these for online delivery. It was recognized within the projects that this approach to learning design needed to be replaced by a more iterative and participative approach in which the academics worked alongside learning technologists to design the materials. However, this approach was problematic organizationally for our Chinese partners, who much preferred to allocate a block of time for the development once the materials were written. In order for collaboration to occur, and to encourage a cross-fertilization of ideas, the approach used for both projects was one in which the academics were put at the centre of the design process and a team of learning technologists were appointed within the School of Education at the UoN supporting them. These learning technologists created design solutions and raised awareness of technical possibilities. A rapid prototyping approach was used, in which ideas were quickly visualized and shared. It was through this process of actually creating materials that the contexts for learning and design were analysed and through which the pedagogic principles emerged.

The Case Studies

The following two case studies provide examples of the outcomes of this participative design approach. They exploit the potential of the chosen platform to store information in its database and to provide a personalized and motivating learning experience.

Case Study One: Making choices — supporting relevance and personalization

The first case study is an introductory activity in the 'Teaching Grammar' module, which was developed as part of the collaboration with BNU and which forms part of a BA programme in English language teaching for experienced middle school teachers of English in China.

The materials aim to prepare teachers in using learner-centred approaches in their classrooms, which is a requirement of the New Curriculum in China that teachers of English must now implement. The challenges pedagogically were to establish the relevance of the materials for the learners and to ensure that individual differences in learner needs were considered. How could this part of the curriculum exhibit an empathetic understanding of each learner's own classroom context and provide a personalized learning experience?

The affordances offered by the technology meant Chinese teachers could be presented talking about their problems in short video clips. Small file sizes were used, and these were created in Macromedia Flash so that they could be played over low bandwidth connections in an Internet browser with the free Flash plug-in. The issue was how to personalize the experience to ensure the teachers could feel that the learning materials were addressing the difficulties they were having in teaching grammar, without their having to admit publicly they needed support with these issues — the potential for loss of face and the fear of being seen as not coping by colleagues needed to be handled carefully. In addition, it was important to ensure that the areas that were covered in the materials were the ones that were related to the teaching context, that of the New Curriculum in China. In the final materials, this was achieved by presenting the learners during the introduction to the unit with a screen that allowed them to access the concerns of individual teachers of English concerning the teaching of grammar (see the top screen shot in Figure 9.1, p. 148). The screen provides pictures of six teachers. Clicking on the tab next to the picture enables the learner to access the short piece of video and to listen to the teacher speak. The learner may choose to read a summary of the teacher's words by clicking on the inverted triangle under the video screen. Thus, the learner can choose to listen, listen and read, or simply read. The learners may also do this as many times as they want. Once the learner has accessed all of the teachers' concerns, they are asked to reflect on which of the problems already mentioned relate to their own teaching, and to rank these in order of priority for themselves as teachers. The ranking is achieved by simply clicking on a picture of a teacher and dragging it to another position so that the two visuals swap places (see the middle screen shot in Figure 9.1). Once the six problems have been ranked in terms of personal priority, the learner saves this screen. This exploits the affordances offered by the chosen platform to store this in the database, which means that they can be accessed by the learner at any time; see the bottom screen shot in Figure 9.1. This allows the particular chosen order of the problems to become the learner's preferred pathway through the courseware. The aim was also to use this information to alter the order in which the six sets of materials covering the six problems was presented to the learners. Thus each learner would be presented with a personalized navigation through the materials which reflected their personal preferences once they had completed this introductory exercise.

Figure 9.1 Three Screen Shots from the 'Problems Choices' Activity

The two key elements in the learning design that support relevance and personalization for the learner are:

1. The affordance of being able to listen to the problems six Chinese teachers face in teaching grammar problems and for the learner to be able to identify the relevance of these to their own practice — achieved through the use of short video clips and their transcripts;

2. The constraint of being able to reflect upon their own practice *privately* in relation to six problems related to classroom practice and the New Curriculum, which then informs the order in which each learner studies the materials — achieved through an online sequencing exercise, the results of which are stored on the platform database for retrieval in the future.

These affordances and constraints were used to provide an attractive and motivating learning environment, ensuring that the learning was relevant and personal. In addition, this supported learners in developing their own capacity for independent learning and self-directed professional development: their capacity for autonomy.

Extensive evaluation of these online materials with a cohort of teachers in Beijing in 2004 confirmed that the learners found this approach highly motivating. This evaluation is reported in detail elsewhere (Chen and Joyes 2005). The teachers indicated that they also had these problems in their teaching and, because of this, they were highly motivated to study the content. The following are indicative comments about this activity from the teachers in the pilot.

> When I started this unit, I felt it is so closely related to my teaching and teaching grammar is something I really want to improve on; therefore, I want to know what the content is very much. I can't help thinking of getting on the course and discuss with others about this issue. So I feel a web-based course should make the learners feel it is necessary (relevant) for them and if so they'll learn it actively.
>
> *Zhao Minqian*

> I like the idea of having some Chinese teachers to talk about their problems in teaching grammar because I also have these confusions in my teaching. I became very interested in finding out what the experts are going to say about how to solve these problems.
>
> *Wen Zhang*

> There are so many new ideas and suggestions, I'm eager to try some of them with my own students.
>
> *Xian Feng*

Case Study Two: The Workspace — *supporting autonomy and personalization*

The logic of education systems should be reversed so that it is the system that conforms to the learner, rather than the learner to the system. This is the essence of personalization. It demands a system capable of offering bespoke support for each individual that recognizes and builds upon their diverse strengths, interests, abilities and needs in order to foster engaged and independent learners able to reach their full potential. (Green et al. 2005: 1)

Early discussions between the academic writers revolved around the need to support the development of learner autonomy and the nature of the functionality that would be required to support this. These discussions led to the notion of incorporating a portfolio. This was not to be a simple record of progress or achievement but a learning tool that would support the process of portfolio development within a course. This was to facilitate reflection on learning and to be linked to peer and tutor review that would provide opportunities for formative as well as summative assessment. The notion was that the tool needed to support a constructive alignment (Biggs 1996) of the learning objectives to the nature of the learning experience and to the approach to assessment. Thus, if, as is the case in the unit on grammar, the learners are to explore new approaches to teaching in their classrooms and are then expected to share and reflect upon their practice, then the nature of the assessment needs to value the collaborative reflection on practice that they have been through: something that is important if learners are to be encouraged to move from surface to deep approaches to learning (Biggs 1999).

It became clear through discussions with learning technologists that the basis of the tool would need to be a personal archive, which would exploit the affordances offered by the platform database to enable storage and retrieval of completed and ongoing work for each learner. If this archive was to be useful, then it needed to store automatically any online interaction in which the learner was involved; for example the outcome of the Problems Choices activity above, contributions to the bulletin board, threads in discussion groups, and so on. Learners would need to upload files (document, image, audio and video) to the archive, to encourage the sharing of practice through a range of media and to encourage the inclusion of these as part of the assessment. In addition, a range of functionality would need to be included to support the nature of learning in HE. One of the features of learning at this level is the need to develop reflective and critical thinking, and reflective writing is an important aspect of this. The distinction between descriptive and reflective writing was seen as an important constraint, as learners can find this a confusing aspect of their work at this level. It was felt that the provision of an online reflective journal, as well as a notebook, would support learners in understanding the distinction. Another aspect of study and writing at this level is the appropriate use of academic referencing, and to support this, learners need to be encouraged to build a digital catalogue of articles and books that they have studied. The inclusion of a bibliographic referencing tool was therefore thought to be useful.

The learning activities and the assessment approaches were to be designed to support learner autonomy, and the functionality discussed above needed to be added to the platform to achieve this. It seemed sensible to incorporate all of this functionality in one plug-in learning tool which was eventually called the *Workspace*. This would enable learners to access their archive, make notes, write journal entries, upload files, share work with peers and tutors and so on, in one online space that could be accessed throughout their studies. It also meant that the *Workspace* could be developed as an open source module that could be integrated into a wide range of platforms, including *Moodle*.

The following provides a summary of the pedagogic affordances and constraints of the *Workspace*. The pedagogic affordances are:

- an online *Workspace* with a comprehensive set of tools for effective online academic working, which include reviewing completed activities/work, note-taking, reflective writing, bibliographic referencing, uploading files (document, image, audio and video), audio recording of messages and feedback, sharing with peers, submitting assignments and getting feedback from tutors;
- personal and private online *Workspace* with opportunities to make selected work public to peers and tutors. This work is available throughout the course and potentially beyond.

The pedagogic constraints are:

- sharing is with registered course members and only happens when the student is ready to do this;
- it separates two types of writing activity — descriptive and reflective;
- does not contain course/module instructions, guides, resources etc., just the results of such activities — it separates module/course from the meta-reflective and critical process of constructing understanding.

So why would the *Workspace* be attractive to online learners? The user needs analysis revealed that both students and tutors wanted a personalized online environment, that they valued the notion of feeling part of a university and of a learning community, and that they valued formative feedback on their work. The *Workspace* concept emerged as the place in which a student would work online and that would attract the student to want to work there rather than from a CD or print-outs of online materials. The functionality would provide a sense of being recognized as a member of an online community of learners.

The premise behind the *Workspace* is simple. If a student is working online then they should be provided with all the useful tools for learning, together with an archive of their work in one online space. A learner can access this from any computer; they do not have to worry about saving files and moving files between computers; they do not have to download or use specialist software: the *Workspace* provides for all their online working needs. This *Workspace* removes some of the organizational and technical barriers that face the online learner and ensures their energies are focused on engaging with the learning materials not the technology. The final developed version even has administration functionality that enables the tutor to hide some of the tools at the start of the learning process, to ensure learners are not overwhelmed with unnecessary complexity.

Figure 9.2 (p. 152) shows a view of the *Workspace* in which the learner has opened the 'Reflective Journal' intending to make an entry. The 'Personal Archive' is open and the Problems Choices task can be seen in this learner's archive, as well as in his or her 'My Bibliography', 'My Notes', 'My Reflections' entries. These can be viewed at any time by the learner, but are specific to a study unit accessed via the 'Select Unit' button.

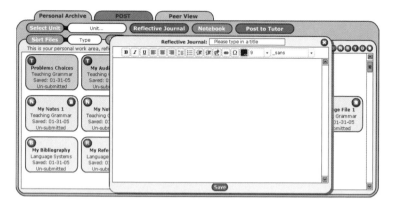

Figure 9.2   The *Workspace:* The 'Reflective Journal' View

Figure 9.3 shows a view of the *Workspace* where the learner is selecting two peers to whom they wish to submit a selected portfolio of their work. This selected portfolio can include anything within their archive, including any uploaded files. The learner selects the items they wish to share for review and comment, and then they select the Post to Peer button. The 'Peer View' tab enables files submitted for peer review to this learner to be accessed and commented on. Sharing or submitting an assignment to their tutor for formative feedback or for marking is a similar process and is achieved through selecting the 'Post to Tutor' button. An assignment might typically include an extensive reflective journal entry or an uploaded MS Word document, together with a selection of items from the learner's archive that are referred to within the submitted assignment document.

The *Workspace* is continuing to be evaluated as part of the *eChina-UK Programme* and is available to try out and download through the *eChina-UK* website, http://www. echinauk.org/.

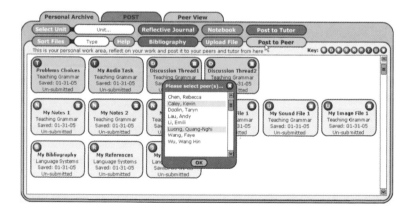

Figure 9.3   The *Workspace:* The 'Selecting Peer Reviewers' View

Conclusions

Online course development is expensive, and it is of concern that retention for online courses is often low, something recognized internationally (Bonk 2001; Cao 2005). Why might learners not value online learning? Perhaps this question should be reconceptualized into how might e-learning value or recognize the learner, so that the learner might in turn value the experience?

The learner's online experience puts in mind the main character in the film *Groundhog Day*. In this film, he wakes up one morning and lives an eventful day, working and socializing in a small town, and at the end of the day he then retires to bed. On waking up to what should have been the next day, he is confused when he finds that he is reliving the same day, which he can respond to in different and new ways. This is quite novel for the first day, and even for the second day, but the fact that his experience continues to be ignored becomes a major tension. Eventually, he realizes that he needs to change something if time is to move on. This, to some extent, is the experience of the online student: they log on and carry out some work; they make some notes, carry out an activity and then log out. If they revisit the online course, it will still recognize them, and it may well be monitoring their presence, but apart from any contributions they may have had to an online discussion, there will be no evidence of the progress they have made and no use will have been made of this to support their learning. Learning is a very impersonal experience. It is clear that the 'something' that will enable time to move on for online students is the ability to design online learning to ensure their experience is a personal one.

Students at the very least deserve some recognition that they have completed something and because, in any case, this is being tracked by an online server, there is no reason why this should not happen. At one level, the history of the student's learning can be tracked, and this can be made available to the student. However, this technological affordance, to monitor everything a student does, can be exploited to become a pedagogic affordance, one that provides potential for action for learning by the students. This chapter has explored two examples of the ways this has been achieved. The challenge is to ensure that the potential for adapting the technologies happens during the design process. This means that the design for learning process must involve a team approach, with academic writers leading on pedagogy and supported by a skilled team of technologists willing to accept the notion that adaptation of the learning environment is part of the development process. This has implications not only for learning design but also for the design of platforms. These need to allow for ease of integration of new tools and for transfer of the archives that form the basis of tools, like the *Workspace*, from one course to another, as well as from one server to another. The archived digital data are personal to the learner, who should have ownership of this, not the institution. At present these data are rarely used to support learning within a course, let alone across courses or across phases of education. This notion of personalized learning, which is at the heart of the UK Department for Education and Skills five-year e-learning strategy (DfES 2005b), is one in which learners can create a coherent experience of learning in diverse locations, collaborate with experts in areas of personal interest, track and review their own learning across different sites and stages of education, have access to resources in forms and media relevant to their language skills, abilities and personal preferences. (Green et al. 2005: 5)

Personalized learning relies on the affordances of technologies being exploited. It is likely that these can only be unleashed through collaborative design processes in which the potential for adaptation of technologies is explored.

Section 4

Managing Collaboration Processes

An important aim of the *eChina-UK Programme* has been to strengthen collaboration between China and the UK. It was hoped that if British and Chinese partners worked together on a common task, there would be a number of positive outcomes for both countries, including the following:

- the emergence of innovative ideas about e-learning design, which could be tested through the delivery of pilot courses;
- a growth in mutual understanding of HE issues in each other's contexts, including those pertaining to e-learning;
- the forging of collaborative partnerships which would extend beyond the life of the programme.

However, effective collaboration does not happen by chance, of course — it needs to be managed appropriately. Martha Maznevski, who has researched diversity in groups in the business context, argues as follows:

> Understanding our differences is the first step to managing them synergistically. (Maznevski 1994: 549)

> The common element in high performing groups with high member diversity is integration of that diversity. . . . diversity leads to higher performance only when members are able to understand each other, combine, and build on each others' ideas. (Maznevski 1994: 537)

The *eChina-UK* project members were diverse in numerous ways (including nationality, academic specialty, professional role, pedagogic beliefs, prior experience of e-learning, level of bilingualism, level of seniority, personality), and all of these factors affected team processes. We found that even that first step of 'understanding our differences' was more challenging than we ever anticipated. This section, therefore, explores some of these challenges.

Spencer-Oatey and Tang, in Chapter 10, take a programme management perspective and discuss the various elements of collaboration that needed to be managed effectively at different stages of the programme. Using as a framework Canney Davison and Ward's (1999) 'best practice guidelines' for leading and managing international teams, they consider the various issues that arose at each stage and the ways in which they were handled. They end the chapter with a set of recommendations for handling future collaborations of this kind.

In Chapter 11, McConnell, Banks, and Lally explore the similarities and differences in pedagogic beliefs and approaches that they experienced in their project. They explain the challenges they faced in developing an understanding of these similarities and differences, the impact that their varying perspectives had on the materials design and development process, and the ways in which they sought to harmonize their viewpoints and achieve a new, intercultural approach.

Motteram, Forrester, Goldrick and McLachlan, in Chapter 12, emphasize the multiple voices within their project team. Using Activity Theory (e.g. Engeström 2001) as a conceptual framework, they draw attention to the crucial role of 'boundary crossers'. They argue that an artefact or a tool can be a helpful focus to discussions and collaborations that attempt to cross boundaries, and they illustrate their argument by describing the role that the Virtual Learning Environment (VLE) had within their project.

10

Managing Collaborative Processes in International Projects: Programme Management Perspectives

Helen Spencer-Oatey and Tang Min

Introduction

Extensive research evidence, especially from the field of international management (e.g. Maznevski 1994; Janssens and Brett 1997; DiStefano and Maznevski 2000; Maznevski and Chudoba 2000; de Dreu 2002; Polzer, Milton and Swann 2002; West 2002) has shown that any kind of diversity in work groups is a double-edged sword: it has the potential to improve creativity, innovation and performance, but if it is not managed effectively, it can have an extremely negative and disruptive effect. This chapter explores the challenges that the *eChina-UK* project members experienced during their collaborations and the ways in which they handled them. The members were diverse in many ways (e.g. nationality, subject-area expertise, professional background, age, level of seniority, prior experience of e-learning, level of fluency in English and in Chinese), but this chapter focuses particularly on the international dimension.

The chapter uses as a framework Canney Davison and Ward's (1999) 'best practice guidelines' for leading and managing international teams. Those authors define an international team as "a group of people who come from different nationalities and work interdependently towards a common goal" (1999: 11), and they maintain, on the basis of their extensive research with such teams (especially in multinational/international organizations), that this four-stage model is easy and helpful for team sponsors, leaders, members and facilitators to work with. The model is illustrated in Figure 10.1 (p. 160), and we use it as a framework to discuss key international collaboration issues that the *eChina-UK* members experienced.

Data for the chapter were obtained in two main ways: from the UK programme manager's systematic written records of the management, collaboration and communication issues of the programme; and from two rounds of in-depth interviews with all of the main *eChina-UK* team members. The first round of interviews took place in the spring of 2004, after the first six to nine months of collaboration; and the second round took place towards

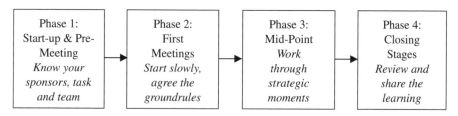

Figure 10.1 Best Practices in the Life Cycle of an International Team (based on Canney Davison and Ward 1999)

the end of the project, between the autumn of 2004 and the spring/summer of 2005. In all, 27 Chinese and 21 British team members were interviewed. All interviews with the British team members were carried out by the British researcher. Nearly all interviews with the Chinese team members were carried out in Chinese by the Chinese researcher, although a few were carried out by the British researcher. Translated versions of the Chinese interview comments are presented here. (For more details on the research procedure, see Spencer-Oatey and Tang 2006.)

Phase 1: Start-Up and Pre-Meeting

Canney Davison and Ward (1999) summarize the first phase as "know your task and team", and they recommend that the key steps that managers and leaders need to take at this point are as follows:

> 1. *Develop and agree the purpose of the team with the sponsors.* "The team leader and sponsor(s) need to painstakingly clarify the mission, purpose, agenda, accountability, time frame, resources available, organisational barriers and key stakeholders."

> 2. *Select the team members.* "Once the purpose of the team has been clarified, the next step is to establish the team membership. . . . The process by which the team members are selected will also have a powerful influence on the subsequent dynamics of the team."

> 3. *Plan the communication technology support.* "Once the geographical location of the team members is established, the project design team needs to assess what communication technology can enhance the interaction of the team for that particular task."

> 4. *Decide if you need an external facilitator, contract with the sponsors and team and clarify the boundaries of responsibility and the facilitator's role.* Canney Davison and Ward suggest that key issues to consider when making these decisions are (a) the extent to which team members come with conflicting agendas, (b) the extent to which the team leader needs to be involved in the technical detail of the task, making it hard also to attend to process, and (c) the level of experience and confidence of the team leader in managing an international team.

> 5. *Interview the key players.* "Once the membership has been agreed with the team members, it is useful for the team leader to start getting them involved, prior to meeting face to face.

This can be done through interviews or sending out a questionnaire to find out how much the team members already understand about the task, their attitude towards, or historical interaction with, each other and their level of commitment."

6. *Plan the first meetings.* "When the above work is done, key team members, the leader and/or facilitator and key sponsors need to go through the agenda for the first meetings. They need to establish who will present what, and check to see that any proposed team building exercises will be new, culturally and organisationally relevant and at the right level of experience." (Extracts from Canney Davison and Ward 1999: 91–94)

For the *eChina-UK Programme*, the purpose of the collaboration was negotiated and agreed by a Sino-UK Joint Steering Committee, which consisted primarily of representatives of the two key stakeholders: the Higher Education Funding Council for England (HEFCE) and the Chinese Ministry of Education (MoE). The aim and objectives of the programme were identified by HEFCE as shown in Table 10.1.

In Britain, HEFCE put out a call for bids to all English universities, and specified these details in the particulars. English universities thus submitted their bids in accordance with these specifications. The selected universities were each informed what their budget

Table 10.1

The Aims and Objectives of the *eChina-UK Programme* as Specified by HEFCE

Aim:	The aim of the Sino-UK e-Learning in higher education programme is to strengthen collaboration between China and the UK in the use of information and communications technology (ICT), and particularly the Internet, for distance and flexible learning in specified areas of higher education.
Objectives:	The objectives for the programme are:

a. To pursue the further development of ICT and the use of academic electronic networks in their application to learning and teaching in higher education, in both countries.

b. To develop and pilot innovative distance education courseware materials, in the selected areas, capable of being delivered through the Internet in the two countries. These national pilot projects will explore:

- the development of new course materials
- the compatibility of Chinese and English platforms
- mode(s) of delivery
- quality assurance
- learning management environments
- student support.

c. To disseminate the generic lessons drawn from the pilot projects, including the benefits and issues of pedagogy, working cross-culturally, and of publishing and intellectual property rights, bearing in mind the desirability of a future agreement on mutual recognition of academic qualifications and credits.

d. To inform the development of national policy initiatives on eLearning in higher education in both countries.

e. To support HE staff in developing their competence in the use of Internet-based learning and teaching.

(HEFCE 2002: 10)

would be and were allocated three years to complete their project. A programme manager was appointed to manage the programme as a whole in the UK on behalf of HEFCE, and to act as a liaison person between HEFCE, the UK members of the steering committee, and the project leaders. Step 1 (developing and agreeing the purpose of the team with the sponsors) was thus carried out in Britain in this way. In China, the MoE selected leading universities in Beijing, and the Joint Steering Committee paired the British and Chinese universities, allocating the subject areas they should focus on. It was not clear, however, the extent to which the Chinese universities understood the aims and objectives of the programme as a whole at that time. No full-time equivalent of the UK programme manager was appointed in China, and this made liaison between stakeholders and project staff problematic both within China and internationally.

According to Canney Davison and Ward's (1999) 'best practice' model, project leaders should then carry out steps two to five. For the *eChina-UK* projects, however, this was impossible, because the British and Chinese partner universities had only been allocated a broad area for collaborative work (e.g. generic pedagogy for primary and secondary school teachers). Ideally, before choosing project members and planning communication support, they needed to meet with their partner members to agree a specific collaborative project that complied with the aims and objectives of the programme as a whole and that was achievable within the time and budget allocated. In reality, however, all each university could do at this stage was to select key staff members who would attend the first joint meetings.

Initially, all the parties felt their collaboration was something of an 'arranged marriage'. In nearly all cases, they had never met each other before, had little idea about each other's backgrounds and interests, and had no sense of each other's goals and motivations for participating. E-mail was used to exchange concrete information such as who would be attending the meetings and brief information about these people's current positions, but this mode of communication is unsuitable for building deeper mutual understanding. The first meetings, therefore, needed to provide the partners with the opportunity for extensive relationship building, as well as for planning their collaborative projects. The British project leaders and key project members visited their partners in Beijing in March 2003 and spent about a week there in order to start this process.

Phase 2: First Meetings

Canney Davison and Ward (1999) give detailed advice as to how the initial meetings should be handled. They recommend that leaders take the following steps:

> 7. *At the first set of meetings, explain the organizational strategy and policies, putting the purpose of the team in context. Jointly identify, prioritise and agree the mission, purpose, objectives and key success criteria.* They give the following advice: "Bad experience has taught us this golden rule: first gain commitment to a common direction, then explore differences. Otherwise un-channelled differences can blow up and land in your face";

8. *Emphasize building interrelationships when face-to-face;*

9. *Consciously explore the cultural similarities and differences and resulting strengths and weaknesses of the team;*

10. *Agree the first set of action plans.*

(Extracts from Canney Davison 1999: 96–100)

When the British teams arrived in Beijing, their first sense was that (in several but not all cases) they were discussing and negotiating with institutional managers rather than academic counterparts. They were expecting to meet other academics with whom they could discuss and agree a specific collaborative project, and so found it disconcerting to be negotiating about academic matters with non-subject experts. In fact, this was due to structural differences between British and Chinese universities in handling distance/online courses. In Britain, online courses are typically handled by academic departments, and so the *eChina-UK* projects were organizationally 'located' in faculties, departments or centres whose academic staff had the relevant expertise (e.g. Faculty of Education). In China, however, the projects were located in special units that were responsible for distance and/ or continuing education. (See Kang and Song this volume, on Online Institutes in Pilot Universities.) These units do not have their own academic staff but rather buy in such expertise from other parts of the university when it is needed. This difference not only made it more difficult for the British teams to negotiate and agree the focus of their collaboration but later led to project management difficulties for some of the Chinese partners.

Despite these initial mismatches, the British and Chinese project leaders were able to agree on foci for their collaborative initiatives and to develop these into formal joint project proposals for submission to HEFCE and the Chinese MoE in July 2003. The proposals identified jointly agreed aims and objectives, project deliverables and key performance indicators. Nevertheless, there were certain elements of the collaboration that were impossible and inappropriate to tie down from the start. For example, the HEFCE documentation stated that the joint teams were to develop innovative courseware. At the beginning, when both teams were unfamiliar with e-learning in each other's contexts, it was impossible for them to anticipate, in concrete terms, exactly how their courseware materials would demonstrate innovation. Moreover, since this was a pilot programme, HEFCE did not want the teams to pre-specify their outcomes too precisely. They preferred an unfolding approach, which would allow the teams to build up their mutual understanding and to follow up flexibly on fruitful new leads if and when they arose. Acquiring valuable generic insights was an important goal of the programme, yet at the beginning no one could be sure precisely what these might entail. So in that sense, it was neither feasible nor desirable to specify the exact success criteria for all of the expected outcomes from the programme.

Having agreed their project plans and gained HEFCE and MoE approval of them, the project leaders were then in a position to select their project members. All of them identified staff to fulfil the following roles: academic developer, instructional designer, graphic designer, Web designer, technical support, e-tutor, project manager and project director. Most of the projects entailed the development of several modules, each requiring different academic expertise (e.g. one project developed modules in educational psychology, generic pedagogy, and e-learning and educational technology), and so the number of people involved was often very large. For example, there were about 35 staff at Beijing Normal University, 30 at World Universities Network (Universities of Manchester, Sheffield, Southampton and Bristol) and 20 at the University of Nottingham working on their respective projects.[1] The large number of people had major consequences for both project management and for collaboration and communication processes.

For project management, it meant that a huge amount of liaison work was required both within and across British and Chinese partner universities, and since there were staff from different sections of the university, internal financial matters also needed to be addressed. Role responsibilities needed to be specified and the amount of time required from each person needed to be clarified. In fact, such project management matters proved very challenging for the larger projects, especially because the requirement for innovation made it difficult to judge the amount of time that would be involved. For example, if managers' experience of developing e-learning materials related primarily to the video recording of lectures (see Gu this volume), or if they had never previously been responsible for the development of any kind of e-learning materials, it was extremely difficult for them to judge realistically the amount of time and range of responsibilities needed to develop interactive materials that incorporated a variety of media and of learning activities. Both in Britain and China, several of the universities underestimated the need for an experienced project manager who would be entrusted with the authority to truly manage the whole project. As a result, some of the team members felt let down by the project management arrangements, as can be seen from the following interview comments:

> Chinese 08: *I think the whole process would be much easier and smoother if we academics, instead of the management, were authorized to lead the project.*

> Chinese 09: *We just knew we were involved in a project, but we didn't know clearly what sort of roles we should play specifically, what kind of functions we should perform, what sort of rights we should have, and what kind of responsibilities we should take. And about those questions, there were no formal documents or anything like that.*

Across the joint teams, two different collaboration procedures were used. Two of the joint partnerships used 'extended stay', whereby a member of the Chinese team came to Britain and worked with the British team for six months (in one case) or for one year (in the other case). This provided the opportunity for extended, in-depth collaboration, yet at the same time, it reduced the breadth of contact between the British and Chinese team members. The reason was that the 'visitor' acted as a go-between between the British team and other Chinese team members, and there was a smaller amount of multiple interchange between British and Chinese team members. In addition, if the British team members could spend only a limited amount of time on the *eChina-UK* project (because of other responsibilities), it could be very frustrating for the visitor, when she or he was concentrating on it full-time.

The other projects used 'exchange visits', whereby small teams of people visited the other country for one or two weeks on a fairly regular basis. In addition, some of the Chinese team members stayed in Britain for longer (one to three months) on a number of occasions. This collaborative method entailed periods of very intensive work, which were very demanding on the teams (especially the host teams, who simultaneously had to handle their ongoing responsibilities), and usually these were extremely productive. However, there was a tendency for things to 'go dead' between visits, and it required a lot of proactive effort by the project directors to keep things moving on.

In fact, communication turned out to be one of the most challenging issues for all of the projects. This involved several aspects, including managing the different modes of communication, developing effective social communication networks, managing language proficiency issues, and ensuring common conceptual understanding among the project members. Most members found face-to-face communication particularly effective. They also found e-mail extremely useful, but writing ideas clearly can be quite demanding, especially for non-native speakers. People's experiences of video-conferencing were less positive, perhaps partly because of the poor connection quality.

> Chinese 11: *I prefer face-to-face talk. It is convenient and you need not bother to write down your opinions. Besides, sometimes words could not express well what one thought.*

> Chinese 13: *I feel face-to-face interaction is best. Many issues can be expressed clearly and directly. If you choose to send emails, you might need more time to achieve the same communication effect as clearly and as fast as face-to-face talk.*

> Chinese 01: *In some circumstances, when a face-to-face meeting is impossible, video-conferencing is also good. But there is one problem with video-conferencing. That is, when many sides are taking part in the video conference, it is not easy to communicate things in depth. . . . It doesn't work very well for multilateral talk, because some things need to be discussed by two partners. In video conferencing, there is less room for emotional interchange, it is more like talk only for the sake of talk. I don't think it is very effective.*

For the large projects, establishing effective communication networks was important, yet it was not easy to achieve, given the numerous practical constraints that everyone was working under. One Chinese project member gave the following evaluation:

> Chinese Researcher: *In your opinion, was the communication effective?*

> Chinese 20: *No, it wasn't. Though both Chinese and British sides had their own project managers, they couldn't do all the communications on their own. We should have embedded different communication mechanisms in the project at different levels.*

One of the module teams within one of the projects used a collaboration platform to discuss topics, assign work, to send out notices and to manage files and work diaries. They found this worked extremely effectively, but since it was all in Chinese, the British partners were unable to participate. This raises the problem of language.

All of the British projects initially relied almost exclusively on the ability of the Chinese partners to speak English. None of them had any Chinese-speaking members at the start of their project, and so the burden of interpreting and translation fell almost entirely on the Chinese partners. For one of the projects in particular, this was a heavy burden. Language affected not only team interaction but also course development and mutual exchange and evaluation of each other's materials (everything had to be translated from English to Chinese, and from Chinese to English, so that the Chinese and British academic developers could give feedback on each other's work.)[2] This significantly increased the workload of the Chinese partners and was problematic in a number of ways. Some people felt quite strongly about this issue:

> Chinese 21: *The working language was English. Due to the language problems, when we couldn't express ourselves clearly, it seemed as though we Chinese were at a disadvantage. But as a matter of fact, the British were thinking hard to get what we wanted to say.*

> Chinese 16: *I think we should show consideration for each other in terms of language. China is now developing very fast; they should know some Chinese to communicate with us. . . . We have learned a lot of English, it's their turn to learn some basic Chinese, as it is two-way communication. I find it weird that they don't know even a word of Chinese.*

As the projects progressed, most of the British realized the importance of having a Chinese speaker to work with them in Britain, and so identified suitable people to bring in on an ad hoc basis. In addition, several of them started to take Chinese language lessons.

All of the project members found that it was vital to spend considerable time reaching a common understanding of 'technical' terms and concepts. This was not a language proficiency issue; it was equally important among native speakers. At first, people needed to clarify use of terms like 'course', 'module', 'unit', 'chapter', and even something like this could be experienced as emotionally challenging:

> British 09: *When I first joined, I spent weeks if not months on a simple practical confusion as to what is a unit, module, what was the other one?*

> British 06: *Activity.*

> British 09: *There was no standard definition, so I was like blocked at the first hurdle, and so I wasn't quite sure how much material I'd got to write, because we were given this notion of how many hours the student would spend, I wouldn't know in which box those hours fitted. . . . I thought I don't understand this, I can't do this.*

The process seemed never-ending: uncovering the nuances of meaning associated with each person's or each group's use of a word, and then developing joint working definitions. There was a continual stream of words and concepts to discuss; for example, blended learning, online learning, formative assessment, summative assessment, forum, e-portfolio, student workspace, evaluation, reflection, criticality, and so on. There was no alternative but to spend considerable lengths of time talking with each other, and gradually building up a common understanding and common language.

Through these experiences, the project members came to realize not only the vital importance of bilingual speakers and their role in interpreting but also the crucial need for cultural mediators. Effective communication depends not only on the accurate translation of linguistic meaning but also on the grasp of pragmatic meaning (which entails the understanding of background assumptions, implicit messages and so on). It was very hard for both British and Chinese members to understand many contextual issues and to pick up a wide range of subtly communicated elements, especially at a distance, and so the role of bilingual, culturally aware individuals who could help facilitate mutual understanding emerged as vitally important. These people were needed to describe and explain a range of issues, including the educational context, pedagogic beliefs and practices, management procedures and ways of working and interacting. They could also advise on best ways of handling such matters. (See also Motteram et al. this volume, on boundary crossers.)

Since the staff were developing e-learning materials primarily for delivery in the Chinese context, it was essential for the British members to acquire a very good understanding of the Chinese educational context. This was not always straightforward, especially in relation to the more subtle elements that do not easily emerge from needs analysis questionnaires or school visits. For example, one Chinese member commented as follows:

> Chinese 12: *They* [the British] *were over-idealistic in terms of professional development. For Chinese teachers, professional development mainly means titles and degrees. We're more realistic. So when carrying out learning activities, the teachers were only doing them roughly. . . . They* [the British] *just simply asked the teachers to watch a video, search for something, or hand in a report. But I think Chinese teachers are not that self-motivated because of the time pressures they are under. So we could only force them* [the teachers] *to learn, we made them fill up an e-portfolio.*

Some of the British developers needed some content-specific information on the Chinese educational context, as well as Chinese research data, in order to write some of their units. They found it difficult to obtain this, and it was not always clear whether this was because it was only available in Chinese (and thus not searchable in English) or because it did not exist. For example, a British developer needing to write a unit on teacher evaluation commented as follows:

> British 02: *I found it was difficult to find specific information in the literature in English. I'd track down articles via the internet, but the abstracts were in Chinese. But after being over there, and talking to the teachers, I began to think that the material on teacher evaluation doesn't really exist. It depends on the area, the school you're in. Maybe people haven't done that kind of research. Maybe it's also a different kind of research. I was looking for something in-depth, teachers talking about how they are evaluated in schools, which there's a lot of now here. But what I could find, and what I was sent, seemed to be very quantitative. There were a lot of figures and graphs. So it's obviously a different kind of research being done, so maybe that's why I couldn't find what I wanted.*

For both the British and Chinese project members it was not feasible to discuss straightforwardly their cultural differences and similarities regarding pedagogic beliefs and practices. People tended to have an implicit understanding of their own beliefs, and found them difficult to articulate in a vacuum. It was only through discussion of concrete tasks that the beliefs and practices began to emerge. In fact, HEFCE anticipated this, and that is exactly why they set up the programme in the first place as comprising a number of collaborative projects with tangible outputs. It meant, though, that plenty of time needed to be allowed for such conscious mutual understanding to emerge, and yet the timescales for the projects militated against this.

Canney Davison and Ward (1999: 130) recommend that international teams discuss and agree working practices, such as how members will make decisions, how they will communicate, and so on. Again, it is not always meaningful to do this in a vacuum; nevertheless, it would have been useful to consider this openly in certain respects. There can be organizational and structural differences that project members need to be aware of, and sometimes these may change during the lifetime of the project. One Chinese leader commented as follows:

> Chinese 22: *The British might think that the Chinese were working inefficiently, but it was because they didn't understand our organizational structure. Particularly, after the restructuring of the school, they should know who was responsible for what and whom they should go to for certain issues. My feeling is that they didn't know so much about this. There were so many people involved in this project on our side, and not everybody was the decision-maker for the big issues, so they should understand this. They should know about our organizational structure, the operational status of the project, our needs and so on.*

In fact, it was not just a matter of organizational/structural differences; there were also clear differences in decision-making practices. British project managers/directors had much greater authority to make decisions than their Chinese counterparts, such as over how resources would be allocated, how many staff needed to be employed, and how plans would be implemented. One Chinese director explained it as follows:

> Chinese 23: *Great differences exist between the working mechanisms in China and in the West. For example, professors in the UK have a major say in the affairs they are responsible for. The Vice Chancellor of the university or the Dean of the Faculty would not interfere too much. But things are quite different in China. Most of the resources are under the control of the university or the department. . . . For example, [name of British project manager] was inclined to think that he had the final say for something. But we couldn't. We have a procedure to go through. We need to conduct investigations and negotiations within our group and for some important things we need to report to the university or the Chinese Ministry of Education. In contrast, the British partners could make their own decisions once they had got the money from the government. So our working procedures, overall circumstances, thinking style and decision-making processes etc. are not all the same.*

Although these comments may oversimplify the situation in Britain, there is clearly a fundamental cultural difference between British and Chinese universities in decision-making procedures and in the relative authority of a project manager/director. These differences inevitably affect the speed with which a project can be taken forward.

There were also differences in protocols around e-mail, management of meetings and initial misunderstandings of each other's styles of interaction, as the following comments illustrate:

> Chinese 02: *Sending mass emails is a good way. But when we send such emails, it will infringe Chinese principles. If I send such an email to a person in a higher position, s/he will feel offended. Nowadays we send various materials by email, but Chinese are special, superiors will feel particularly insulted. . . . Sending emails to superiors is not a good way, because it shows no regard for status differences between people. Some superiors dislike equality, so the best way to communicate with them is to submit a report, either in written or oral form.*

> Chinese 14: *When we were in the UK, we found that the British side had a very clear cut meeting arrangement, like how often an update meeting should be held. And the plan was strictly carried out. . . . I think this working pattern was quite effective and efficient. In contrast, a regular meeting system was impossible here in China because each member had so many things to do and so little time for regular meetings.*

> Chinese 06: *The UK colleagues are more likely to raise issues directly. Their logic is that issues should be raised first, then they'll try their best to find solutions. Even if they couldn't solve the problems immediately, at least they would know what the problems are. It's their culture, I think. But one part of the Chinese culture is that we are too shy to open our mouths to talk about certain things. . . . Sometimes the UK project manager sent some suggestions to us. When we got the suggestion, we usually got nervous and wondered 'must we do it immediately?' or 'are they commanding us to do this?'. . . But working together with them for a while I gradually realised that I could voice my opinions too and take time to think. It wasn't a big problem.*

Phase 3: Mid Point

Canney Davison and Ward (1999: 100) argue that the mid-point phase is often characterized by "bursts of activity followed by periods of stagnation and poor momentum in which problems arise, the hidden agendas missed at the beginning can emerge and create . . . strategic moments". They advise taking the following steps:

> 11. *Work through strategic moments;*

> 12. *Make sure that everyone is involved and uses the feedback tools established at the beginning;*

> 13. *Keep a check on the timing, space the milestones and use the time together and time apart to its full potential;*

> 14. *Communicate what is being achieved and broadcast successes as they emerge;*

> 15. *Reduce the presence of the facilitators and promote team self-management and accountability.*

(Extracts from Canney Davison and Ward 1999: 100–107)

About one year after starting their collaborations, several of the projects needed to think through their underlying rationale for developing the e-learning courseware materials. As can be inferred from Table 10.1 (p. 161), HEFCE's implicit rationale was that it was a means of achieving the following:

- mutually beneficial collaborative partnerships, whereby each would learn from each other;
- insights into a range of issues associated with e-learning and with working cross-culturally.

HEFCE hoped that the materials would be useful in themselves not only to the Chinese partners but also to the British partners; however, their primary focus was on the generic insights to be gained rather than the materials per se. The Department of Higher Education in the Chinese MoE, on the other hand, originally hoped that the projects would develop innovative full courses that could be offered on a public good basis across China, and that would thereby contribute to the 1,500 'Quality Courses' （中国精品课程） being competitively developed and selected for free access and use throughout the country.[3] At the beginning, HEFCE and the British universities were unaware of this MoE objective. Meanwhile, the Chinese universities had their own agendas that differed from that of the MoE. They wanted to offer the courses developed on a fee-paying basis, partly to recoup the costs they had encountered and partly for commercial reasons. The British universities had varying agendas. The demands of the UK 2008 Research Assessment Exercise[4] meant that many British staff wanted (and needed) to gain research assessable publications from the collaboration, and their attention was therefore focused on the applied research associated with their project. However, there was also interest in developing collaborative degree programmes (beyond the scope of the *eChina-UK Programme*) and/or professional development courses that both parties could offer.

In principle, there is no contradiction between the development of course materials and a focus on applied research; they can easily go hand in hand. However, when money and time are limited, the balance can easily become problematic. Two of the projects agreed to develop master's level modules, and another project agreed to develop bachelor's level modules. It was clear from the start that it would be impossible to develop the full set of modules needed for the complete degree programmes. From a British perspective, this was not problematic, because developing a relatively small proportion would provide the British members with most of the benefits they were looking for. For the Chinese partners, however, it was much more problematic because they would be left with an incomplete degree course or even incomplete modules. These mid-term realizations led to some extremely painful strategic moments for some of the projects. Their differences came to the fore and resulted in either outbursts of anger and complaint, or stony silence and withdrawal.

Needless to say, such moments needed to be handled extremely sensitively, and the effectiveness with which the projects were able to work through them was largely dependent on the amount of trust that they had built up between project members during the earlier phases of the collaboration (cf. Phase 2 Step 8 of Canney-Davison and Ward's [1999] model). Members of all of the projects spent considerable amounts of time getting to know each other socially — having meals together, going on sightseeing trips, meeting each other's families and chatting about a wide range of topics — and this relationship building was a key factor that enabled them to work through their strategic moments effectively. Their differences were gradually resolved, and fruitful outcomes were achieved.

Members were then able to start communicating their achievements. Joint workshops were held both in Britain and in China and attended by as many staff as possible from all the *eChina-UK* projects. The workshops were found to be extremely effective for the cross-fertilization of ideas, for the motivation of staff and for the promotion of collaborative working. Staff from HEFCE and the MoE also attended these workshops and commented how impressed they were by the immense dedication of the joint teams, the depth and range of insights emerging, and the quality of the project outcomes.

Phase 4: Closing Stages

Canney Davison and Ward (1999) give the following recommendations for the final phase of a collaboration:

16. *Make sure everyone stays involved to the end;*

17. *Review the learning within the team;*

18. *Celebrate the success and plan for the future;*

19. *Pass on what has been learned to the rest of the organization (sector).*
    (Extracts from Canney Davison and Ward 1999: 107–110)

They point out that a project needs to "review its process in a fairly formal way using all the background information to sort out what went well, what could be improved on, and to record specific intercultural problems and guidelines for other teams" (Canney Davison and Ward 1999: 107). This is what the *eChina-UK* project members are doing at the time of writing. This reflection has been far more challenging than anticipated because during phases 1 to 3, they were concentrating primarily on the task at hand (the joint development of materials) and did not always keep formal records of their strategic moments, their strategies for resolving them, and the generic learning they were acquiring. Nevertheless, there is a unanimous sense that both individual project members as well as universities have gained tremendously from the collaboration in a variety of ways, including understanding of e-learning, the development of professional friendships and partnerships, and intercultural understanding. (See the Professional Learning section of our website: http://www.echinauk.org/) As one person put it, *"It has opened a window for me."*

In terms of international collaboration, some key lessons we have learned are as follows:

a. It is wise to *keep a project small in scope*, at least in the initial collaboration. If the task is too large and disparate, it will require the involvement of a large number of different staff and different organizational sections. That will give rise to major project management challenges, which may reduce the number of high-quality outcomes that can be achieved.

b. *International collaboration is extremely time-consuming*. If true collaboration (rather than superficial co-operation) is to take place, staff need to have the time to 'start slowly' rather than immediately focus on the task. They need to build mutual trust and understanding, so that there is 'glue' to hold them together when pressures later arise, and they need to learn about each other's contexts, professional viewpoints, ways of working, and so on, so that they can complete the task more effectively. Reducing or severely limiting the timescale of projects in order to save money is thus highly counterproductive; it may well shipwreck the partnership completely.

c. It is critically important to appoint a *competent and experienced international project manager*, who can liaise effectively with academic and technical staff as well as with international counterparts, and who has the authority to direct the project meaningfully. This is an appointment that is frequently overlooked in educational contexts, or regarded as unnecessary, yet is vital for the success of complex projects.

d. In bilateral collaborations, it is essential that *both parties have bilingual speakers* as members of their projects. It is both inappropriate and ineffective to rely on just one party to provide all the translation and interpreting that is needed. Moreover, *each party needs to have a cultural mediator* who can provide intercultural insights and who can act as a go-between when necessary. Such a person is particularly helpful when there are issues that one party does not understand, or when there is an impasse that needs to be bridged.

e. At an early stage in the collaboration, project members should seek to *understand the organizational set-up in each other's institution* and identify who is responsible for what. This is not as easy to achieve as it may seem, as relevant information is often not available in written form, and people tend to have an intuitive rather than explicit understanding of their own institution's set-up. Members also need to *establish acceptable ways of working*, such as decision-making procedures and protocols for handling e-mail.

f. When selecting project members, people's expertise, availability and personal goals all need to be considered. *Their roles and responsibilities should be identified as clearly as possible* (although innovative working will always involve a considerable degree of uncertainty) and they should be 'bought out' of current responsibilities if they already have a 'normal' workload. Any changes in personnel during the lifetime of the project should be kept to a minimum.

g. *Sustained, good quality communication is vital* and needs to be promoted actively. Despite advances in technology, *regular face-to-face meetings are essential* for complex discussion and negotiation, and for relationship building (which is fundamental to the success of any collaboration) (see Maznevski and Chudoba 2000 for research into communication strategies used by global virtual teams).

h.   *Extended exchange visits by key project members is cost-effective and fruitful.* However, it can have a gatekeeping effect by limiting the breadth of contact with the partner institution.

The project members are disseminating their outcomes (including lessons learned) in a variety of ways, including 'normal' channels like conference presentations and academic papers. However, we have chosen to focus on two: this book and the *eChina-UK* disseminator site (http://www.echinauk.org). We hope that interested parties will engage with our reflections, reports and samples, and send us feedback comments. Our mutual learning will thereby continue.

Concluding Remarks

Canney Davison and Ward (1999) developed their 'best practice' model from their experiences of working with many large multinational and international organizations, both in the public and private sectors. Although the set-up phase of the *eChina-UK Programme* was more complex than their model suggests, perhaps because of the many stakeholders involved, their broad division of phases was very applicable, and much of their advice was very relevant. Nevertheless, some fundamental questions remain:

*   Is it feasible for similarities and differences in professional beliefs and practices to be explored in advance, or is it necessary for collaborative partners to start working together on a concrete task before they can emerge?
*   Is it feasible for communication and collaboration protocols to be agreed in advance, or is it necessary for partners to start working together in order to develop awareness of what they prefer and what is needed?

Our experiences in the *eChina-UK Programme* indicate that a tandem approach is needed. It is impossible to gain a deep understanding of each other's professional beliefs and practices, or preferred protocols for communication and collaboration, prior to starting the task. Yet it is unwise to ignore such issues until serious problems emerge. So we recommend that engagement with the task, and reflection on the process and perspectives of those involved, go hand in hand every step of the way, each continually informing the other and each continually moving the other forward. This is very time-consuming, and stakeholders need to be fully aware of this, yet only in this way can synergy truly be created and the richest outcomes be achieved.

11

Developing a Collaborative Approach to e-Learning Design in an Intercultural (Sino-UK) Context

David McConnell, Sheena Banks and Vic Lally

Introduction

This chapter focuses on the processes of intercultural collaboration that occurred during a strand of the *eChina-UK DEfT* Project (*Developing e-Learning for Teachers*) (see Table 1.1 [p. 6] and Motteram et al. this volume, pp. 189–201). This part of the project involved staff from the University of Sheffield and Beijing Normal University (BNU) in jointly developing e-learning materials for a master's level module in Educational Technology and e-Learning.[1] One of the goals of the *eChina-UK Programme* as a whole is to develop understandings in both countries of cultural change and exchange in e-learning pedagogy (see Spencer-Oatey this volume, pp. 3–9 and Spencer-Oatey and Tang this volume, pp. 159–173), and we (the members of the UK team involved in the Sheffield–BNU module) were particularly interested in this objective because it offered the opportunity to incorporate two different educational cultures into one programme. In this chapter, we explore the collaboration issues that we experienced, and discuss the ways in which we made progress in being able to understand our different approaches to e-learning pedagogy and practice. The Chinese Ministry of Education has introduced curriculum reform about new methodologies related to student-centred learning, group work and teacher-student interaction, and this was a strategic driver of the project. As a consequence, the Chinese team were particularly interested in gaining knowledge of collaborative e-learning as practised by the UK team.

Effective collaboration processes are key to the success of all joint projects (Ngor 2001; Burnard et al. 1999), because collaboration can be complex (De Laat and Lally 2003). In this project, part of that complexity was the national diversity of the members. Such diversity can confer benefits when "the inherent dimension of nationality is legitimized as a source of information and thus becomes a role-related source of diversity" (Maznevski 1994: 534), in that it can result in enhanced creativity and problem-solving (McLeod and

Lobe 1992; Ling 1990; both cited by Maznevski 1994). However, good collaboration rarely happens by accident and, as Maznevski points out, cultural diversity can pose barriers to effective interaction. In our collaboration, it was certainly true that working across national boundaries on the joint development of e-learning materials, with the additional complexities of differing languages, presented us with real challenges (Banks et al. 2006). Despite this, we were successful in that we moved to a second phase of collaboration. Our collaboration with BNU became a process through which we were able to grow in our understandings of each other, share our respective pedagogic ideas and expertise in e-learning, and build on these to develop new ideas.

The main argument of this chapter is that an 'intercultural' approach to educational design, that draws on differing pedagogies, theories and collaborative action, can emerge from e-learning initiatives such as the *eChina-UK Programme*. We are particularly keen to illustrate how the theoretical perspectives that underpin our work in the UK (social constructivism and constructionism, situated learning theory, experiential learning, action learning and research, and community theory) informed the pedagogical design embedded in our Educational Technology course development, and how they were also adapted to meet the requirements of the Chinese educational context. On the one hand, our approaches informed the processes of our collaborative work, and, we argue, enhanced the quality of project outputs; on the other, engagement with the issues associated with implementing e-learning in a Chinese context also had an impact on our own practice. In the following sections, we provide examples of these processes.

Conceptualizing Educational Design: From a UK Perspective

The challenge of educational design

The fundamental focus of our work in the UK is 'educational design'. Education itself is about planned intervention in the learning processes that are constantly occurring in individuals and groups of people. These processes include emotional and social processes, learning processes, and teaching processes.

Systematic intervention in the development of these processes requires planning, and this is the central aim of educational design as pursued in this project. 'Design', then, in its educational sense, involves the production of plans, templates and frameworks that help structure, co-ordinate and support learning and teaching activity. This includes learning tasks, of course, but also the work that needs to be done to create and maintain the social and physical environment within which learning and teaching take place. This *may* seem relatively straightforward but is complicated by the dynamics of the teaching and learning process.

By engaging in design, we are attempting to nurture a shared direction for the development of teaching and learning processes, while acknowledging that human processes are too complex to be 'controlled'. The challenge, then, is to develop theory-informed educational practice, by design. In our *eChina-UK* project, this required us to achieve mutual understanding at a very deep level of our respective pedagogic ideas of e-learning, both as researchers and as practitioners, and to span the two cultural contexts of the UK and China. It was also important that we had the opportunity to meet potential learners (Chinese teachers) so that we could understand their needs. This helped us to bridge the divide between theory and practice (see Goodyear, De Laat and Lally 2006 for a more detailed account of how theory and practice can interact to support effective educational designs).

Theoretical approaches underpinning e-learning designs

We have argued that 'educational design' for e-learning requires a theoretical basis and this theoretical basis informs our intercultural collaborative work. We have stated that, for successful intercultural collaboration to occur, it is necessary to achieve a deep and mutual understanding of the pedagogies and practices of each partner. So before looking at the practicalities of design in detail, we will briefly outline some of our underpinning theoretical ideas, as an example of the 'weave of theory' that we brought to our collaboration with BNU.

Many teachers and trainers, including our BNU partners at the start of the project, approach e-learning from the viewpoint of Instructional System Design (ISD). ISD views learning as a linear activity, and conventionally it is based on four key concepts or assumptions (You 1993). Courses developed using the ISD method have the following characteristics:

Linear: Specific learning objectives determine what is to be learned, and each step in the learning process is predetermined and builds on the previous step.

Deterministic: Learning patterns have directions that can be defined in advance and are difficult to change.

Closed: The learner is obliged to think and act only within the firmly set boundaries that have been imposed by the instructional systems designer.

Negative in their feedback: ISD courses often employ negative feedback mechanisms to ensure that learning and teaching outcomes 'fit' with predetermined goals. This is problematic, because it means that there is little possibility of change during the learning process in response to what the learners achieve.

The approach of the Sheffield team contrasted strongly with that of the BNU team. One of the key aspects of our theoretical approach is a 'social-constructivist' view of learning that also considers the situativity of learning processes. This leads us to focus on developing online discussions in which participants link new knowledge to their prior knowledge, and actively construct new internal representations of the ideas being presented (Boekaerts and Simons 1995). We also draw on ideas about the meaningfulness and situativity of learning. We view learning as a set of processes by which the learner personalizes new ideas by giving meaning to them, based upon earlier experiences. Meaning is also indexed by experience (Brown et al. 1989). Therefore, each experience with an idea, and the environment of which that idea is part, becomes part of the meaning of that idea (Duffy and Jonassen 1992). Learning is therefore understood and viewed by us as situated by the activity in which it takes place (Brown et al. 1989; Lave and Wenger 1991). This is the view held by the UK team, developed from earlier research and practice (Banks, Lally and McConnell 2003).

In our thinking, we also draw on a body of work that has focused more explicitly on the social or group dimensions of learning. Influenced by the work of Vygotsky (1962, 1978), many authors (Lave 1988; Lave and Wenger 1991; Resnick 1991; Wertsch 1991; Moll et al. 1993; Smith 1994; Lave 1996; Levine et al. 1996; Salomon and Perkins 1998; Dillenbourg 1999; Goldstein 1999; Wegerif et al. 1999) discuss the role of the group in shaping and driving individual cognitive (i.e. learning and tutoring) processes (group-mediated cognition). Key aspects of this view include the suggestion that, in a group meeting, the situation itself may exert a strong mediating effect on individual cognitive and conceptual processes; in other words, the thinking of individuals is influenced by the group in which they are working. The merger of psychological and social processes is another fundamental feature of group-mediated cognition. A third key feature is the tension between the conceptual structure or understanding (of the problem or ideas under discussion) of the group and that of the individuals within it. These individual understandings may vary from each other as well as from the group. This tension may be the driving force for the collective processing of the group.

Another perspective that we have drawn upon is sociocultural theory. Whereas the social-constructivist perspectives makes a distinction between the individual cognitive activities and the environment in which the individual is present, the sociocultural perspective regards the individual as being part of that environment. Accordingly, learning cannot be understood as a process that is solely in the mind of the learner (Van Boxtel et al. 2000). Knowledge, according to this perspective, is constructed in settings of joint activity (Koschmann 1999). Learning is a process of participating in cultural practices, a process that structures and shapes cognitive activity (Lave and Wenger 1991). The sociocultural perspective gives prominence to the aspect of mutuality of the relations between members and emphasizes the dialectic nature of the learning interaction (Sfard 1998). Construction of knowledge takes place in a social context, such as might be found in collaborative activities of the Educational Technology module (see McConnell 2000 for a much more detailed exploration of collaborative learning).

In summary, we (in the Sheffield team) contend that this complex synthesis of theoretical ideas, drawing on social-constructivism, social-constructionism, sociocultural theory, and ideas about situativity and collaboration in groups, is necessary in order to take account of the complexities of individual and group processes in the learning context that are the focus of the designs described in this chapter. Furthermore, we try to indicate how, together, they direct us towards a focus on individual and group processes, towards the interactions between these, and towards learning and tutoring. These ideas had an impact on the way in which the two project teams in the UK and China collaborated to produce a master's module in e-learning.

The Collaborative Design Process

Starting points

As indicated in the previous section, the two project teams — Sheffield and BNU — started with two very different conceptions of e-learning (currently being investigated further in a follow-up *eChina-UK* project on *Intercultural Pedagogy*). The BNU team had considerable experience of developing e-learning with Educational Technology as the subject and ISD as their pedagogic model. In addition, they had an appreciation of collaborative learning and wanted to learn more about how to achieve this in practice. The Sheffield team's experience, on the other hand, was of developing e-learning as collaborative learning through online groups and communities, with a weave of social theories of knowledge construction as the basis of a pedagogic model. We were keen to learn how this could work in a Chinese context. Our collaboration focused on sharing our two approaches to e-learning and exploring whether it was possible to use design features from both models in the development of the online course (Banks et al. 2006).

Both Sheffield and BNU had experience of distance learning and teaching, and of supporting off-campus learners. The Sheffield team had experience of 'fully' virtual teaching through the *WebCT*^{TM} Virtual Learning Environment (VLE). BNU's experience was of blended learning, in which some of the course was online and some face-to-face, delivered in local learning support centres (see Kang and Song this volume, pp. 11–32). BNU was in the process of developing its own VLE to support online collaborative learning (*WebCL*) (see Motteram et al. this volume, pp. 189–202).

Our views on e-learning production were also different. According to Cao, Wang and Tang (2005), the dominant production process in the Chinese context can be summarized in the following way. A key textbook is used as the source of content for each course. This is 're-appropriated' for the online learning setting: instructional designers prepare the content of the book for presentation online (cf. Gu this volume, pp. 37–55). Tutors, who have not been involved in the development of the course content or in the learning and teaching processes to be pursued in the course, are recruited to teach the learning material. Students are expected to focus on 'learning' the content, largely on their own. Assessment is by a final examination, the content of which is determined by the teacher. Learner support is not provided in the BNU system (Ding 2005). An aim of course designs of this kind is to economize in the production process and in the use of academics' time.

Design for learning that is non-linear, interactive and occurs in social settings, such as groups and communities, requires us to engage in a qualitatively different approach to the design process. We argue that we are led to ask the question: what social engagements and processes provide a context for learning in professional development contexts? When we look at learning through the lens of ISD, it may seem that many teachers see learning as the acquisition of propositional knowledge. What happens, then, to practice, when learning is viewed as social co-participation and knowledge building? From this perspective, learning is a process that takes place in a participation framework, not solely in an individual's mind. Learning is a way of being in the social world, not only a way of coming to know it (McConnell 2006).

The production process in this model focuses on students developing their professional practice in the context of the academic course. The course is developed collaboratively by a team of academics and Web technicians, each of whom brings resources, expertise and professional practice to bear on the design process (Barab et al. 2006). The academics involved in designing the course also tutor on it. Students are expected to learn collaboratively in the community with others. Assessment is also a collaborative process, involving the student, group and tutors. The quality of the course design, the learning and teaching processes, and the outcomes, are assured through institutional mechanisms. These include course evaluation involving students and tutors, institutional measures such as the involvement of external examiners, and national governmental mechanisms (QAA 2001). This course design process has a cost in terms of people's time, the use of human resources and in the development of rich resources for the learners, but the model has the potential to lead to quality products and learning outcomes.

The Sheffield team thus took the view that, when designing sustained, purposeful e-learning that takes place in groups and communities, it is necessary to adopt a view of learning that requires a participatory design. Such a view involves:

- emphasis on collaborative and co-operative learning;
- learning through dialogue and group work within a community (of learners, of practice);
- interaction with online materials;
- collaborative knowledge production;
- major use of VLEs (e.g. Web-CT™ or Blackboard) to create and share learning resources, and to enable student-to-student, and student-to-teacher communication.

In contrast, we understood the BNU team's approach to be as follows:

- the teacher is the expert;
- there is a high dependence on instructional design;
- the transmission/dissemination model is dominant;
- theory is not readily related to practice: there is a gap between academics and practitioners;
- there is a skills-based focus in courses;
- peer-to-peer interaction is undervalued.

Developing a shared educational rationale for designing e-learning that supports groups and communities

In order to collaborate, both teams needed to start by sharing our respective beliefs and practices in the pedagogic design of e-learning. This helped us to see what we could learn from each other and how our different ideas could be incorporated into a joint design for the module. Our respective beliefs about e-learning were the focus of our joint project meetings. Ideas and understandings of e-learning terminologies, issues and practices, were constantly discussed, revisited and renegotiated through the process of developing and producing joint e-learning materials.

During these meetings, it was clear that, although we used similar terminologies, their meanings often differed (cf. Spencer-Oatey and Tang this volume). We found that we reached agreement on the meaning of terminologies but then frequently had to revisit our understandings at later dates, and, because of this, we had to rework ideas and materials in the light of new understandings. During these meetings, Sheffield academics presented information and evidence about how to design for online groups and communities. BNU academics presented case studies of existing online Educational Technology modules that demonstrated their approach to educational design, based on their concept of a knowledge framework using Bloom's taxonomy of knowledge. In addition, a member of the BNU design team spent time in Sheffield to learn more about our practice, producing design templates, and both BNU and Sheffield ran trials with online learners in China. We found this process of exchange absolutely essential for reaching a basis for collaboration and agreement on a joint design, although it was very time-consuming. It was also essential that the meetings were bilingual.

In this collaboration we addressed a number of key questions:

- How do we design for online group work and learning communities in a Chinese context?
- Can a learning design developed in the UK work in China?
- What adaptations need to be made to this learning design for it to be effective in China?
- What are the design implications of adapting to the Chinese learning and teaching context, and the challenge of scalability?
- What will each team learn from this in terms of their practice and knowledge?
- How can we achieve the professional development of teachers so that they can successfully practise these new, collaboratively developed (intercultural) methods?

The development of learning designs for communities and groups

Fairly early in the project (December 2003), the Sheffield team travelled to China for a project meeting at which we presented a discussion paper on theory and practice in networked collaborative e-learning. We suggested that the course should involve students in peer learning, in sharing resources and learning tasks, in co-operation rather than competition, in group work and knowledge construction, in working with multiple perspectives and diversity, and in managing their own learning. The BNU team were particularly keen to learn more about collaborative learning, and in fact the ideas in this presentation were to form the basis of discussion of the eventual design of the joint course. We all agreed that there should be a greater emphasis on learning processes rather than the traditional emphasis on 'content'.

In the UK and Europe, 'networked collaborative e-learning' is the generic term for the process of bringing together students via personal computers linked to the Internet, with a focus on them working as a 'learning community', sharing resources, knowledge, experience and responsibility through reciprocal collaborative learning.

This form of e-learning foregrounds the educational need for students to work in social learning environments that emphasize both the 'situated nature' of learning and the importance of co-production and co-participation.

Within this virtual learning community perspective, students can have opportunities for a wider choice of the content and direction of their learning, and its management. They may also co-operate with others in their learning, through processes of negotiation and discussion. The students (who were to be school teachers in China) would be encouraged to take a critical perspective on their learning and to focus on their own learning and development from a critical, reflective perspective, combined with an understanding of relevant concepts and ideas. The architecture of most VLEs can be used to support students working in groups in this way. We agreed on the incorporation of the following supportive structures in the module, to facilitate these principles:

■   An action learning/research cycle

Action learning/research (see Figure 11.1) was implicit in the overall design of the module. We wanted students to be active in their learning; to consider why they were learning and what they were trying to learn about; to carry out some activities that supported their learning, and then to reflect on what happened in carrying out those activities, and the outcomes of their learning. This was to be achieved in small social e-groups.

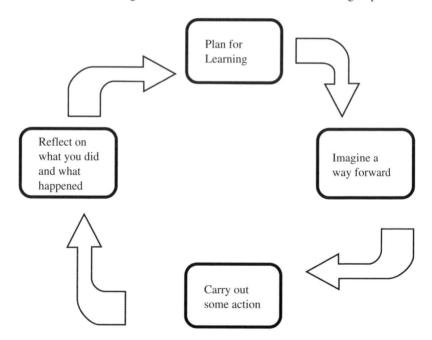

Figure 11.1   Action Learning and Research: A Cycle

■ **Knowledge building**

Students would be encouraged to go beyond 'merely' learning course material, and to co-operatively build new understandings of knowledge, based on group discussion, critique of what they had learned, and analysis of ways in which they could take their learning into their classroom practice.

■ **Scaffolding of group work and learning**

We aimed to support learners in moving to this new way of learning, by incorporating a wide range of interaction opportunities, including the following:

- community spaces: e.g. plenary networking, reviews, presentations;
- group spaces: e.g. e-seminars, collaborative projects, personal assignments, self-peer-tutor review and assessment, scaffolded discussions, free-ranging discussions;
- workshop reviews: during which there was collective evaluation and design;
- café areas: for chatting, sharing photos, exchanges;
- resources: journal papers, photos and biographies, Web links, library.

We scaffolded learners' experience of these features in a range of ways. For example, we provided a structure for each section of the module that was initially highly visible but became less visible as the module progressed. With regard to resources, we provided much more specific guidance regarding follow-up reading for the early units than for the later units. In ways such as this, we aimed to help learners move towards more autonomous, self-managed and group learning.

Of course, this design has implications for the role of the e-tutor, the person who is responsible for 'orchestrating' the collaborative activities of the students as they engage in the processes outlined above. The following list gives some examples of the task requirements of the e-tutor on this type of online course:

- help to organize the group;
- provide the scaffolding for the cohesion and development of the group, and the skills of the group members;
- consult with group members;
- guide group members where appropriate;
- provide resources;
- ask good questions and model this skill;
- design the learning experiences (not just content);
- understand how to work in asynchronous learning/discussion;
- reflect on his or her own practice;
- see the learning potential of openness/chaos at times;
- take care not to lecture the students;
- have an 'approachable' presence online;
- communicate effectively via text; i.e. have 'presence' online.

We all acknowledged that Chinese online learners would need considerable support to become effective collaborative learners. This insight revealed a gap in the provision of effective e-tutor training, particularly to help teachers to manage the change from teaching face-to-face to teaching online. As a consequence, the development of an e-tutor training programme has become an objective for the follow-up projects of the *eChina-UK Programme* (cf. Joyes and Wang this volume, and Afterword this volume).

Achieving Intercultural e-Learning Design in Practice

In this section, we briefly outline the structure of the module that emerged from our intercultural collaboration.

Many of our initial discussions were about the purpose and level of learning appropriate for a master's module, as we had different views. Sheffield thought that the purpose of the module should be to enable the learners to link theory and practice, through reflection on their practice, and thereby to develop perspectives as research practitioners. BNU wanted the focus to be more practical, to support the teachers in effective decision-making about using e-learning technology and to develop associated skills in using it. Both partners argued that their approach promoted deep learning. We managed to reach consensus on this by using the bridge of 'problem-based learning'— a methodology popular in China as a vehicle for collaborative learning that provides an authentic context for reflective practice, and this has been embedded in the way online Tasks and Activities were presented.

The feedback from the BNU team in response to our first drafts of unit prototypes indicated that they thought the design was too loose, unstructured and abstract to meet the needs of Chinese learners. The emphasis on process rather than content meant that their main impression of the unit was that it was too theoretical and did not therefore meet their requirements for problem-based learning. By comparing our first unit prototypes with examples of existing course materials from BNU, over the timescale of several project meetings, we were able to adapt our design by using some elements of Chinese design. It was essential that we did this, in order to respond to the challenges of the Chinese context, such as scalability — the large number of learners allocated to one tutor. So we adapted our learning design to enable group work and communication to be an integral part of staged tasks and activities, leading to specific learning outcomes within each Unit. We added specific objectives and outcomes for each Unit. The Chinese team used Bloom's taxonomy of educational objectives as the knowledge framework, as adapted by Pi (1998), as the basis for designing activities for different types of knowledge. We found this difficult to fit into our social-constructivist model because of the requirement to predetermine knowledge. Therefore, we tried to frame the learning outcomes in terms that acknowledged individual learning and understandings. The tasks and activities were linked to key content, readings and website links, case studies and, in some instances, the use of video triggers.

For example, Unit 1 is an introduction to e-Learning and Educational Technology.[2] This tries to combine the Sheffield and BNU team members' conceptions of e-learning. As previously stated, the Sheffield team's conception of e-learning was the use of technology in learning to facilitate online knowledge construction. The BNU team's conception of e-learning was that educational technology is a subject in its own right. We therefore provided content about the use of technology and experiences of technology, as well as socially constructed group learning. In order for the learners to understand something about the learning platform they are using and communicating via the Internet, we provided resources about using VLEs and good practice in computer-mediated communication. These two documents were linked to staged tasks during which learners were required to post specific messages in the VLE to communicate with other learners and to reflect on their practice. Learners were also required to watch a video trigger demonstrating use of ICT in classrooms, and to use this as the basis for group discussion about how ICT was being used in some school classrooms in the UK. Learners watched the video, and their responses formed the basis of a group discussion about e-learning. Although we provided case studies and examples of e-learning from a Western context, we found it very difficult to use examples from a Chinese context. There are few examples of Chinese practice available in English, but this is now being resolved by providing examples/case studies in both English and Chinese and by giving annotations to Western resources.

Another important design issue was assessment. We acknowledged that assessment was essential as a means of motivating learners, but the Sheffield team had a preference for formative assessment while the BNU team preferred summative assessment. Both teams were interested in using e-portfolios. The assessment finally proposed for the module was a combination of formative and summative assessment, with assessment of learner participation in computer-mediated communication.

As the two teams gained experience of working with each other and sharing ideas, the process of decision-making around the design of e-learning became much easier. Eventually, it was possible for one partner to present draft prototypes of module units to the other, and decisions about adaptations to be made and implemented quickly. This speeded up the process of e-learning production and helped the two teams feel they were working as one. The pedagogic framework that was subsequently used for the module incorporates design elements both from Sheffield and BNU. For example, it uses some characteristics of the organizational framework for a Web-based curriculum developed by Huang and Zhou (2005) with the learning community model developed by McConnell (2006). Needless to say, there is scope for further integration and refinement, in the light of learner experience, and this is being explored in our follow-up project.

Reflections on the Development of an Intercultural Collaborative Approach

Reflections around key themes of a small number of members of both the Sheffield and BNU teams were analysed in a phenomenographic summary of their personal experiences (Banks et al. 2006). These revealed both similar and different perspectives, based on a complex mix of cultural, linguistic, institutional and practice differences.

Initial expectations of participation in the project revealed a mutual wish to understand the different cultures of team members and the processes of e-learning in each context. However, there was a difference between the Sheffield and BNU teams in goal orientation: "the pressures to produce a product are much stronger among our Chinese colleagues, products that can be used with students, whereas the Sheffield team was more interested in developing a dialogue around a course design that was built on student collaborative learning and collaborative work" (Banks et al. 2006). The difference in goal-orientation can to some extent be explained by the perceived external influencing factors, such as policy at national and university level, expectations of stakeholders in the broadest sense, leadership style and organizational culture (cf. Spencer-Oatey and Tang this volume).

The practical reality of two teams of people working between two contexts and cultures was difficult and complex, and this had an impact on the management and outputs of the project. Time needed to be allowed for joint working in Chinese and English. It became clear that there was often not a high level of shared understanding arising from discussions, so understandings of concepts and terminologies had to be constantly revisited and renegotiated. Both sides had 'different agendas' which were not acknowledged publicly, at least initially, partly because of difficulties in communication. One of the senior members of the Chinese team commented: "the understanding of e-learning in UK differs from university to university" and "maybe the personal epistemological belief is a more decisive factor for e-learning course development, and the revolutionary change in education caused by ICT doesn't lie in how the learning materials are created or delivered, but rather in how the concrete learning activity is organized and who has the final decision on how to organize it" (Banks et al. 2006). We realized over time that a complex mix of cultural, linguistic, institutional and practice factors were coming together to mediate collaboration. This slowed the process of implementation, but it also meant that the teams developed pragmatic skills of response and adaptation which helped to maintain collaboration and achieve project goals.

A further complication was that the BNU and Sheffield teams had different styles of working. A member of the Sheffield team commented: "there was a high degree of hierarchy among members of the Chinese team, and only the leading person was able to make decisions and others carried them out" whereas in the Sheffield team "we try to come to a decision through consensus". Another Sheffield team member noted that "the Chinese would focus on what to do, while UK people would be concerned more with the process, i.e. the when and how to do".

Both BNU and Sheffield colleagues acknowledged that their underpinning educational philosophies were different and that this affected the design of the different module units. In terms of e-learning course design, there was agreement that the BNU team was concerned about content, while the Sheffield team was more interested in learning processes. In an analysis of the module units from three dimensions, a member of the BNU team identified the differences as follows: *course structure:* content-focused versus process-oriented; *learning activity:* teacher-centred versus student-centred, *assessment:* external assessment by teacher versus assessment by students, with the BNU units tending towards the former and the Sheffield units to the latter. ISD was a dominant feature of the BNU team's thinking, whereas in the Sheffield team a research-informed, student-centred approach that emphasized reflection and had less structure was the basis of thinking. The process of collaboration in the project, nevertheless, was sufficiently successful for the two teams to move into a follow-up project, and for the number of universities participating in the project, both in the UK and in China, to be expanded.

Discussion and Conclusions

In this chapter, we have discussed the collaborative development of an e-learning module by two teams of academics — one based at the University of Sheffield, UK, and the other at Beijing Normal University, China. The work entailed the joint development of an online master's level module in Educational Technology for Chinese high school teachers, and it required collaboration between two groups of academics whose cultural contexts are different and who are operating in different educational paradigms. We have attempted to illustrate how challenging it is to translate complex theoretical ideas that underpin educational designs into practical course designs that can cross cultural boundaries. In trying to achieve this process, our respective teams commenced and developed a conversation in which our differing pedagogical foci — on process and on content — were moved towards a more intercultural, shared understanding of pedagogy, in which we were creating designs that build upon all of our experience and expertise.

A truly collaborative approach to e-learning design is based on complex processes that we are only just beginning to uncover and investigate. Fundamental lessons that we have learned so far are as follows:

1. Intercultural collaboration is demanding and time-consuming, and requires mutual trust. To build trust requires the participants to have time, bilingual capacity, and a shared 'locale' in which to develop interest in the participating cultures. Moreover, trust needs to be based on shared project aims, or at least mutually supportive aims.
2. In order to develop and maintain intercultural collaboration, it is essential for all parties to reflect critically on their respective beliefs and practices of teaching and learning, and to be committed to adaptation.
3. Participating in intercultural interaction in itself helps people to critique their own habitual practices and 'taken for granted' perceptions, and thus fosters the social construction of teaching and learning in ICT contexts. It can thereby influence existing practices as well as foster the emergence of new ones.

There are many other aspects of our learning around intercultural collaboration that we do not yet fully understand. If we can deepen our understanding of how academics from different cultural contexts may work together, and if we can model these processes, then we may have the basis for much productive Sino-UK academic collaboration in education, for the mutual benefit of our higher education systems. Our current follow-up project is aiming to contribute to such understanding.

Collaborating across Boundaries:
Managing the Complexities of e-Learning Courseware Production in a Joint International Project

Gary Motteram, Gillian Forrester, Sue Goldrick and Angela McLachlan
on behalf of members of the WUN project team[1]

Introduction

The *DEfT* (*Developing e-Learning for Teachers*) Project was a two-year collaboration between the School of Networked Education (SNE) (now School of Continuing Education and Teacher Training — SCETT) at Beijing Normal University (BNU) and the Worldwide Universities Network (member universities involved were Bristol, Manchester, Sheffield and Southampton). The Schools of Education at the Universities of Manchester and Sheffield[2] were responsible for creating the e-learning courseware with BNU. Bristol and Southampton Universities were responsible for conducting the initial needs analysis with BNU and the subsequent formal evaluation of the courseware produced. In response to the Chinese Ministry of Education's (MoE) policies to improve the provision of basic education[3] in China, this project aimed to develop high-quality, bilingual master's level e-learning courseware for in-service secondary school teachers in China

The *DEfT* Project had the following aims and objectives:

a. to establish an effective and agreed model of e-learning suitable for the Chinese context;
b. to develop high-quality, collaboratively produced e-learning courses (or modules, as they are frequently called in the UK) based on the agreed model;
c. to establish a working relationship for continued collaboration.

In this chapter, we focus on the practicalities of developing collaborative working relationships.

When embarking upon collaborative international projects, one might assume that the development of productive working relationships, the realization of project objectives or the eventual success of the project as a whole could be impeded by what are typically referred to as 'cultural differences'. Holliday (1999) uses the terms 'large' and 'small' cultures to distinguish between broad-brush cultural differences, such as between different nationality groups, and the more fine-grained differences, such as between different communities of practice. So in the context of the *eChina-UK Programme*, where the collaboration was between UK and Chinese partners, it could be assumed that differences in 'large cultures' might prevent effective progress because partners were not able to fully understand each other's ways of working, their educational systems and practice, or because political systems and governance are so different.

The existence of 'large cultures' can certainly complicate the development of a project partnership, yet focusing on difference rather than embracing similarity can be detrimental to effective progress. From our experiences in this project, we found that it is not so much the large cultural issues of which we need to be mindful; rather, it is awareness and appreciation of the more complex 'small cultures' that significantly facilitate the successful realization of outcomes. For Holliday (1999), small cultures are the micro-issues that make up the matrix of any new sociocultural endeavour. The materials writers, e-tutors, project managers, academics, graphic designers and technicians involved in the *DEfT* Project found that it was generally relatively easy for them to relate effectively to others in their own discipline areas. For example, Chinese and UK academics from the same subject disciplines could fairly easily come to an understanding of the issues involved in creating the courseware; similarly, the Chinese and UK technical teams could explain concepts to each other. However, the negotiation between the academics and the technologists (see Joyes this volume),[4] for instance, or between academics and school teachers, was more difficult because, as Holliday suggests, it is more problematic to bridge the gaps between different small cultures. So we propose that overcoming the differences among the small cultures is vital for successful outcomes.

Our experiences of working in the highly complex situation of international project work has enabled us to conclude that the focus should be at the level of small cultures, along with the utilization of particular artefacts which fruitfully assist in generating an understanding of the issues in hand. Activity Theory (Engeström et al. 1999; Engeström 2001; Centre for Activity Theory n.d.) offers a framework to illustrate how these artefacts can help to provide the necessary links, so that dialogue can take place between team members and progress can be made. Focusing on the particular artefacts facilitated discussion across the small cultural boundaries and is arguably a useful model for other similar collaborations, in China or elsewhere.

We suggest that, for effective collaboration to occur, two elements need to be in place: the presence of artefacts that enable a focus for debate and development, and the willingness and capability of at least some team members to 'cross boundaries' and thereby to create the necessary bridges for work to proceed. In this chapter, we explore the sociocultural dimension of a number of our project's small cultures, and we take Activity Theory and Boundary Crossing as theoretical frameworks to explain how the complexities of e-learning courseware production can be effectively managed.

Teams and Voices

Team composition and organization

The teams that worked on this project were aiming to create educational materials for a virtual learning environment (VLE), and so a large team of people with a broad and diverse range of skills was needed. It required academics who were well versed in distinct areas of education, and consultants who could advise on content and review the units. It also required people with specific technical expertise who could advise on and develop the platform and manage the VLE; this included people with skills in computer programming, graphic/ Web design, e-learning pedagogy and who could offer technical support when required. Instructional designers were responsible for designing a suitable template which could be used by the materials writers, and they advised on e-learning pedagogy and materials design. The composition of the teams was at the discretion of the two project managers, who sought to obtain available staff with the range of skills required to achieve the project aims and objectives. A range of people (as outlined above) were thus brought into the project at different stages, depending on their expertise and as the requirements of the project necessitated.

The composition and organization of the Manchester and BNU teams were somewhat different. In China, it is common for there to be a large technical team whose job it is to create the materials. The SCETT has three divisions: one for marketing, one for pedagogy and instructional design, and one for technical support. Materials are created on the basis of market research and government initiatives, suitable academics are found to create videoed lecture courses (cf. Gu this volume), and additional text material is created in conjunction with the instructional design team to support the videos. The academics' role is simply to provide the input; all the technical aspects are dealt with by the relevant division. This is seldom the case in non-open universities in the UK, where materials are often both created and added to VLEs like *Moodle* or *WebCT™* by academics, with little or no support.

Collaborative teams, Activity Theory and multiple voices

Activity Theory (Engeström 2001) analyses human behaviour in terms of activity systems. It maintains that people engage in historically situated, goal-directed behaviour or activity, and that a number of elements interact together to form the dynamic context for the activity: subjects, objects, instruments, community, rules, and division of labour[5] (see Figure 7.2 in Joyes and Wang this volume, p. 117). Engeström argues that activity systems are always multi-voiced:

> An activity system is always a community of multiple points of view, traditions and interests. The division of labor in an activity creates different positions for the participants, the

> participants carry their own diverse histories, and the activity system itself carries multiple layers and strands of history engraved in its artefacts, rules and conventions. The multi-voicedness is multiplied in networks of interacting activity systems. (Engeström 2001: 136)

In our project, there were three main voices: those of the academics/materials writers, those of the technical support staff, and those of the target teachers. Each of these had their own perspectives on the activity of developing the materials, including their own goals for it, and each can therefore be treated as the subject of the activity system.

The technical support team see their responsibility as the installation and maintenance of the online systems. They view this within the constraints of university policy and against the backdrop of national debates on such issues, and they are interested in how the tools work and perform in different circumstances. Their agenda may also include a desire to push for a change in current policy, or to find a way of implementing new systems, in that by demonstrating a specific need, they may be able to leverage more funds from their institution. They are interested in whether any modifications would make the technology work more effectively, and whether they have the necessary capacity on their servers to support the number of people accessing the materials. They may well also be interested in pedagogic issues. All these technical matters are a very important aspect of any e-learning development, as, without the necessary technologies, e-learning cannot work. If we are involved in a collaborative project that involves different technical systems, then the technologies in the two different systems must also be compatible. So, this raises questions of interoperability and reusability of learning objects. The technical teams in both Manchester and BNU were aware of these issues. This is the first voice in this discussion.

The second voice is that of the academics. In fact, the academics are likely to have multiple voices because of the impact that different disciplines may have on conceptions of teaching and learning. In our teams, there were specialists in a range of educational disciplines, as well as psychologists. Academics also vary in their degree of experience with e-learning. Teaching and learning online is a new experience for many university lecturers both in the UK and China. Although academic staff increasingly make use of various forms of ICT in their teaching (e.g. PowerPoint, Internet-based references, electronic access to journals, interactive white boards etc.), far fewer have experience of using a VLE to support students studying at a distance. Many academics may have quite strong ideas about what, and how, content should be delivered, may be keen to try out new pedagogic ideas, and may have particular views of what teachers in schools need. Yet they may not understand how the different elements of e-learning work, and they may not realize the constraints that they will put on the system by requesting it to do certain things. This can cause problems in dialogues with technical support teams. Conversely, the technical colleagues need to understand the requirements of the materials producers and of the tutors who will support the learning and the learners themselves.

The third voice is that of the recipients of the training: the teachers. These are the experts in classroom teaching, who may be involved in continuous professional development activities on their own account, or because of a requirement from the government or local authority. They have their own ideas about practice and may not see things in the way that academics do. They may be interested in finding out how e-learning works, yet the technologies available to them may not be compatible with what is going to be delivered. The academic writers and technical staff need to get feedback from this target audience of in-service teachers (in our project these were senior high school teachers), in order to gain insights into whether the materials are suitable, whether the technologies work, and whether the teachers are in favour of learning in this way.

The Collaborative Process

The first step in materials development was for the academic developers from both BNU and Manchester to spend time together to discuss at length the curricula content and the pedagogic approaches to be adopted in the materials (see McConnell et al. this volume). The units were divided among writers according to their area of expertise and interest, and a design template was developed collaboratively and specifically for this project by the instructional designers (Goldrick and Wang 2005). Materials writers then initially worked on units independently and in their own language. Draft units were shared within their own teams and then passed to consultants and other materials writers for feedback. Next, they were translated and passed to materials writers in the other team for comment. Technical staff liaised with instructional designers (and sometimes with materials writers), providing a range of technical skills, support and advice on e-learning design and development. When the content and design had been agreed and finalized, materials were uploaded to the VLE. Some of the Manchester team uploaded their own materials to the VLE, because they had received training to do so. Later, as they developed a better understanding of e-learning processes through practice, they also modified them. In contrast, the BNU materials writers passed their units to the technical team who uploaded the units to the VLE on their behalf.

This development process that we used in our project is very different from that traditionally used in China. As explained above, it is common in China for there to be a large technical team whose job it is to create the materials. The academic's role is simply to provide the input, and all the technical aspects are dealt with by the relevant division.

How, then, could the teams bring coherence to these different procedures for developing e-learning materials, and at the same time ensure that everyone's voices were adequately heard? We suggest that the notions of borders and boundaries within Activity Theory are helpful for conceptualizing this process.

Activity Theory, Borders and Boundaries

Third Generation Activity Theory

Engeström (2001: 134) argues that, in the current stage of development of Activity Theory, which he labels third generation,[6] there is a need "to develop conceptual tools to understand dialogue, multiple perspectives, and networks of interacting activity". He summarizes current perspectives in terms of five key principles (Engeström 2001: 136–137). Two of these[7] are particularly relevant to this third-generation perspective.

(a) "Contradictions [play a central role] as sources of change and development. Contradictions are not the same as problems or conflicts. Contradictions are historically accumulating structural tensions within and between activity systems."

According to this principle, contradictions occur, for example when a new idea is introduced into an activity system. It can create problems but it can also lead to innovations in practice. These innovations in practice may not necessarily be initially of great impact but may eventually lead to an overall change in the practice of an activity system and potentially the creation of one or more new activity systems. Certainly a variety of tensions emerged in the *DEfT* Project that were probably exacerbated by the marked background differences in the initial activity systems. However, as the later discussion will show, the resolution of these tensions led to a development in understanding of the interests of the different professional groups involved in the project.

(b) "Expansive transformations can take place in activity systems."

The idea of expansive learning is that the learning not only results in changes to the subject or subjects but also to the system. In other words, learning occurs at both the individual and the group level, and systems are changed as the participants interact with each other. The changes in the system in turn bring about change in the individual in a constant cycle. It is clear that many of the professional groups involved in *DEfT* learned a considerable amount from this project. Despite all of the difficulties that they faced, the production of the materials was successful and they were deemed generally appropriate by the groups of teachers who took part in the pilot course (Forrester et al. 2006). Changes were also made to at least one of the VLEs as a result of the activity that occurred during the first pilot (see below for more detail), and at Manchester University there is increasing interest in the use of *Moodle* (see below) as an alternative to the adoption of expensive corporate solutions like *WebCT[TM]*. These changes occur when members of activity systems transfer their knowledge to other places as the cycle of learning continues to expand.

In our project, there was a whole range of shared artefacts that helped us achieve expansive learning, but a number stand out. Firstly, a template was developed by the instructional designers for the creation of the materials; and secondly, different VLEs (namely *WebCL* and *Moodle*, explained in detail later) were used in the two different pilots. Below we focus on just one of these artefacts, namely the VLE and its role in enabling dialogues about e-learning to occur across three small cultures. But before doing this, it is necessary to consider the related issues of borders and boundaries which can occur between the different activity systems and which can be overcome by having people who are prepared to cross these boundaries in order to develop the shared objects.

Borders, boundaries and boundary objects

Borders and boundaries have a particular significance for *DEfT*, because of the large range of different types of borders and boundaries that were faced. At the most obvious level, there were the physical country borders that we crossed on numerous occasions to make the project happen. There were also the boundaries between our 'different' ideologies; however, the key focus here is on the facilitative nature of the boundary. As Lamont and Molnar put it in a review of boundaries in the social sciences: " . . . boundaries are conditions not only for separation and exclusion, but also for communication, exchange, bridging, and inclusion . . . " (Lamont and Molnar 2002: 181)

The term 'boundary object' as a metaphor for 'communication, exchange, bridging, and inclusion' was first developed by Star, in a study with Griesmar (Star and Griesmar 1989), of the working practices of the various staff at Berkeley's Museum of Vertebrate Zoology. The fundamental issue at the heart of her theory is that, in order for scientific work to occur effectively, it must bring together groups of people with different motivations but who are all working to the same end: " . . . actors trying to solve problems [who] come from different social worlds and establish a mutual *modus operandi*" (Star and Griesmar 1989: 388). The boundary object 'sits in the middle' of such a group of actors and serves to co-ordinate their various perspectives in achieving a common goal. It can pass across groups and facilitate the process of collaboration. In our project, a number of artefacts functioned as boundary objects, and without them, the process of materials development would most likely either not have occurred or would have occurred without any joint working. This is a useful lesson for similar future projects.

Boundary crossers

In order for the boundary objects to be effective, they need to be taken across the boundaries and understood by a range of people in the different small cultures. They therefore need to be interpreted by people who have a foot in two or more of the small cultures. These people are our interdisciplinary carriers and who Wenger (1998), in his exploration of Communities of Practice, refers to as 'brokers'. Good brokers are able to create new meaning in new communities of practice:

> Given enough legitimacy, visitors with a carefully composed paraphernalia of artefacts can provide a substantial connection indeed. (Wenger 1998: 112)

In our project, a number of people played the role of brokers, including the project managers, the template designers, some academics, and the technicians who set up the systems. Clearly, without these brokers working on and interpreting the artefacts and then taking them to others, the project would not have been successful. In any project, it is a key task, therefore, actively to identify people who are willing to cross borders. If there are no people to take on these roles, then it is very unlikely that a project of this nature will have any chance of success.

We now move on to consider how these ideas were borne out in the practice of this particular project.

Boundary objects and brokering in action

We have chosen to illustrate our thesis by focusing on activity around the VLEs. This is because the VLEs had a direct impact on all of the activity systems and the small cultures that were within the larger activity systems. The data used below come from questionnaires and interviews conducted during both pilots and in-depth interviews with key actors, conducted at the end of the project by the UK project manager.

The VLEs

One of the original aims of the *eChina-UK* joint steering committee was for the same e-learning platform to be used across all the different *eChina-UK* projects. The motivations for this in both countries stemmed from existing national policies that saw these developments as being important for the expansion of the higher education (HE) sector. In both the UK and China, although large sums of money had been invested in the production of a national VLE, in neither case have these attempts so far been successful (see Conole et al. 2006 for a discussion of the UK perspective). The attempts to agree on a single VLE at the steering committee level continued for almost nine months, when it was finally accepted that this it was not going to be possible. The committee therefore decided to allow each project to make use of a suitable local VLE. The outcome of these negotiations for *DEfT* was the utlilization of two VLEs. The delay of this important decision and the need to move materials between systems may have made it more difficult to create 'innovative' materials. We would argue, however, that ultimately the delayed decision enabled the teams to gain a better insight into the different ways that e-learning material can be produced, and come to a better understanding of the strengths and weaknesses of the different processes. For a collaborative international project of this type, this is a useful outcome, particularly when development histories can be so different and can be motivated by a whole range of social and cultural developments. Finding the right artefacts that can act as boundary objects can enable a variety of dialogues to occur that may well help a project of this nature to be successful. In a time when there is increasing collaboration between UK and Chinese universities in the delivery of courses and programmes, an understanding of the differences by which materials are produced is an important consideration. Because of the complex nature of e-materials development, the focus on the VLE enables the small cultures to give voice to their concerns through a neutral object. We are no longer focusing on our different large culture backgrounds but focusing on an artefact that everyone can express a view about. Views expressed can be very strong but, because the object of discussion is not personal difference, collaboration can be maintained.

The debate concerning the use of VLEs in the project is in Engeström's terms a 'contradiction'. The initial idea that there would be one VLE for the whole *eChina-UK Programme* was not a good starting point for the development of collaborative understanding between complex HE institutions. Each institution had its own platform and had often made substantial investments in the development of the platform. Labelling one platform as deficient offended all sorts of sensibilities, created unnecessary conflict between institutions, and affected the development of the materials. The process of trying to choose a single VLE for all the various projects meant that valuable time that could have been spent focusing on what was best for each of the projects was lost.

Nevertheless, although initial progress regarding the VLE was slow, the project team members were eventually able to gain experience of two different VLEs, one Chinese (*WebCL*) and one international and open source (*Moodle*). This enabled valuable debates to occur between the technical teams and the academics about how VLEs might best meet the needs of both the academics and the teachers who would be piloting the materials. It also enabled academics to gain a much broader and more thorough understanding of the capabilities of different VLEs, as well as their limitations and how these could potentially be overcome. The teachers who piloted the materials used only one VLE, because *WebCL* was used for the first pilot and *Moodle* in the second. However, the materials development and technical teams worked with two different VLEs, and this helped them acquire a broader understanding of how e-learning can work in HE.

The pilots

The two pilots that were conducted during this project had different aims and purposes. The first was conducted with a group of 32 chemistry teachers in Fujian who were following an 'upgrading' course at the local Institute of Education. The pilot demonstrated that it was possible for a group of regular classroom teachers to access the materials, undertake online tasks and to interact remotely, using a number of different tools. It also indicated that adjustments were needed to the amount of material that could be delivered in English, that the amount of material we were presenting in each unit might need reducing, and that assessment needed to be embedded more appropriately (see Forrester and Motteram 2004). Even more significantly, it showed how much work was needed in training online tutors appropriately (see Joyes and Wang this volume). The second pilot was more complex and involved over 100 English language teachers in schools in Beijing and in Shenyang in Liaoning Province in northern China. English language teachers were specifically chosen as participants, so that UK materials developers could take part in the online tutoring and so that they could evaluate their materials in action (Schön 1983). A full report on the two pilots is available on the *eChina-UK* website (http://www.echinauk.org/papers/reports/reports.php).

■   *WebCL*

The two VLEs used during the pilots differ in their mode of operation and have different features. *WebCL* was developed at BNU by a team directed by Professor Huang Ronghuai. It is used not only for delivering e-learning to groups of teachers at BNU and elsewhere in China but also as a tool for research. However, it was not the platform being used by SCETT at the beginning of the project, even though Huang Ronghuai was a vice-dean at that time.[8]

As *WebCL* is a research tool, new functionality is being added regularly, and the platform now has a very wide range of features. For example, it has what their development team call a Blog embedded in it — something that is not common in most of the products used in UK HE. Our use of *WebCL* in the first pilot enabled both teams to envisage how the VLE/e-learning might work. It helped us to begin to cross necessary boundaries and to build confidence in each other's ideas and skills. Moreover, Huang Ronghuai's team were able to get feedback on *WebCL* being used in a rather different learning configuration, and this led to changes being made, particularly in the user interface. *WebCL* also needed to be able to present materials bilingually so that UK tutors could interact with it and upload materials.

The materials that we were developing for the proposed master's programme were rather different in nature from those that had formerly been developed at the SCETT. Prior to the start of the project, their materials had been mainly videoed talking heads with some supporting documentation, chiefly in PowerPoint. The materials in the *DEfT* Project had much more text and used video as a stimulus for reflection rather than for knowledge transmission. The development team were therefore not sure how these new materials would be received by potential students who were much more used to a transmission model. This was expressed in some reservations about how the first pilot might go:

> *I didn't feel at all confident that we could manage the piloting issues well, WebCL, the VLE, the content, the tutoring, all of those things. (BNU project manage)*

However, it was agreed that we should go ahead using this VLE, and the first pilot was considered very successful both by the *DEfT* team members and the participants, with some very positive comments about *WebCL* itself:

> *It is a powerful platform, which provides us with valuable learning material. It also expands my vision in learning and teaching and offers a platform for mutual communication. (Pilot participant)*

The successful use of *WebCL* during the first pilot was significantly aided by a number of people who were able to act as boundary crossers. These people were able to inhabit the multiple activity systems, even if only on the peripheries, and since they had sufficient understanding of these various systems, they were able to broker activity between them. The key boundary crossers with the VLEs were the project managers, but there were also other people who aided that process, including some of the materials developers and the instructional designers. These boundary crossers were able to act in positive ways to promote the development of the materials, and were to provide feedback to the *WebCL* project development team. The Chinese project manager commented in the following way:

> *Huang Ronghuai ...tried to improve [...] WebCL using our ideas, before upload[ing] the materials I t[old] them that it should be [...] modified, [there needed to be an] English version [...]. this was certainly done, not by himself, he asked the students to do that. This was achieved in a very supportive way . I asked his student to come to my office and we talked about what was needed. (BNU project manager)*

In discussions we had during the first pilot with two of Huang Ronghuai's research students, who were also developers of *WebCL*, we discovered that they had already embedded some new features, following comments we had made earlier. These included visit statistics and the beginnings of an e-portfolio. Our discussions then ranged over a number of topics, including the issue that students new to the system might well feel daunted by this wide range of facilities.

This use of *WebCL* boosted team confidence, helped to bring people closer together and facilitated general working practices for the remainder of the project. It also meant that, when we were asked to switch to *Moodle* (see below), there were fewer uncertainties. Although there was some initial resistance because it had taken a while to get to know *WebCL* and because *Moodle* was less fully featured, the teams were convinced that they would adjust quickly in the light of their experiences with *WebCL*. In Engeström's (2001) terms, there had been 'expansive learning'. In fact, new understandings were ultimately created out of the 'contradiction' of having to change VLEs mid project. Whereas such change might have potentially been seen as a failure for the project, it in fact enabled us to approach development in different ways and to have a deeper and wider ranging experience of e-learning.

Moodle[9]

Moodle was introduced into the project by the head of the technical support section of the SCETT[10] and was used for the second pilot. Following the reorganization of the school, there was a proposal to introduce a new VLE, and *Moodle* was suggested as an interim platform to enable the running of the second *DEfT* pilot, as well as the Nottingham-BNU *eELT* pilot (see Joyes, and Joyes and Wang this volume). *Moodle* also offered the SCETT an opportunity to work with a very different kind of platform. One of the key differences between *Moodle* and *WebCL* is that, if academic developers receive some limited training, they are able to access *Moodle* directly, without the need for too much technical mediation. This, it was hoped, would enable discussion to occur between the technical staff in the SCETT and the academic developers who were from other departments in the university, and who needed to work with them to produce e-learning materials.

Moodle proved to be a success on a number of levels. We were able to put up the materials bilingually and to allow the Chinese English language teachers and their tutors to select the language they preferred to use on a given occasion. This also meant that a larger number of tutors on both sides could be involved in jointly observing the interaction that took place. When we collected data from the pilot participants, tutors and other stakeholders in the project, we were able make use of artefacts like the VLEs as a focus for our discussions.

With *WebCL*, all the materials were uploaded by the technical support team or by the Chinese project manager. With *Moodle*, this was also the case on the Chinese side — the materials were dealt with by the technical support team and the instructional designer. However, on the UK side, two of the materials writers experimented with putting their own materials on to *Moodle*. As a result, it was possible to demonstrate how tutors could potentially interact directly with the online materials and update them as necessary while participants were interacting with them. In interviews that were conducted near the end of the project, one of the Chinese tutors expressed disappointment that the conversion of the learning materials on to the *Moodle* had been done too quickly for him to get involved. He commented that the 'developer should join in translating the materials into *Moodle*', thus showing an interest in being more directly involved in the uploading and editing of materials directly in the VLE.

Both of these production models, the more industrialized Chinese model and the more craft approach we used at Manchester, have their proponents and their detractors. From our perspective, looking at and exploring the different methodologies enabled further debate to occur about what might be useful practice in both contexts, and both sides began to recognize the strengths and weaknesses of the different systems.

Arguably, the VLEs functioned as tools to enable greater understanding and to facilitate the ongoing debate. They also gave the online tutors significant insights into e-learning that would inform their future practice. Although *Moodle* is an international VLE and has a social-cultural history embedded into it that is said to reflect the current Western orthodoxy of 'constructivist learning' (cf. McConnell et al. this volume), it still allowed us to deliver material suited to Chinese local contexts and to have constructive debates about the way forward. The fact that the Manchester team had also had experience with *WebCL* meant that there was more balance to the discussions. In addition, as a result of using Moodle, more members of the teams were able to begin to cross boundaries in ways that seemed unlikely at certain stages of this project. Although *Moodle* was not introduced in order to allow us to have these debates, it certainly provided the vehicle. It has not been adopted fully into the SCETT, but people who were involved in the project have gone on to make use of the ideas in other parts of their teaching, thus demonstrating expansive learning.

The tutors in both teams were able to articulate in an informed way their changed understanding and attitudes towards e-learning. The following comments from two tutors are illustrative of the new kind of thinking that the project engendered:

Chinese Tutor

> *Before participating in this project I thought that distance learning was only about the different place where you could study materials. But now I think distance learning is quite different from face-to-face and that the idea of distance is not very important at all. I think*

this is a different learning way of learning. For example in our University and in one middle school the participants can learn the materials especially produced for our project they can learn it at different time and the different distance, especially for example they can learn at noon and they can learn the materials in the mid-night in his home. This is the distance learning and this is very convenient.

British tutor

In fact I would probably say that had I not been involved in eChina-UK we wouldn't have WebCT now because [. . .] I knew very little and from being involved in eChina-UK it kind of opened your eyes a little bit to what you can do — these different things that in the case of the MEd it is going to be something that augments what we do face-to-face which is fine. It is never going to replace the MEd face-to-face interaction with the students but it will be something that will enhance their learning experience, I am sure. Without having participated in eChina-UK I don't think I would have even gone down that route. So in that sense it has opened that door and it will hopefully, fingers crossed, it will help the students this year.

Concluding Remarks

The VLE is just one example of the facilitative artefacts that were deployed within this project. It has been selected because of its centrality to the process of e-learning. Members of the three small cultures (academics, technical staff, and teachers in schools) were able, with the help of boundary crossers, to have meaningful conversations around it, and through this to surface the issues that are core to the design and development of materials for e-learning. The artefacts themselves helped to draw out the issues that are important and relevant for taking a project forward. As Lambert explains: " . . . the focus is on the context-boundedness of knowledge and skills and the need to reconstruct them afresh in each context" (Lambert 2003: 234). We would recommend, therefore, that teams identify early on the artefacts that can promote discussion, act as a common object for debate, and that can generally facilitate the process of international collaborative working.

Section 5

Addressing Policy Issues

This last section of the book turns to issues of policy. Policy forms the backdrop to all of the other issues explored in the book, and this section illustrates the close interplay between policy and practice.

Chapter 13 focuses on intellectual property (IP). In any collaborative venture, the creation, management and use of intellectual property need to be agreed among the various members. However, this can be a challenging task, especially for e-learning teams who have little experience of handling IP issues. When the collaboration is a cross-national one, it is even more complex. In this chapter, Windrum reports the experiences of the *eChina-UK* project members in relation to this, and concludes with a suggested schema for people to address IP rights issues in future collaborative ventures of this kind.

The next two chapters turn to policy initiatives. In Chapter 14, Huang, Jiang and Zhang explain the policy of the 'Informationization' of higher education (HE) in China. They identify the initiatives that the Ministry of Education has taken, they report the impressive progress that China has achieved in applying information technology to HE, and they indicate why all of this 'top-down' policy implementation is so important in China. The final section of their chapter identifies the challenges that China currently faces in bringing about the informationization of HE in China.

In the final chapter, Conole and Dyke take a very different perspective from Huang et al., arguing that e-learning initiatives should move away from top-down, large-scale commodification, to more local, context-sensitive co-modified developments. They start by describing the massive changes that have taken place globally — in society, in education and in technology — and they maintain that these changes have had an impact on educational policy and practice. They identify three main shifts within education: a shift from a focus on information to communication, a shift from a passive to more interactive engagement, and a shift from a focus on individual learners to more socially situative learning. They argue that e-learning initiatives need to promote more personalized and localized developments.

13

Managing Intellectual Property Rights in Cross-National e-Learning Collaborations

Caroline Windrum

Introduction

Technology-enhanced learning — or e-learning — is considered to hold significant promise for educational transformation. Potential benefits are argued to include the provision of more stimulating educational environments for learners, combined with more efficient, effective and scalable models for conducting the 'business' of education. Educational designers are involved in the production of, or look for access to, what are considered good quality resources as part of the educational offering. This is particularly the case in networked education, where heavy demands are placed upon making available pedagogically rich resources.

The growth of digital technologies has accelerated the ease, pace, scale and affordability by which works may be copied, transmitted, shared or disseminated. Equally, the various forms of new media are helping to achieve improved levels of quality or fidelity in the derivative text, audio- or visual-based materials (Stamatoudi and Torresmans 2000). The upshot of these developments is that the use of works is not so easily tracked, monitored or controlled by the owner as in the past. Herein lies the dilemma. The creation of innovative e-learning materials requires major upfront investment of time, effort and expertise. At each point of the educational design process, forms of intellectual property (IP) are created, disseminated and used. What claims may individuals involved in materials production make upon their works, how do they regard the outputs of their effort, and what are the implications for the subsequent management, maintenance and use of these materials? These issues are brought into even sharper relief in the context of cross-national e-learning materials development collaborations, where different legal IP frameworks, institutional and cultural practices are in operation.

The *eChina-UK e-Learning Programme* brought together academic groups from different universities to work together in teams in order to create high-quality, innovative teaching and learning materials. In all cases, it was envisaged that the materials would benefit from the collaborative design process and be used in subsequent educational programmes in the respective Chinese institutions. The programme comprised four distinct collaborations in the initial phase, each tasked with the design and development of educational materials in a particular area (see Table 1.1, p. 6).

This chapter explores the topic of IP within the collaborative e-learning projects, based upon team member accounts of how they encountered and sought to resolve issues. First, it addresses how the interviewees perceived and accounted for IP issues. Second, it considers the forms of agreement that the teams reached regarding the ownership and use of IP. Third, it seeks to highlight the ways in which teams managed these agreements during the course of the programme. Finally, there is an opportunity to reflect upon what these insights might reveal about the processes of addressing IP in cross-national e-learning collaborations. The implications for future developments in this area are also speculated upon. (Further information on IP in the *eChina-UK* projects is available on the programme website: http://www.echinauk.org/.)

Before turning to these issues, however, it may be helpful to sketch out what is meant by IP.

What Is Intellectual Property?

IP provides a legal definition to the outputs of human creativity, invention and innovation and conveys ownership to the individual who generated the creative work. There are various forms of IP; patents, copyright, trade marks and design rights are the main ones.

Traditionally, the notion of IP Rights (IPR) is viewed as an attempt to strike a balance between two competing interests: private and public. It is argued that society (the users or consumers of IP) benefit by gaining access to new ideas and knowledge generated by individuals (the creators of IP). In turn, individual creators (or originators) need to receive some form of incentive to stimulate and encourage them to share their ideas and knowledge with others. Rewards can take various forms for the individual: personal recognition, financial return, or enhanced reputation (McSherry 2001).

Copyright is the principal form of IP contained in educational materials. "Copyright protects the labour, skill and judgement that someone — author, artist or some other creator — expends in the creation of an original piece of work, whether it be a literary work, a piece of music, a multimedia programme, a Web page, a painting, a photograph, a TV programme, or whatever" (Oppenheim 2004: 1). It entails different categories of work, e.g. literary, dramatic, sounds, image, which may be contained within different forms of media e.g. print, digital etc. Table 13.1 (p. 207) provides an overview of these dimensions.

However, copyright does not offer the owner a monopoly right to do something; it is merely a right to prevent others undertaking certain actions; e.g. to copy, distribute, sell, rent, broadcast etc. — the so-called 'restrictive' acts. For example, in written work, a reader may read, enjoy, talk about it with friends, and use the ideas contained in the book, but the reader may not copy, reproduce, lease, adapt, or amend the original work without

Table 13.1
Copyright Framework

Categories of Copyright Material	Main Media Channels	Nature of Restrictive Acts
Literary work	Print media	Copy
Dramatic work	Digital/online	Issue copies to the public
Musical or artistic works	CD-Rom	Rent or lend
Sound recordings	DVD	Perform, play or show the
Performance	Satellite	work to the public
Films	Audio	Distribute
Broadcasts or cable	Video	Reproduce
programmes		Broadcast
Typographical arrangement		Amend
of published editions		Adapt, e.g. translate
Software		
Database rights		
Additionally in China:		
Quyi [Traditional		
performance arts]		

clearance or the owner's permission, for the duration of the copyright period. Thus, copyright protects the expression of ideas in their material form, but crucially, not the ideas directly.

Cross-national aspects

IP law is complicated and the subject of continual contest and redefinition (Withers 2006). Both China and the UK are signatories to the main international IP conventions as outlined in Table 13.2 (p. 208). The greater challenge facing these nations is the assertion of that law. It is generally acknowledged that China has moved rapidly to establish an internationally recognized IPR regime (CBBC 2004). This signals a national desire to ensure the IP of citizens in China, while respecting the right of those from other signatory nations who seek to operate within its territory. Understandably, cultural practices and norms will take time to evolve.

The Ministry of Education has moved quickly in advancing reform designed to safeguard all forms of IPR in higher education (HE), with a view to enabling innovation and economic development (MoE 1999). Universities are being strongly encouraged to set up structures and mechanisms to raise awareness of, and protect IP, and to find viable models for working internationally (MoE 2003, 2004).

In cross-national e-learning programmes, the key differences between the respective national IP codes may be summarized as: in the UK, the employing organization owns the

Table 13.2

IPR Legal Framework and Key Differences

IPR Context	China	UK
International Agreements	1886 Berne Convention (1971, 1979); 1952 Universal Copyright Convention 1996 WIPO agreement The Copyright Law (1990, 2001)	1886 Berne Convention (1971, 1979); 1952 Universal Copyright Convention 1996 WIPO agreement Copyright, Patents and Design Act (1988) Various EU Directives
Ownership	Author owns; but priority right to exploit reserved by employer	Employer owns; but special exceptions/traditional practices
Scope and Duration	Registration optional: registration required for published works; Life of author + 50 years	No registration required: Life of author + 70 years (for literary works)

(Sources: PR China State Intellectual Property Office and HEFCE/ JISC Legal)

IP of its staff, though, as many will recognize, certain exceptions and traditional practices in the HE sector appear to run counter to this. A clear distinction is made between the ownership (the employer) and authorship (the employee) following the creation of the work. In China, by contrast, the creator remains the owner unless special provision is made, such as a form of employment contract. In other words, academics retain ownership of their work (State Council 2002).

Method

A series of interviews were held with key members of the project teams, either individually or in groups, and where appropriate with other institutional members. In the context of the current discussion, informants were asked to reflect upon two key themes: (1) IPR issues in setting up the collaboration and (2) IPR issues in managing the collaboration. The twin themes were useful in addressing participants' current understanding of IPR, their knowledge of any explicit institutional IPR policies and practices, and the nature of issues confronted and how they were resolved.

Interviews were held in English, or via a translator, as it proved difficult to locate and recruit local interviewers in China who felt comfortable enough with the subject matter to lead discussions. Admittedly, this is a weakness of the current research; however, informants in both the UK and China were encouraged to be frank about their reflections, given that identities would remain confidential. Generating a sense of privacy was perhaps further enabled in that the interviewer was not directly involved in the materials development projects, and may have been viewed in a more impartial way.

Initiating a conversation about IPR is seldom easy, and it needed to be approached in a non-threatening manner. Informants may feel vulnerable, exposed or perplexed by the line of questioning, and therefore, at the outset, each was invited to raise issues of an IPR nature which they felt were pertinent to their individual or team experience. Once initial concerns, if any, were aired, a semi-structured interview schedule was used as a way to guide discussion, thereby covering aspects of IPR which had not been considered previously. The adoption of a more grounded approach to these discussions was felt most appropriate. In addition, it was recognized that Chinese and British members might not necessarily perceive the same issues, nor characterize them in a similar fashion, and therefore it was important not to enforce a rigid UK-centric framework of potential concerns. Further to this, it must be recognized that individual informants may not have represented team opinion, as experiences within teams could vary.

The timing of various interviews was also important. Meetings were held once the projects were well established, so that the design team members had a chance to reflect around what was happening within the project and give a more authentic account of emerging practices. Any earlier, and the approach might have been viewed as a form of unwarranted intrusion or surveillance.

The four case studies help illuminate the issues for these particular teams at certain stages. Specific attention is paid to those issues which were apparent across at least two projects. An interview coding system of (C:x) and (B:x) denotes Chinese and British interviewees respectively and incorporates an indication of their role or status within the programme, e.g. academic director, academic developer, project manager, etc.

Findings and Discussion

This section considers three aspects of the accounts reported by the design teams:

1. cross-national perspectives on the issues of IPR;
2. setting up or formalizing the collaboration;
3. managing IPR within the collaboration.

Cross-national perspectives on the issues of IPR

■ **Member perspectives of their own IP**

How aware or concerned were team members about the IPR issues? How did they regard their own IP and that of the partnering team? Did they agree? What were the reported drivers and barriers in the process of e-learning collaboration? Was the concept of ownership an appropriate construct for thinking around the materials development process?

Chinese views of their own intellectual property

All members were aware of the concept of IP, but the extent to which individuals were able to articulate their views reflected to a great extent their prior experience of dealing directly with IP issues and/or collaborations of this kind. The more senior members of staff, especially those with managerial responsibilities, displayed a greater confidence in engaging in this form of conversation.

The most clearly defined comment on the relationship between academic and institutional interests captured the following tension: *"Universities 'own' academics' time in the classroom . . . The university pays you for your teaching and will pay for your research . . . but privately you own the research but the university gets the benefit by your reputation. . . . It will support and underwrite you"* (C:1, academic director). However, when pressed as to what this might mean in relation to the creation of teaching materials that would be used by others, as might happen with the *eChina-UK* materials, an uncertain status of online and other e-learning material emerged. In respect to who owned the e-learning materials being developed by the *Chinese* members, two related factors became apparent: (1) that there was an implicit understanding that the online institute owned and could control and exploit the resulting online materials, in that *"the students are registered to the university not the academic or school — it is the university that is the awarding body, so there is understanding . . . that courses are put in perspective . . . [The] University must own as the students are registered to it"* (C:1, academic director); and (2) that this position was further influenced by the nature of the works to be produced in the programme. A clear distinction was made between 'content authoring' and 'courseware production': this distinction formed a critical driver within the process of programme development.

Content authoring was very much viewed as forming the heartland of academic interest. It entailed two clear aspects: published and unpublished works. The possibility for state-regulated, formal publication, especially textbooks, was considered a very strong pull, given that royalties could be earned. *"In our experience, what we look for . . . is hard copy course works* [e.g. textbooks] *. . . All* [university] *teachers want to write what students would like to have. As staff, we consult with peers and at conferences to write a book on certain things"* (C:3, senior academic). In relation to unpublished works, e.g. course teaching materials, presentations, or general resources that formed the basis of the content being developed, views indicated its 'clear division' as a secondary driver — one which was more overtly aligned with institutional ownership, in that *"If it's* [the courseware] *that good, others can use it . . . we would be glad"* (C:4, senior academic). It was considered that unpublished content would serve to enhance academic reputation by still retaining the academic's name, even though the named academic would not receive any subsequent direct financial benefit for producing the teaching materials.

By contrast, courseware production incorporated the wider aspects of producing a course or unit of learning activities, and necessarily involved a wider team of developers who had programming, development and other skills. In this case, *"the courseware team* [are] *employed exclusively for production . . . these people have a 'naming' right . . . but don't own it* [the material]*"* (C:2, academic director).

In the context of Chinese online institutes/schools which have to operate on business principles, the need to own materials was widely recognized; however, the blurring between private individual and organizational boundaries was a necessary precondition and incentive for academic staff to become involved in content authoring outside of their particular school. Mutual benefits were gained. While great care was taken in these interviews not to invoke a concept of ownership, it was clear that academics in particular felt strongly attached to their works, and this acted as a significant driver and motivator for Chinese staff to become involved in e-learning developments locally. A sense of ownership — either by academics of their own works or institution — was expressed fairly consistently across the projects.

British views of their own intellectual property

Although British academics were aware of IPR issues, many tended to talk about it in a somewhat abstract manner. The topic of IPR could be invoked, but unpacking what this meant, how IPR positions might be negotiated, and the implications of institutional ownership was rarely elaborated freely without prompting. Member accounts indicate there was great uncertainty as to how to deal practically with IPR; hence for some, it became *"something that gets so problematic, you go into denial mode . . . [you] try to block it out"* (B:6, academic developer). Moreover, a number of academics expressed frustration that IPR did not afford them some *"form of protection for our ideas and concepts"* (B:7, academic director). Other complaints revolved around the apparent lack of direct reward to individuals for engaging in this cross-national activity: *"It is about time that somebody stood up and started saying that the university should get realistic about this . . . . all this extra work . . . we should be paid additional sums to do this"* (B:2, project manager). Aside from the issue of staff incentives, which were fairly prominent in a couple of projects, most respondents reported that involvement in the programme had heightened their sensitivity to IPR issues and they welcomed the opportunity to discuss the issues.

Generally speaking, members in the British teams acquiesced in the knowledge that their employing institution had some form of claim over their IPR. Many seemed unaware of, or unconcerned about, the current UK sector-wide debate regarding the status of teaching materials within institutions (HEFCE 2003, 2006; Casey 2004). In general, universities across the UK are increasingly seeking to assert institutional ownership and control over online teaching materials, on the grounds that university resources have been deployed in their development. A distinction is therefore being made between teaching resources and research publications, where it is customary practice for universities to waive their rights in favour of the academic. As with Chinese colleagues, the customary practice of academic freedom in publication was considered a vital incentive, though the British teams' overriding interest was to generate research publications in particular. Support staff who were involved in the production process were acknowledged in the materials as members of the design team, but were not viewed as having any form of ownership in the resulting products.

Several members of the British teams stressed the efforts they had gone to in order to establish what they considered to be good IPR practice. This was evidenced in a general avoidance of third-party material due to concerns over infringement, e.g. works produced by outside parties were not used, and in a couple of instances, such materials were removed because their origin could not be established. In another example, *"We have avoided a lot of these issues* [third party] *by designing the stuff ourselves . . .* [there is a] *couple of graphics we still have to sort out . . . but copyright has not been a big issue for us"* (B:2, project manager). However, this reluctance to include external works in their materials may not have been the most cost-effective route but was justified on the basis that developers felt they could not guarantee how such works might ultimately be used. In those cases when third parties were used, e.g. external consultants, students or external writers, a range of documents such as assignment agreements or requisite licences were reported as being put in place in order to maintain UK institutional ownership.

■   **Team perspectives of the collaboration**

Effective collaboration requires a combined effort in pursuit of a common goal. How did teams view each other's IP, and what insights might be gained from a better understanding of the issues which were reported by interviewees?

From the outset, all members struggled with what was to be developed in their particular project. It took a long time for most teams to narrow down and reach agreement on what was required and how best this could be achieved in the time frame and with limited funding. As one member stated, *"I think it would have been very difficult for us to lay down things, particularly when we were not clear about what we were producing . . . The actual final products are not that sure and what they will get used for in China is far from clear, on our side, it may be different* [in the other projects]*"* (B:2, project manager).

However, it was recognized that both sides had learned from each other, as evident in the British comment that *"by weaving into it* [the materials] *a whole load of ideas and processes that patently weren't there and creating something that we hadn't got before, and that they didn't have; so that it was new . . . but contained their content, our joint collaboration and a whole load of pedagogical design ideas that were new instantiation for us as it is in a different context"* (B:7, academic director) was highly regarded and considered deeply satisfying. Thus, as another stated, *"we had to get into the mindset that there were so many things you could not control e.g. platform . . . just focus on what you could do . . . but over and above that we were developing a relationship with Chinese colleagues . . . that was what motivated us"* (B:8, academic developer), irrespective of any IPR concerns.

Similar opinions were evident on the Chinese side. Individuals welcomed the opportunity to be involved in a prestigious initiative of this kind, but some respondents perceived they were at a relative disadvantage in dealing explicitly with IPR issues compared to their British counterparts. It was assumed that the British teams would be more attuned to the issues surrounding IPR and would therefore help identify and resolve any issues which needed to be addressed. *"It is natural for you* [British] *to worry about it* [IPR]*; we haven't thought* [about] *it yet"* (C:3, senior academic). However, this arguably exposes a deeper-seated issue — one which was present on both sides. There was a genuine uncertainty concerning what might be characterized as the nature of 'risk' in becoming involved in this programme. One British respondent stated that what he feared most was that the *"Chinese take up these ideas . . . and we lose control . . . maybe* [leading to loss of] *reputation or misuse of* [British] *work"* (B:4, project manager). Ironically, a comparable sentiment was expressed by a senior member of one of the Chinese teams, who commented *"It* [was] *very difficult for us . . . we need mutual understanding . . . it is very important for us"* and when probed further as to why, the response was given that, in general, *"we are afraid that we* [the Chinese] *will be cheated"* (C:5, senior academic).

While underlying concerns existed in relation to the intentional or accidental misuse of their work by the other party, these reservations were not allowed to surface directly during the various collaborative project discussions. In one instance, the refusal of permission to incorporate a particular resource which had already been developed within one of the Chinese institutions perplexed the British members: *"I really struggled to understand why we couldn't take the* [resource] *and adapt it and use it"* (B:2, project manager). Therefore, the level of control that individual academics (admittedly senior) within the Chinese system had in specifying terms of use for their creative works was novel to the British way of thinking. Indeed, some British members for whom it was the first time to work alongside Chinese colleagues, expressed surprise — even *"shock"* (B:5, academic director) at the safeguards which were used by the Chinese institutions in the use of control measures within their online environments. Restricted access to online systems, authentication procedures, user passwords, and anti-piracy tactics which were evident in the Chinese projects served to challenge a number of stereotypes among the British members of what it would be like to collaborate with colleagues in China.

Overall, IPR was an intermittent issue that permeated early discussions but gradually rescinded in significance for individual team members as teams got into the process of design, development and piloting of materials.

Formalizing an agreement

The foregoing discussion has provided a backdrop against which to consider how the teams went about setting up the arrangements for dealing with IPR across the projects. This section addresses: (1) members' accounts of how they went about drafting and formalizing the agreements, the extent to which they could call upon institutional or other sources of advice to help these discussions, and (2) the resulting strategies which were deployed to deal with these issues and the nature of the IP instrument used to embody the collaborative arrangement.

■ Reaching a form of agreement

The evolving nature of the *eChina-UK Programme* and the time required to crystallize the aims and goals of the individual projects tended to mitigate against a rapid move towards an identification and resolution of IPR issues. To some extent, there was also a sense on the British side that there would have been a stronger move to assert rights and protect positions if, institutionally, the materials had been considered to be of high intrinsic value to British interests, or that the materials would be used outside of the anticipated purposes of courseware development in China. As it was, the British teams reported that their participation in the programme was grounded in the aim of developing collaboration and learning with Chinese colleagues, which in turn they felt might yield future benefits. Over time, the goalposts of the programme had shifted to reflect this wider context.

So, how did the teams initiate a conversation around the issues of IPR in the midst of evolving relationships and malleable project boundaries? Who took responsibility for holding discussions? What support, if any, was there to call upon? In some cases, as one member stated, *"All knew that it needed to happen but no-one took responsibility"* (C:6, academic developer). This was a difficult process, and other members have commented on the tensions and uncertainty that were felt in raising this topic in cross-team discussions, especially among those who had little prior experience of negotiating positions and agreements of this kind. Ultimately, it was the project directors/managers who took responsibility for this in the main, though in some instances, personnel roles within the teams were themselves evolving.

According to collective team accounts, the presence and clarity of institutional procedures on both sides for arranging collaborative projects of this nature varied markedly. Certainly, the involvement of personnel with some knowledge and experience of agreement negotiation, especially within a cross-national setting, was critical in how swiftly and with what ease a collaborative agreement might be formulated. In the early stages of project formation, a number of UK groups produced short papers on possible IPR strategies, co-ordinated by the then UK eUniversity. However, the extent to which these documents were circulated or proved useful is unclear. Similarly, there was high-level discussion on the Chinese side. Both Chinese and UK design team members commented on the need to have improved sector-wide advice or guidance support. However, upon further investigation, while information may have been available and even accessed, particularly in the British context, it was not in a format that the design teams felt readily able to engage with.

On the British side, there was a mixed experience of the ease by which institutional IP procedures, advice and support could be accessed. All the British institutions had some form of IP office or expertise which could be called upon. Typically, this was located in a central support unit, often related to a research/procurement office function. This form of unit has been on the increase within British universities for a number of years. The use made of such services met with varying degrees of success and enthusiasm. In some instances, their input in terms of IP advice, document drafting, support at meetings, professional safeguards was gratefully received, while others commented less favourably on the perceived level of support. Comments ranged from *"they were great . . . they dealt with everything"* (B:3, project director) through to *"Our experience . . . is that you have to deal with it* [agreements] *yourself. They* [central support services] *can be obstructive . . . it's not their core business"* (B:4, project manager)

Similarly, on the Chinese side, some design team members attested to the difficulty of knowing how best to reach a principled agreement between the parties. As one respondent put it: "[There is] *no standard law in China . . .* [over collaboration of this type, and that you] *need to do by agreement building on a case-by-case basis . . . We consulted our lawyers"* (C:2, academic director). However, it was clearly recognized that cross-national institutional agreements had to be signed at a senior level within the organization. The protocols for achieving this appear to be more complex on the Chinese side than in the British case, not in relation to the final signing authority but more in the status and position of individuals to lead, negotiate, review, draft and approve documents. As with the British examples, senior managerial sign-off was required at the level of *"Maybe the Dean or Vice Dean for a normal contract . . . it has to be authority of university"* (C:5, senior academic) or indeed, at the most senior levels.

■ IP strategies and instruments

Across all projects, institutional discussions quickly gravitated towards a strategy of joint ownership for the materials to be produced. *"We discussed IPR between* [British] *and* [Chinese] *institutions; whatever would be produced would be jointly owned"* (B:8, academic developer). It was considered the most practical solution to the difficult issues pertaining to IPR, bearing in mind that the ultimate intention was to exploit the products of the various collaborations in educational programmes to be offered by the Chinese institutions, and perhaps jointly with the British.

This strategy was perceived as offering a principled basis for how the materials developed as part of the collaboration would be regarded by both parties. Typical terms invoked were guided by three principles: (1) that the contributing party would ensure it held title to the materials it brought to the collaboration, (2) that each party would recognize and respect the IP of the other party, and (3) that each party would be entitled to use the joint materials developed through the project collaboration. The strategy of joint ownership was taken to represent the most equitable and transparent arrangement for all parties concerned.

Generally speaking, the British lead institutions took responsibility for drafting documents which were then shared with the respective collaborating partner/s for approval. The purpose of the agreements was to express the principles and nature of the collaborative arrangement between institutions. The issues of IP ownership and use formed key clauses within these documents. Other issues related to the contexts, planned use and aims of the courseware.

These were frequently difficult exchanges, for, as one British interviewee commented, *"any form of legal terminology . . . we came to realize we have problems of understanding language . . . they* [Chinese] *were suspicious of it . . . they mistrust you; words like 'vesting' . . . it is important to use it but they are still suspicious"* (B:9, project manager). This was borne out in conversations with some senior Chinese colleagues who treated such documents with equal unease, given the documents' typically unappealing and obscure legal and/or technical language.

The final instruments drafted were unique to each of the projects and ranged from a formal collaboration agreement to lighter forms of agreement. Despite protracted discussions around the nature of the collaborations, not all of these agreements were signed. However, this was not always due to problems or issues along the UK-China axis but sometimes unresolved issues between partnering British members, or a relaxing of attitude in that *"It's about the debate, dialogue and establishing good working relations . . . IPR has featured in discussions when we signed up . . . but even if we had signed up something, things have moved, where does that leave us?"* (B:2, project manager). In those instances when agreements were not signed, the process of design team collaboration and interaction was not hindered or impeded; rather, the lack of a formal signed agreement was considered more a source of embarrassment than concern.

Managing IPR

Arguably, reaching a form of group consensus is a critical step in ensuring a successful collaboration, with or without the presence of a formal agreement. To what extent did the teams rely upon these provisions to steer their design routines? How important was the presence of agreements in determining activity or resolving any IP problems that might arise? Moreover, what other IPR issues, if any, might the teams likely encounter on the basis of other examples of cross-national (e-learning) collaboration?

Once the agreements were approved (if not signed), or at least a form of *modus operandi* established, little explicit monitoring, audit or reporting of IP provisions of ownership and use took place, according to most members. This perhaps reflects a lack of awareness of, viability, usefulness or regard for ensuring that each partner was meeting their undertakings to secure ownership of IP through creating, licensing or gaining permission for the materials which they deployed in the collaborative development process. Arguably, supporting procedures were not in place to help orientate members cross-nationally as to what was required of them to monitor and control rights issues in the materials they were jointly creating. Design progressed under good faith, and issues of copyright clearance, on the UK side at least, were subject to internal institutional procedures but, generally speaking, these protocols were not made transparent or communicated to the Chinese partners.

While academics on both sides felt that scholarly codes of practice would ensure that relationships would proceed fairly smoothly, the issue of academic publication came to the fore in the majority of interviews. This was most effectively dealt with by agreeing a principled basis for the sharing, inclusion and ordering of names in publication, although this was not always achieved.

From the broader perspective, might we anticipate any potential issues which might surface in the longer term? Based upon the experiences of other (Sino-UK) examples and in discussions with other collaborative projects and interested parties (Williamson et al. 2003; CBBC 2004; JISC 2005), the following points are highlighted as areas to which teams should be sensitive.

■   Joint ownership

While the concept of joint ownership would seem a sensible and practical solution, legal opinions point to the slippery nature of the concept. In UK legal terms, 'joint' is taken to mean indivisible, so that the individual contributions of design teams could not be differentiated but are deeply entwined. In practice, this did not characterize the development process, as workloads and responsibilities were carved up between respective teams, and individuals could point to their particular piece of work. Moreover, consideration needs to be given as to whether any form of discussion was required to make use of jointly developed materials. Teams seem to have given scant regard to whether they had to request permission or keep their collaborating party or parties informed of their intended or actual use made of the materials. As happened on a number of occasions, the use of the newly developed joint resources by a party could occur without the prior knowledge of its partner(s). When such activities subsequently came to light, they did arouse concerns, though these were not always surfaced or expressed for fear of losing goodwill.

■   Legacy issues

Individual members had not considered what claim, if any, they would have on the materials if they chose to move to another institution. Similarly, if the institution sought to change or alter the materials developed by a member, for example, what recourse would that member have to retain their name on their material content? Under such circumstances, authors retain certain 'residual' or 'moral' rights in the materials which they have created in either Chinese or British jurisdictions. These 'rights' include the right to be identified as the author; or to ensure that work is not distorted or misrepresented in any way as to be prejudicial to the reputation of the creator. Few team members seemed to be aware of these issues.

■   Rights management

Some of the resources contained in the developed materials have associated licenses and permissions, which are most likely time-bound. There was little evidence to show how these arrangements and rights were being managed in the longer term, or even if this was a cause for concern. Interestingly, some British members had suggested that all materials should come under an open source policy, but this was rejected by most others on both the Chinese and British sides.

Implications

Standing back from the detail of the individual case studies, what lessons might be learnt from the programme about managing IPR for those who are responsible for promoting, funding, participating or benefiting from cross-national, e-learning materials development programmes of this kind?

The issue of staff training in IPR

In both national jurisdictions, IPR legislation and institutional policies and practices are changing. Greater attention should be paid to support design teams' understanding of national and international perspectives of what constitutes IP. Raising awareness is just the first step, and even though IP legal professionals are best placed to negotiate agreements, it is arguable that academic staff will be better prepared for collaborative programmes if they have an enhanced sense of how the products of intellectual capital are regarded and maintained in society.

Protecting each other's interests

Design team members in both China and the UK recognized that the failure to sign off agreements was not good practice. If a collaborative project had failed, there were no jointly agreed provisions as to how to deal with this. The recording of some form of understanding between parties should ideally be sought on all occasions.

Key points for guiding IP discussions

In summary, Figure 13.1 (p. 219) provides a basis for differentiating between two key aspects of IPR for those embarking upon such programmes: background and foreground rights, and the key concepts of ownership and use.

Conclusion

This chapter has attempted to characterize the dynamics that arose between the Sino-UK teams with respect to the approaches adopted in relation to IP creation, management and use of materials in the *eChina-UK Programme*. Three aspects are apparent. First, the IPR regulatory framework with both countries has been outlined. However, the rich interplay of institutional practices, local customs and cultures mediated how IPR was perceived and regarded within the team contexts. Second, the *eChina-UK Programme*, in general, helped to surface concerns around IPR, making the topic more visible within discussions among the teams, though there was often uncertainty about how to deal with these issues. Third, teams made every possible good effort to reach a principled understanding about the IPR arrangements, but it still remains to be seen how effective these provisions might be when the materials developed within the programme are maintained and used over time.

It is difficult to tell just how pressing these issues were considered to be within the programme. Teams preferred to focus upon innovative pedagogical approaches in materials design rather than the regulatory environments within which these materials might sit. Informal ways of working won over formal specifications of rights. So, what implications might be drawn from this for future reference? In particular, we need to identify new ways of supporting cross-national partnerships to build greater understanding of each other's perspectives and the reasons why certain positions and assumptions are held. Effective

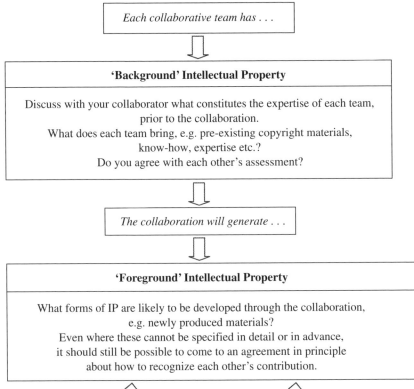

Figure 13.1 Schema for Addressing IPR Issues

communication and trust lie at the heart of this. For example, the funding models within HE in both countries greatly determine the nature of staff contracts and expectations, and the economic values placed upon academic outputs. Finding time to explore such contextual issues might help illuminate some of the complexity and deep-seated cultural values held around the products of human activity. As such, this offers the promise for deepening the nature of mutual understanding between teams. Finally, the materials developed within the programme were designed to form an integral element in the future educational experience of Chinese students. Ultimately, this will determine the true value of the materials.

14

The Informationization of Higher Education in China: Present Situation and Challenges

Huang Ronghuai, Jiang Xin and Zhang Haishen

Introduction

China has achieved significant advances in social and economic development in recent decades. In 2005, the Gross Domestic Product (GDP) reached 18.23 trillion RMB,[1] and Premier Wen Jiabao pointed out in his 2006 Work Report that "China has entered an historic stage where we should rely more on technological advances and innovation to boost our social and economic development, and should place the acceleration of scientific and technological development in a more paramount strategic position." *Informationization* is the term used in China to refer to this process of applying information technology widely throughout society. The aim is to enhance productivity and work efficiency so that the quality of every citizen's material and cultural life can be improved. The introduction and integration of information and communication technology (ICT) into the education system is known as *educational informationization*, and the Chinese government regards this as essential for transforming the heavy population burden into valuable human resources (Chen 2003–04).

China's main strategic aim is to invigorate the country through science and education and through human resource development. Clearly, education has played, and will continue to play, a crucial role in China's social and economic development and its sustainable development. For this reason, a breakthrough is needed now (Zhang J. 2005) in terms of increasing investment, maintaining balanced educational development, improving the infrastructure and implementing systematic reform, because all these efforts will contribute to the improvement of overall labour quality and skills, the construction of a civilized and harmonious society as well as the application of modern technology. Only in this way can China's education system undertake its current responsibilities and fulfill its historic mission.

Higher Education in China at Present

China's educational system is composed of five levels: pre-school education, basic education, special education, higher education and continuing education. In higher education (HE), the main forms of study are regular HE, adult education, self-study HE examination,[2] and distance education. There are 2,004 institutions of higher learning at present in China, and HE is set to grow very rapidly in the near future. The educational arena in China is thus complex and multilayered, meeting a range of different student needs and set for continued growth and change.

The expansion of higher education and widening participation

HE is currently expanding at a phenomenal rate. As Table 14.1 shows, the number of students at regular institutions of higher learning[3] jumped from 3.409 million in 1998 to 13.335 million in 2004, and the gross admission rates rose from 9.8 percent to 19 percent. In 2004, the number of regular institutions of higher learning reached 1,731, and combined with institutions of adult education this gave a total of 2,236. The total number of enrolled students surpassed 20 million (13.34 million at regular institutions of higher learning), and the number of enrolled postgraduate students in these 20 million students reached 3,263,000, an increase of 574,000 on 2003 and a rise of 21.35 percent.

Table 14.1
Number of Regular Institutions of Higher Learning and Enrolled Students

	Number of regular institutions of higher learning	Growth rate	Number of enrolled students at institutions of higher learning (million)	Growth rate
1998	1022	0.2%	3.41	7.4%
1999	1071	4.79%	4.13	21.27%
2000	1041	-2.80%	5.56	34.51%
2001	1225	17.68%	7.19	29.31%
2002	1396	13.96%	9.03	25.63%
2003	1552	11.17%	11.09	22.72%
2004	1731	11.53%	13.34	20.29%

Despite this expansion, there are still regional differences in HE, just as there are regional differences in China's social and economic development. If we look at the figures for the number of enrolled students per 10,000 people in different regions from 1999 to 2001 (see Table 14.2, p. 223), it can be seen that there is still a problem of poor geographical distribution of HE resources (Chen 2005).

Table 14.2
Number of Enrolled Students per 10,000 People
in Different Provincial Regions from 1999 to 2001

Year	1999	2001		1999	2001
Entire nation	32.80	56.30	Shanxi	22.55	43.39
Beijing	169.48	208.28	Hebei	20.53	42.92
Shanghai	111.34	140.96	Guangdong	24.46	42.51
Tianjin	80.73	124.47	Jiangxi	21.00	41.36
Liaoning	46.45	78.16	Gansu	19.99	37.70
Shaanxi	40.51	73.35	Anhui	15.52	37.52
Jilin	45.88	71.83	Ningxia	16.63	36.54
Jiangsu	35.62	66.22	Inner Mongolia	16.66	35.72
Hubei	34.12	64.81	Henan	14.26	35.01
Heilongjiang	31.72	62.44	Sichuan	16.44	34.96
Fujian	24.36	52.35	Guangxi	15.12	33.03
Zhejiang	26.83	52.14	Qinghai	15.83	31.50
Xinjiang	25.29	47.57	Hainan	16.46	29.86
Hunan	22.64	46.75	Guizhou	9.91	28.12
Shandong	24.53	46.38	Yunnan	13.60	27.83
Chongqing	25.74	46.34	Tibet	12.23	26.37

(Sources: Chen 2005 and National Bureau of Statistics of China 2004: 777–805)

Despite these continuing problems of differences in regional provision and uptake, it is important to note that China has made great achievements in the following five aspects in developing China's HE (Zhang X. 2005). First, the number of enrolled students has increased and universities have expanded. There are over 20 million enrolled undergraduates and postgraduates in China's colleges and universities. The number of students is three times higher than that in 1998. Second, a mechanism for sharing the costs of HE expenditure has been developed. Of the total investment in HE, government investment now forms a smaller proportion than social investment. Let us take the 2004 investment as an example. The government invested 93 billion RMB, while there was 120 billion RMB of social investment, including tuition fees. Third, new laws have been enacted. New laws and regulations such as *Higher Education Law of the People's Republic of China* have been brought into force, and these have laid a sound foundation for China's long-term and sustainable development in education. Fourth, the ongoing educational reform is well underway and the HE quality assurance system is improving gradually. A number of initiatives, such as the 'Revitalize Education in the Twenty-first Century Initiative', the '211 Project',[4] and the '985 Project',[5] have been undertaken to promote reform and the quality of HE. Finally, academic research and social services have been boosted. Within the ten-year period from 1994 to 2004, the outlay for scientific research increased nine times from 3.21 billion RMB to 3.44 billion RMB. The number of laboratories, scientific and technological results, as well as academic papers, has also risen.

Higher education as an integral part of the national innovation system

Institutions of higher learning not only play a very important role in training thousands and thousands of talented and enterprising graduates and specialists; they also have a unique and historic responsibility for constructing an innovation-driven nation. Chen Zhili, former education minister, pointed out that "training qualified people is a fundamental task for institutions of higher learning and they must play a major role in the construction of the national innovative system". This framework for a national innovation system via universities is now taking shape.[6]

The system consists of three hierarchical structures, known as pyramids, and one platform. One of the pyramids is the knowledge innovation system. At the top level of this system are national laboratories and large research centres which aim to achieve international renown; at the middle level are key national laboratories; at the bottom level are key provincial-level laboratories. Another pyramid is the engineering innovation system. At the top level of this system are major national engineering research centres and future national engineering laboratories; at the middle level are national engineering research centres, and at the bottom level are provincial-level engineering (technology) centres. The third pyramid is the knowledge dissemination system, which comprises schools and universities conferring different levels of degrees and with a lifelong education programme open to the public. An innovation platform is a platform for the transformation of scientific and technological results, as well as for services, which includes university science parks and technology transformation centres.

At the start of the second phase of the '985 Program', the Chinese Ministry of Education (MoE) clearly gave top priority to the construction of this innovation platform and requested that 65 percent of the funding be spent on constructing such a platform. So far, 252 platform elements have been built, and these are helping to accelerate scientific and technological innovation in institutions of higher learning. Statistics (Zong 2006) show that these institutions of higher learning are now becoming a very powerful force for national basic research and are carrying out cutting-edge high-tech research. As a result, there has been an improvement in the resolution of key scientific and technological problems associated with national economic and social development.

Higher education and the lifelong learning system

The 'Action Scheme for Invigorating Education towards the Twenty-first Century' (MoE 1998) stipulates that the goal of "building a lifelong learning system and making due contribution to the national knowledge innovation system and modernization" should be fulfilled by 2010, which is in less than four years. The building of a lifelong educational system involves administrative systems, legal processes and their implementation, quality assurance mechanisms, improvement of non-governmental organizations and inspection mechanisms (Xu and Li 2001). Joint efforts need to be made to widen participation in HE, improve the abilities and academic qualifications of thousands and thousands of working people, offer occupational training to the unemployed to enhance their job opportunities, and gradually to standardize the professional qualification certification system.

Informationization Development in Higher Education at Present

The rapid growth of the Internet in China has laid a solid foundation for educational informationization. "The Statistical Survey Report on Internet Development in China" released by the China Internet Network Information Center (CNNIC 2006) in January 2006 shows that the total number of Internet users[7] in China has increased to 111 million and that there are 49.50 million computers connected to the Internet. There are approximately 2.6 million domain names and 690,000 websites. The total amount of bandwidth for international access is 136Gbps, and the number of the IPv4 websites in China is more than 67.1 million.

The Chinese government has realized that educational informationization, which is an important component of national economic and social informationization, can facilitate the formation of a modern national educational system, enabling every citizen to enjoy more opportunities for better education and resulting in a learning and lifelong learning society. So, the government has formulated the policy of "speeding up the pace of educational informationization and of boosting educational modernization through educational informationization".[8] A number of remarkable advances in the overall development of educational informationization in HE have already been achieved, as the following sections explain.

The development of the infrastructure for educational informationization

The China Education and Research Network (CERNET) and the satellite-based network, CEB-sat, now cover the whole nation and are interconnected, and thereby constitute an initial integrated transmission network for modern distance education. CERNET covers over 200 cities all over the country, including 36 provincial capital cities. It includes a national network centre, 10 regional network centres, and 28 major provincial network hybrids, and connects more than 1,300 organizations and over 800 institutions of higher learning. More than 300 institutions of higher learning are connected at an Internet speed of 100Mbps. There are 5 million networked servers and 15 million academic and student users. China's main network of CERNET2, the next generation Internet network, has been completed and began business operations in 2004. At the same time, ChinaGrid, which is a powerful platform that can integrate numerous resources for education and research, has been applied in its initial stage.

CEB-sat supplies multiple information transmission services for the entire country as well as surrounding nations and regions. It can provide eight digital TV channels, eight digital audio broadcasts, and eight VBI-IP data broadcasts. The programmes that are available can be categorized into traditional TV programmes with information, courseware and VBI broadcasts. The service covers educational administration and help-the-poor programs in the west of China; distance education by China Television University; satellite English classroom and farming programmes; and distance education for military personnel. The total size of audience now exceeds 2 million.

Different kinds of campus networks have been established in more than 1,600 institutions of higher learning (Li 2005), in over 30,000 K–12 schools, and in over 5,600 secondary vocational schools. Learning sites using CD-ROM materials, satellite programmes or computer classrooms have been set up in thousands of rural K–12 schools. An overall infrastructure for educational informationization has thus been widely established across the country.

The development and sharing of plentiful digital resources to widen the application of modern information technology in the educational system

The Chinese MoE has made a series of efforts to increase educational reform in institutions of higher learning, to promote educational resources sharing, and to enhance the quality of training to produce qualified people. In 1999, the MoE launched the 'Online Curriculum Construction Program for the Twenty-first Century', calling for 321 development projects in online curricula for HE, as well as digital resource databases (a materials database, a case studies repository and an item bank). By the end of 2003, all these projects had been evaluated and accepted. During that period, there were nearly 100 colleges and universities participating in these projects, and there were approximately 10,000 academics and technicians involved in the technical development. This programme has played a critical role in speeding up the informationization of HE.

In 2003, the MoE initiated a Quality Curricula Programme to assure teaching quality and practice reform in institutions of higher learning. One hundred fifty-one quality curricula were selected that year, and the teaching plans of these curricula went online so that others could access them.[9]

The CALIS (China Academic Library and Information System), a component project of the '211 Project', is building a public service system. It aims to construct an open-ended digital library for China's HE and to provide efficient and comprehensive documentation services. Over the past few years, the Chinese government has invested 142 million RMB in building a three-level documentation network platform, and a complementary 1 billion RMB has been invested by universities. The platform is made up of a national centre, regional centres, and university libraries, and can provide such functions as public retrieval, borrowing of books in participating libraries, documentation transfers, co-ordinated sourcing, and online co-operative cataloguing. In 2004, there were 584 participating university libraries. Two hundred two databases had been purchased, and nearly 20,000 foreign electronic academic journals had been introduced. All this has supported teaching and research in colleges and universities.

Furthermore, the 'College Digital Archive Program', which was started in 2001, has attracted a great deal of attention. There are 18 such digital archives being developed, covering disciplines such as geology, archeology, shipping, medicine, arts, humanities and architecture. Based on CERNET, an interconnected information service platform has been built and a resource-abundant knowledge treasure-house for information-sharing is taking shape.

Breakthroughs in research into key technologies and standards

During the period of the 'Tenth Five-year Plan', the Ministry of Science and Technology, the National Development and Reform Commission, and the MoE set up research projects into network-based educational technology, and tackled many difficult problems in numerous key technologies that were holding back the development of modern distance education. These included combinations of different kinds of networks, interconnectedness and intercommunication, and online teaching, and the outcomes from these projects have provided the technical foundation for the all-round, in-depth development of distance education in China.

As a result of the rapid expansion of online education, a number of international standardization organizations, such as ISO, IEEE, etc., are concentrating their efforts on formulating the standards and specifications. In 2001, the MoE established a Modern Distance Education Standardization Committee, and in 2002 it was approved by the Standardization Administration of China to become the Chinese e-Learning Technology Standardization Committee (CELTSC). The establishment of these standards can help consolidate quality assurance of online education and promote its development in a healthy manner. It also helps to maintain orderly competition, facilitate the interoperability of systems and promote the repurposing and sharing of materials.

In 2002, the MoE issued the following standards: the 'Modern Distance Education Technological Standard System and 11 Trial standards, Version V1.0' and 'Metadata Standards of Teaching Resources for Basic Education'. These emphasized the specifications for courseware production and for the distance education interface. So far, CELTSC has revised and/or established more than 40 standards that are appropriate for conditions in China,[10] 10 of which are being examined and approved. This endeavour is helping to construct a China e-Learning Technological Standard (CELTS) and has made it possible for structurally diverse systems to become connected and to have resources integrated.

Major developments in higher distance education

Now that information technology and especially Internet technology and multimedia technology are developing so rapidly, modern distance education that includes interactive online learning has made impressive progress. Since the MoE authorized 68 universities to experiment with modern distance education (see Kang and Song this volume), higher distance education has grown from nothing to an integral part of lifelong education in Chinese HE.

In 2004, there were over 3 million registered students in these universities, 97.4 percent of whom were on-the-job learners (Zhang W. 2005). These pilot universities set up more than 3,000 off-campus learning support centres, and there were over 200 teaching units in the military. The rapid development of distance education has boosted widening participation in HE. So far, the distance education pilot programme of the Central Radio and Television University is the largest among similar programs offered by all these pioneering universities. The university has 44 provincial-level broadcast and television universities, 841 city-level branches of these universities, and 1,742 county-level working stations. All of this has contributed to the formation of a modern distance and open educational system.

With regard to instructional modes, these pilot universities are capable of offering computer information technology, with a variety of multi-transmission network technologies and with digital multimedia technology. These include the Internet, wide bandwidths for local networks, a digital communication satellite system, video-conferencing, audio-conferencing, teleconferencing and cable TV network; there is no longer just a single technical means and instructional mode. The platforms for online teaching and teaching administration are constantly being updated and can satisfy the needs of both online teaching and teaching administration.

The development of higher distance education is not only promoting the application of information technology in teaching and academic research; it is also helping the educational information industry. It is stimulating the development of online-based resources for HE and is promoting the establishment of a system for sharing good quality resources. It is also expanding the channel for delivering quality educational resources to west China, to rural areas and to the military. Distance HE is thus taking the lead in the informationization of HE and is playing a crucial role.

The training of qualified personnel for informationization

Information science and technology has become a basic compulsory course for first-year and second-year undergraduates. Computing is taught as a specialized field in over 500 colleges and universities, and at the end of 2003, there were over 1.2 million undergraduate students enrolled as majors on computer science and information technology degree courses. Among these 1.2 million undergraduate students, there were approximately 300,000 students from four-year colleges and universities majoring in computer science, and over 600,000 students from junior colleges and from four-year colleges and universities enrolled as majors on computer-related courses. Moreover, 35 colleges and universities were authorized by the MoE to establish pilot software institutes in order to train different kinds of qualified software engineers with practical skills. By the end of 2003, there were more than 30,000 enrolled students, of which over 17,000 were undergraduate students (including those taking a double major degree) and 13,000 graduate students (Wu 2005). In November 2003, 35 colleges and universities were approved by the MoE to run pilot vocational software technology colleges. These colleges are attracting qualified educational resources from both home and abroad, as well as encouraging links between industry and colleges and between colleges and enterprises. They stress the importance of training qualified people who have good applied technology skills. In addition, 15 universities set up courses to train integrated circuit engineers so as to provide a national pool of talent in this field. By 2004, there was a total of over 10,000 enrolled students. Of these, there were over 5,000 undergraduate students, over 3,000 graduate students, over 600 doctoral students and 15,000 graduate students.

All these figures demonstrate how much attention has been paid to the training of computer professionals. Such training not only pushes forward the informationization of HE but also helps provide the range of skills needed for the informationization of society as a whole.

Challenges in the Process of HE Informationization

The informationization of HE will face the following challenges in the next phase.

The speeding up and enhancement of resource development and application

There is an acute shortage of educational resources, especially information resources in key disciplines, and this has resulted in a failure to meet the development needs of key disciplines in HE. There is a huge gap between China and the industrialized world in the resources in these important disciplines. Most of the information resources in the natural sciences originate from famous foreign websites; there are few database resources, electronic journals and software applications for which China owns the intellectual property rights.

Up to now, campus networks have primarily been used for routine educational administration; academics and students have typically only used information technology to look for teaching materials, to communicate with peers, and to access college or university information. In other words, network use for teaching purposes has been less developed than its use for administrative and service purposes. According to a survey (Zhao 2004), reasons for the inefficient, low use of the network are rated as follows (from most important to least important): lack of sufficient teaching equipment (67 percent), lack of sufficient teaching resources (67 percent), lack of an effective teacher training program (63 percent), increase in academics' workload in that preparation is too long (56 percent), high costs of use of teaching equipment and maintenance (54 percent), slow network speed (51 percent), and lack of an effective encouragement and reward system (47 percent). All seven of these barriers (including hardware, resources, computer literacy, and administration) act as significant constraints on the effective application of information technology to teaching.

The need for a rational and effective investment process

At present, there is an imbalance in the elements of HE informationization that receive investment. Jiao (2006) reports that, as far as the scale of investment is concerned, there was a steady growth in investment in the informationization of HE between 2003 and 2004. Yet if we look at the elements that received investment, we can see very clearly that hardware received the greatest amount, accounting for 78.3 percent of the total investment, whereas software and services received merely 17.3 percent and 4.4 percent respectively. Yet Jiao's (2006) survey of college students showed that students had many complaints about the campus network services. Many students pointed out that network connections were often interrupted, throwing them offline. In addition, the security of the campus network needed to be improved, and this had a negative impact on the use of the network for teaching and research.

The power to purchase educational resources is controlled by e-learning education institutions or information centres at a range of levels. Policymakers (officials of the bureaus of education, administrators of universities) and users of these resources (academics) tend to work in isolation, unaware of the users' needs, and so they are unable to satisfy them. There is also very little inspection of how the system is operating and how far users' needs are being met, indicating that market administration needs to be strengthened. The use of below-standard products is also very widespread, which is another consequence of the lack of an effective system of inspection. Clearly, there is still a lot that needs to be done to improve the overall service environment.

Expanding and implementing quality assurance

In the process of widening access to HE, it is essential to strengthen the quality control and inspection processes in education so that a good quality assurance system at HE level can be established. This system should deal with relationships between scale, effectiveness, quality and development; between 'higher enrollment rates' and 'tough graduation standards', learner autonomy and self-discipline; between acceptance of societal and governmental supervision and HE institutions' quality control, as well as between 'retention of unique features' and resource sharing, between localization of the design of the resources and promotion of the efficient use of good quality teaching resources (cf. Conole and Dyke this volume, pp. 233–248).

The increase in student enrollments has led to a shortage of academics across the country (at present there are 970,000 teachers, and the proportion of students to academics is 16:1). There are particularly few talented, innovative and outstanding pedagogic teams, especially from colleges and universities in west China, and there is a shortage of quality teaching resources. Furthermore, there are low levels of efficiency in the application of educational technology and in the amount of sharing of large instruments and library resources. All these problems result in poor quality teaching and education as a whole. Skills and qualities such as innovation, communicative competence, team spirit, and independent learning still need to be fostered more effectively in students. There is, therefore, an urgent need to take advantage of both information technology and the application of advanced modern educational technology, so that we can keep pace with the development of HE and improve the quality of teaching and education as a whole.

The challenge of adequate investment

The Chinese government's goal is to commit four percent of GDP to national-level investment in education. However, such an amount is unable to meet the demands of such a rapidly developing sector. In HE, for example, there are currently over 2,000 colleges and universities and 20 million enrolled students, and it is thought that, by 2020, the number of enrolled students could reach about 35 to 40 million (China's Distance Education n.d.). If we look at the growth from a traditional perspective, this means that about 1,500 to 2,000 new universities, each with 10,000 academics and students, will have had to be built by 2020. About 450 to 600 billion RMB will have had to have been spent on construction costs, and 1,500 to 2,000 billion RMB will have had to have been spent each year on the nurturing of people's skills and competences. This will require 600 billion RMB of funding every year, yet it is predicted that, by 2020, the funding allocated to education will be 2000 billion RMB (five percent of the GDP). So, if calculations are made in this way, it can be seen that there will be a deficit in construction funds of around 450 to 600 billion RMB and in annual training expenditure of 900 to 1,400 billion RMB.

It is evident, therefore, that HE cannot be developed in this traditional way. It is essential to explore new ways of acquiring learning facilities and teaching resources.

Equality and educational informationization

Educational informationization is committed to equality and inclusion. This is a core mission of educational informationization and an opportunity for development. Academic circles and governments have recognized the importance of balanced educational development and the key role that this can play in building a harmonious society. Education is "a balancer and stabilizer of social development. It is also a regulatory device for social redistribution" (Yang 2005). After many years of an examination-based and selection-based educational system, and the rejection of the discredited 'educational industrialization' approach, the return to a balanced, equitable educational approach has already become the theme of our times. Educational informationization can fulfill the dream of educational equality through resource sharing. The sharing of educational resources and the digital learning support services will become intrinsic driving forces in this new phase of promoting informationization.

HE is an integral part of the national innovation system, and HE itself needs to keep innovating and adapting itself to new environments, new tasks and new roles. As the declaration from the World Conference on HE (1998) points out, society is increasingly knowledge-based, and such societal changes are posing great challenges for HE, requiring unprecedented reforms and innovations. The informationization of HE is both vital and inevitable, but exactly how it can assist us in achieving innovation remains to be further explored.

15

Complexity and Interconnection:
Steering e-Learning Developments from
Commodification towards 'Co-modification'

Gráinne Conole and Martin Dyke

Introduction

Education has changed dramatically in the last thirty years as a result of a number of factors. This reflects a more general wider societal change and has been fuelled by national policy directives as well as technological changes. This chapter provides a critique of the context within which e-learning occurs and considers how this shapes and directs practice. The central argument of this chapter is that contextual factors have a significant impact on the directions of e-learning activities, and hence an understanding of these factors is important for both policy decisions and practice. The chapter highlights some of the key shifts which have occurred in society, such as the increased impact of technologies, changing norms and values, the shifting and contested nature of knowledge, and discusses their impact on education. It will reflect on the potential role of e-learning in addressing the needs of this complex, constantly changing society. It argues that there are three main shifts occurring in education which need to be taken into account: a shift from a focus on information to communication, a shift from a passive to more interactive engagement, and a shift from a focus on individual learners to more socially situative learning. It considers how new technologies can support these shifts.

Oliver et al. argue that there have been a number of important changes in the way we view 'knowledge'. They suggest that:

> Although the terms 'knowledge society' and 'knowledge economy' (Drucker 1994) have become a kind of journalistic short-hand for a profoundly complex shift in world-view, they nevertheless serve to encapsulate this new ideological context. The new status of knowledge in society is related in complex ways to developments in the technologies of knowledge. (Oliver et al. 2007: 19)

This chapter aims to address the complex and interconnected relationship among knowledge, technology and society and the impact of this on educational practice, focusing in particular on e-learning in this context.

The chapter begins with a critique of the current state of e-learning, touching on the key catalysts which have defined its emergence as an important aspect of educational practice in recent years. It considers some of the reasons cited for using e-learning. It then outlines the range of factors influencing education, highlighting their impact and demonstrating the complex interconnections among these. Finally, it outlines some of the mechanisms used to make sense of this complexity and some of the research issues that are currently being addressed, using a case study example from the *eChina-UK Programme* to illustrate this.

A central issue explored in this chapter is the extent to which developments are seeking to package e-learning into discrete and fixed commodities. It is suggested that an alternative design would be to encourage a more organic approach to e-learning, in which the learning entities can be adapted by learners and teachers and can thereby be more responsive to individual and contextual needs. Such an approach would require flexible and open e-learning material and environments that enabled ongoing modification or 'co-modification' by teachers and learners; in other words, adaptations that met their specific situation. This approach is contrasted with proprietary closed e-learning materials and environments that are packaged as commodities or fixed programmes that cannot be adapted by teachers and learners, either in content or in learning approach. When e-learning is engineered and programmed at such a high level, adaptation by other stakeholders is also not a realistic prospect. So, should the emphasis in e-learning be on the front-loaded design and production of fixed materials and learning experiences, or on the provision of enabling frameworks of rich e-learning experience that people can adapt and co-modify to a particular niche and need?

Whether such a 'co-modified' approach, through joint collaboration might be more appropriate, particularly in international developments, in which local, cultural variations need to be taken into account, remains to be seen. We argue that a production-driven approach to application of e-learning, one that could be termed 'Fordist' in nature (Brown and Lauder 1992), may produce e-learning that is inappropriate in other cultural settings. To use Raymond's analogy, e-learning could be developed less as a 'cathedral' and more as a 'bazaar' (Raymond 1999); it could adopt the principles of open source and open content, providing flexible frameworks where stakeholders can develop the learning experiences jointly and adapt to their own needs and shared sociocultural and historical contexts.

In essence, information and communication technologies (ICT) can be used to support either the presentation of material or the fostering of communication. Early e-learning developments tended to focus on the former, whereas more recently there has been a shift to utilizing the communicative aspects of technologies, particularly with the emergence of podcasting, wikis, blogs and other forms of social software which enable the creation of new forms of online communications (Weller 2007; see also Conole 2005 for a review of technologies and their impact on practice; and see Conole and Oliver 2007 for an overview of contemporary perspectives on e-learning). Coupled with this, we argue that there has been a shift in approach to the creation of e-learning opportunities, which emphasizes co-modification rather than commodification of materials and their use. The open source movement (in which software is developed and shared jointly by the community) has now extended to the development of virtual learning environments (VLEs). For example, the Open University in the UK, a major provider of distance education with over 200,000 students, has adopted *Moodle* as its VLE.[1] This shared, joint development approach is also being mirrored in content production, through the worldwide Open Content Initiative, in which content is being produced and made freely available, with an aspiration to encourage a community of shared use and re-purposing[2] (cf. Joyes and Wang this volume). The Open Content Initiative demonstrates that the emphasis on education should be on process rather than content, reflecting the three key shifts (social, communicative and active) which we suggest are currently happening.

The Rationale for e-Learning

It could be argued that e-learning, more than any other type of intervention on educational practice, is *the* key catalyst for change in education. Large-scale technological implementations are commonplace in the business sector (for example, with online banking and shopping). In contrast, despite a long tradition of distance education, educational institutions have been slower to take advantage of the potential of new technologies to support their teaching, research and administrative procedures (Jochems, Van Merrienboer and Koper 2004). e-Learning is highly political, surrounded by a plethora of hype on its benefits and the ways in which it might transform education on the one hand, and apocalyptic scare stories of the associated dangers on the other (Nobles 2001). Carr-Chellman (2005: 1) states that "online education has been heralded as the next democratizing force in education".

The most obvious reason cited for using e-learning is its potential pedagogical benefit: the 'anytime, everywhere' flexible and student-centred argument. However, there are also administrative and political reasons for its use. The potential cost-benefits of e-learning have long been a central argument for its introduction, through the benefits of economies of scale and effort. This is particularly true with e-assessment, in which electronic marking is seen as an effective means of reducing tutor marking time. However, e-learning *per se* does not necessarily lead to economy gains, as the human resource effort of producing good e-learning materials or e-assessment questions is both a skilled and significant task. Use of discussion fora as a means of communication does not necessarily lead to a reduction in tutor involvement and indeed can significantly increase it. Political imperatives are also important — many institutions have now developed e-learning strategies, which stipulate how much and in what way the institution plans to use e-learning. In some instances, this can be translated at department level to e-learning 'targets', with percentages set on the number and amount of courses which will be made available online or developed in the institutional VLE. But the rationale for e-learning is not just top-down; practitioners have also fuelled its increase as individuals have experimented with the potential of new technologies in their courses. The emergence of VLEs was a significant factor in this respect as, for the first time, relatively easy-to-use software was available, which the practitioners could use themselves rather than needing to depend on technical support for the development of materials.

Our Changing World

The changing nature of society

Many believe that there has been a fundamental shift in the nature of society, that the world in which we live is dramatically different from that of our grandparents. As a result, the nature and purpose of education has changed, in part in response to the changing nature of society and in part given the changing perspective on what education in a modern context is for. This sits within a wider context of modern society which is in a constant state of change. Technological developments are one of the key catalysts at the heart of this change. Castells argues as follows:

> In the last quarter of the twentieth century, three independent processes came together, ushering in a new social structure predominantly based on networks: the needs of the economy for management flexibility and for the globalization of capital, production, and trade: the demands of society in which the values of individual freedom and open communication become paramount; and the extraordinary advances in computing and telecommunications made possible by the micro-electronics revolution. Under these conditions, the Internet, an obscure technology without much application beyond the secluded worlds of computer scientists, hackers and countercultural communities, became the level for the transition to a new form of society — the network society — and with it a new economy. (Castells 2001: 4)

Land (2006: 1), drawing on the work of Viroli, Adams and Erikson, argues that 'the defining characteristics of early twenty-first century society, and an increasing source of its hazards, is its relentless acceleration and compression of time'. Kearns states that

> The conjuncture of the impact of globalisation, information and communication technologies, and the accompanying shifts in the economic, labour market, and the operations of enterprises have led to fundamental changes in the economy and society that have profound implications for the role of education and training. Policy for ICT in education is positioned at the frontier of this transition to an information society. (Kearns 2002: ii)

Giddens, Castell and others argue that we now live in a globalized, networked society which has fundamentally changed societal norms and values. It is a new world which is continually and rapidly changing and is unpredictable. Nothing is certain anymore; the only thing that we can predict with any certainty is that this change will continue. Giddens argues that modern life is fraught with unintended consequences and manufactured risks, which are a result of our impact on the environment (Giddens 1991). Modern society is culturally rich and diverse, and norms and traditions which have been the bedrock of society are now contested. Standard metrics of society — the family unit, national identity, the nature and status of professions — can no longer be taken for granted. Kuhn's (1996) notion of 'paradigm shift', originally used to describe the way in which quantum shifts in scientific thinking and frameworks occur as a result of a disjuncture between current discourse and practice and irreconcilable new findings, can be broadened and applied in this context. In many ways, we are in the midst of a paradigm shift, as we come to terms with new ways of thinking and dealing with this unpredictable, risk-ladened and constantly changing world, and as technologies develop in sophistication and become a more integral part of our distributed cognition (Salomon 1993). The information revolution has produced vast amounts of new and often contradictory information that forces people to reflect on experience and make decisions (Dyke 2001). Dyke et al. (2007: 87) argue that, within this context, therefore, "e-learning needs to be extended beyond behaviourist principles; to nurture initiative, provide students with opportunities for experimentation, dialogue, reflection, 'higher level' conceptual thinking and reasoning". If this view is accepted, there is a real need to ensure that this intention is instantiated in policy and practice.

Thus our environment is that of a networked *and* information society: we have the potential for global communication through a range of mechanisms (e-mail, chat, video conference, mobiles, etc), and we live in a world that is rich in information and that provides access to events immediately, as they happen. Many current sociological thinkers (such as Beck 1992; Lash and Urry 1994; Castells 1996; Giddens 2000) suggest that our modern society is also characterized by changing norms and values, with fragmentation of the traditional religious held across the globe (leading to some parts of society essentially being irreligious while others have become more fundamentalist), with changing views on marriage and the family, and with the breakdown of the class divide.

The changing nature of education

Mayes and de Freitas (2004) divide learning theories into three groups: 'associative' (learning as activity through structured tasks), 'cognitive' (learning through understanding) and 'situative' (learning as social practice). Dyke et al. (2007) suggest that there are three core elements of learning interwoven across many of the commonly used categorizations of learning approaches, namely learning through 'thinking and reflection', learning from 'experience and activity', and learning through 'conversation and interaction'. An important shift has occurred in recent years away from a focus on individual isolated learners and a focus on content, towards learning in context and in social settings, which places more emphasis on the processes of learning and on the dialogic and reflective nature of learning. This change mirrors shifts in technological developments which have arisen as a result of the phenomenal impact of the Internet and the associated networked society, and more recently on emergent social software. The emphasis therefore has shifted in both educational and technical terms from the 'information' to the 'communication' aspect of ICT.

It is argued (Beck 1992; Giddens 1991) that, in our contemporary risk society, individuals are forced to respond reflexively to rapidly changing information, in order to make pragmatic decisions about a range of issues related to their behaviour, lifestyle, health, security, career and family life. These are aspects of living that they may have traditionally taken for granted. There is a nexus between these conditions of late modernity and approaches to learning that can be of benefit to our learners. Learners increasingly need to navigate their way through a world of rapidly changing information, to turn information into knowledge that can enable them to make more informed decisions and guide their action. It can be argued (Dyke 2006) that learning that nurtures reflection, learning by doing, and learning in the company of others corresponds with the needs of learners in late modernity. e-Learning offers the potential to facilitate such learning. Dyke et al. (2007) argue that learning is complex and multifaceted and that there is an inherent risk of e-learning adopting an almost positivistic, commodified perspective which claims to apply particular theoretical positions to design that is expected to simply manifest itself in the learner's experience. Such an approach would suggest that, if a practitioner takes an e-learning 'model', applies it to their practice then 'hey presto', this will bring about the intended learning approach implicit in the model. Dyke et al. (2007) argue that a more holistic, organic approach is needed, taking theoretical positions as a starting point from which designs can then be developed, applied, reflected on and adapted in the context of a wider community of practice. A more open approach is needed, in which designs are applied in practice, and modified in the light of experience and in response to learners' needs. Such an approach will produce an e-learning experience that may be significantly different from the aspirations the designer started with.

The changing nature of technology

There is a growing belief that we are entering a new phase in the development of technologies, instantiated in what is being referred to as 'Web 2.0'. This change reflects the shift away from information and content towards the communicative affordances of technologies (Conole and Dyke 2004). There are a number of fundamental markers in the history of technological development, such as the emergence of personal computers, the Internet, and mobile technologies. New forms of working and learning are arising as a result. Cook et al. (2007) chart some of the key developments from the seminal paper by Bush in (1945) through to the maturity of Internet technologies today. They cluster closely related words or phrases which are widely used in relation to e-learning, and typical technologies which support them, and define seven categories of use:

- *Independent, flexible, self-directed, blended, open, online, resource-based and distance learning* — Reusable learning objects, Virtual Learning Environments, Managed Learning Environments, Learning Design

- *Group and team work, Computer Supported Collaborative Learning* — Social software, asynchronous learning networks
- *Assessment, drill and practice* — Computer-assisted assessment, item banks, automatic text analysis
- *Motivation and engagement* — Multimedia, virtual reality
- *Discovery learning* — Hypermedia, simulations, games
- *Personalisation* — Adaptive learning environments, portfolio systems
- *Informal Learning* — Mobile learning, ubiquitous computing

(Cook et al. 2007: 53)

Technologies are now beginning to be used in a rich range of ways to support learning. We are seeing the emergence of technology-enabled spaces, and adaptive technologies which offer new and exciting opportunities in contextual, ambient, augmented, distributed and social networked learning. While much of the early focus of activity in Internet developments was on content (and ways of creating, storing, retrieving and managing information), more recently interest has shifted towards the social potential of technologies. This is reflected in the emergence of wikis, blogs, and podcasting and other forms of social software.

The speed of development of technologies is frightening: mobile and ubiquitous technologies now abound, and nearly universal technological connectedness has almost become the norm. Technology is now an integral part of our everyday lives, to the extent that some, like Virioli, present a compelling apocalyptic version of the future, contending that the speeding up of society and the major dependency we have on technology for all aspects of our lives is not necessarily a good thing. Land (2006) quotes Virioli as stating that:

> the dromocratic[3] condition serves to compress time and space such that users of networked communication are rapidly approaching a point where they will all operate instantaneously in real time. This can only lead to the collapse of space and the death of Geography.

(Virioli [2000], cited by Land 2006: 3)

Virioli sees global interactivity as eroding difference and diversity, and removing human prioritizing and agency. He forewarns that we are heading towards inevitable disaster on an unprecedented scale, in that when (not if) technological disaster strikes, it will affect all of us instantly; the breakdown of the global communications disaster will soon lead to societal breakdown.

Thus the potential of technologies and their impact is clear, but bittersweet — offering tantalizing promise of new and exciting ways of working and learning, while also having potentially disastrous and unintended consequences. This is perhaps the most compelling illustration of Beck's (1992) notion of the complex modern 'risk' society in which we live.

Complexity and Interconnections

The changing nature of society, education and technology outlined above are intimately interconnected. Figure 15.1 highlights this, foregrounding some of the key factors that are currently shaping society at four broad levels: societal, national, institutional and individual.

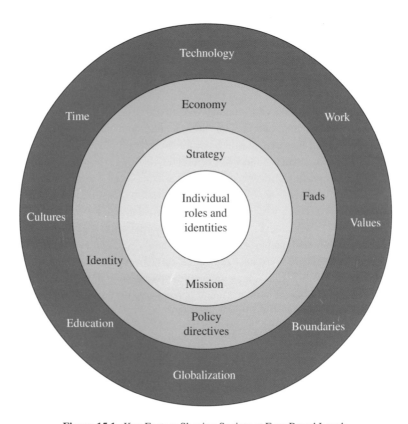

Figure 15.1   Key Factors Shaping Society at Four Broad Levels

Conole, Oliver and White (2007) have suggested that one of the most evident indicators of the impact of technology is the way in which professional roles are changing. This includes the emergence of new roles as a consequence of the development and implementation of learning technologies, as well as changes to existing roles. A review of the impact of tools (Conole 2005) demonstrates how even common applications such as Microsoft Word™ have had a dramatic impact on practice. The most obvious example of this is the demise of the secretary, as there is now no longer a need for dictating and typing. Traditional roles are changing both in support services and academia (Conole 2005). Job titles and structural units within support services have been in a constant state of flux in the last few decades, as institutions struggle to keep up with the impact of changing technologies and try to introduce appropriate structures and roles to provide support for teaching and research activities within the institution. Conole, Oliver and White (2007) argue that, in addition, an academic's focus of work is now different from what it was two decades ago; in particular, there is a much greater emphasis on managerial work than there used to be (Henkel 2000). Academics are less likely to view themselves simply as researchers but are instead required to undertake a multifunctional role with an emphasis on research, teaching and attracting external funding through grants or consultancy. The modern academic is also expected to work more closely with staff in support services. There has also been a noticeable rise of the role and importance of support and administrative staff, as the nature of universities has become more complex and multifaceted.

Learners are also changing. They enter education with very different expectations from those that students had in the past. They have grown up in a networked society, in which the use of technologies is pervasive across all aspects of their lives. They are no longer passive recipients of knowledge but active, demanding 'customers' who expect and want an education tailored to their individual needs. Technology is not seen as an 'add on' luxury but as a central tool for supporting all aspects of their study. These changes are very evident in the emergent findings from recent studies of students' perceptions and use of technologies in the UK (Creanor et al. 2006; Conole et al. 2006). As one Chinese student states, "I think that technology is becoming more and more important for my studies". She goes on to explain that the Internet is her first point of reference for information to support her studies, and she highlights the benefits of technologies as a means of communicating with her tutors and peers. She demonstrates a sophisticated and varied use of technologies to support all aspects of her studies. Technology for her is an integral part of her tool set.

Policy Directives

Conole, Smith and White (2007) argue that institutions are influenced by a range of drivers, of which e-learning is only one, and that these drivers can act as perturbations or catalysts for change. They argue that current drivers include widening participation, accessibility, access and inclusion, lifelong learning, quality assurance, development of competences, and globalization versus maintenance of local culture. They suggest that external drivers on institutions include current national policy and funding opportunities and that more broadly, national and government directives have a bearing; examples in recent years include the increasing impact of quality imperatives (see Oliver 2005; QAA 2004), accessibility (Seale 2005 and other authors in that special issue), economic imperatives and the development of the workforce, lifelong learning (see, for example, Government of Ireland 2003; DfEE 1998; Council of European Union 2002; OECD 1996) and widening participation (see Selwyn and Gorard 2003 for a critical review of widening participation and e-learning).

e-Learning is seen by many as one means of supporting these agendas and as an essential element in delivering higher education efficiently and effectively to a diverse, mass audience. This is in part driven by economic imperatives but is also driven by beliefs in 'open access', democracy and social inclusion. An understanding of the external environment is important in terms of how this informs and shapes local context. In particular, current policy drives and external funding opportunities will have a significant impact on institutional strategic priorities and hence, in turn, on e-learning developments.

Policy directives in China

China is experiencing an intense period of change, and this is particularly evident in education. China has put in place an ambitious programme for change in education, within which e-learning is seen as playing a central role.

ICT has been a central part of the Chinese government's rhetoric for a long time, with a focus on providing an ICT infrastructure across the whole country. ICT developments in China are thus very much driven by top-down directives (see Huang et al. this volume, pp. 221–232). This approach is echoed by the following UNESCO website statement:

> The Chinese government believes that modernisation of education by applying information technology, a process referred to as educational "informationization" is essential in order to transform the heavy population burden into valuable human resources. (UNESCO n.d.)

Kang and Song (this volume, pp. 11–32) provide an overview of e-learning in higher education in China, and Huang et al. (this volume, pp. 221–232) describe the implementation of a technological infrastructure for China and the phenomenal growth in the number of students entering education. Cai et al. (2006) report that the Chinese government is planning to improve compulsory education throughout China through curriculum reform, aimed at moving from a model of knowledge transfer and testing to a more student-centered approach that promotes lifelong learning, problem solving, team building and communication (see also Conole forthcoming). Cai et al. (2005) mirror this, citing the fact that, during the tenth five-year plan (2001–05), the government aims to complete the reconstruction and improvement of the teacher education system, gradually forming a three-level system (diploma — bachelor — master).[4] The policy is targeted at all new primary school teachers holding at least a diploma, at junior secondary school teachers holding a first degree, and at some senior secondary teachers within metropolitan or medium-sized cities who hold a master's degree. The government also aims to increase the capacity to provide MEd programmes and courses for the training of bilingual teachers in primary and secondary schools. China is also experiencing the highest broadband subscription increase in the world; one-third of the broadband development in China is now attributed to the education sector. The massive growth in broadband take-up has the potential to increase the sharing of knowledge, resources, interactivity and communication in teaching and teacher training.

Nevertheless, it is important to contextualize this rapid change in the education system in China in terms of the Chinese approach to and philosophy about education. There is a complex relationship between power and cultural tradition in China, within the context of China wanting to be a global world leader. As part of this aspiration, there is a need to increase the skills of the workforce — education, and in particular e-learning, are seen as central to this process — as is evident in the policy directives outlined below and in particular the e-learning policy directives outlined by Kang and Song (this volume, pp. 11–32). Their overview of e-learning developments in China illustrates the impact of e-learning policy initiatives and the phenomenal growth of the use of ICTs across China.

Case Study: The *DEfT eChina-UK* Project

The first half of this chapter has outlined the nature of e-learning and argued that this occurs in a complex and changing technological and societal environment. We will now consider this by reflecting on the evaluation of a policy-driven educational intervention, the *DEfT eChina-UK* Project, and reflect on how the findings of this evaluation echo many of the central arguments made in this chapter. A more detailed account of the evaluation is provided elsewhere (Cai et al. 2005).

Through this case study, we consider the broader factors outlined above, reflecting on how this international e-learning initiative was undertaken and to what extent some of the key themes described earlier are reflected. We focus on two main questions: (a) to what extent was the initiative essentially producing either fixed 'one-size fits all' e-learning commodities, or e-learning materials that are available for ongoing co-modification as they are utilized by practitioners in different context with different learners; and (b) how are the three shifts in the use of technologies (from information use to communication, individual focus to social dimensions and passive to interactive) mirrored in the initiative?

The *eChina-UK Programme* consists of a series of projects in which Sino-UK joint teams have been developing innovative e-learning courseware to train teachers at secondary and tertiary levels in China. The *DEfT* Project (for more details of this project, see Motteram et al. this volume; McConnell et al. this volume; and the Case Study section of the *eChina-UK* website, http://www.echinauk.org/) was part of this wider initiative and focused on the development of master's level e-learning materials for in-service teachers from secondary schools in China, concentrating on three areas: methodology, educational psychology and educational technology. The project aimed to develop high-quality exemplars of e-learning practice, and a greater understanding of intercultural practice, which included the establishment of an effective and agreed model of e-learning suitable for the Chinese context. We illustrate how the findings from the evaluation reflect many of the wider contextual influences and the trends in education, and in particular the use of e-learning outlined above.

The trainees taking part in the project cited their key motivation for being involved as a desire to improve the quality of their teaching and personal self-development. They said that they wanted to learn new methods to improve the quality of teaching, and to improve their online learning skills, their level of English, and their computer skills. They wanted personalized e-learning experiences that would enable them to work with others to address the here-and-now problems they faced in their classrooms. Other reasons included communicating and exchanging experiences and opinions with other teachers, flexibility with time, and a general interest in finding out more about adopting an independent and flexible approach to learning. These motivations that were cited by the participants reflect the general shift in educational practice from a focus on the sole learner and fixed content to the more socially situated and constructivist learning outlined earlier. It also aligns with the general shift in society towards a more pragmatic orientation to lifelong learning and a need for continuing professional development, as individuals attempt to keep up with the rapid changes in knowledge in their field.

There were also participants who reported being motivated by personal interests or the opportunity to gain a qualification. In contrast to those with intrinsic motivation, there were also a number of the participants who reported that they were required to learn these modules by the school authority, demonstrating an institutional directive towards engagement in these types of activities. These factors mirror the generic pedagogic, administrative and political benefits of e-learning cited at the beginning of this chapter.

The trainees held specific expectations about support from tutors: they expected timely feedback, good guidance and regular face-to-face tutorials. This emphasizes the importance of the communicative aspects of the use of technology; as outlined earlier, there is a general shift in focus from the use of ICT to providing access to information, to its use in fostering communication and collaboration. But the desire to have face-to-face interaction with their tutors raises interesting questions about the purpose of e-learning and the ways in which it can be used to support the learning process (cf. Marsh et al. this volume, pp. 95–107).

The courses were developed jointly by international teams, drawn from the UK and China. One of the key issues for projects of this kind is how to develop successful frameworks for international collaboration, and this case study provides some insights into this issue along with indications for future research. A central tenet of the approach adopted was to encourage a student-centred participative approach to learning. However, the participants of the *DEfT* Project often only engaged partly in the tasks, and the allocated time for each activity was deemed insufficient. There are likely to be a number of reasons for this. Firstly, the level of participants' academic English might not have been of a high enough standard to engage with the materials or to participate in the online forums. Secondly, learners were not used to adopting a student-centred and participative approach to learning, and hence lacked the necessary skills and understanding to take full advantage of this approach.

Supporting the participants effectively in the *DEfT* pilot proved to be a challenging task, as well as a learning experience for the e-tutors, despite their previous experiences in supporting students online. It emerged that there was a gap between the developers' and tutors' perceptions of their academic level and the reality of the Chinese participants' skills. Moreover, the induction programme did not prepare the trainees well enough for the nature of the course nor in the key skills (of independent learning and critical reflection) required to make the most of the course. The e-tutors found that trainees particularly needed more support in undertaking collaborative activities, and in understanding the objectives of the learning tasks and steps to completing them. A stronger tutor 'presence' in the early stages emerged as an important means of achieving this.

However, the e-tutors noticed improvements during the progress of the *DEfT* pilot. At the end of the six-week trial, some participants had become more independent, reflective and critical. The e-tutors came to the following conclusion:

> In order for e-learning to be a truly effective method, the introduction to the materials that participants receive should really be more comprehensive and provide them with the appropriate study skills to properly engage in the virtual learning environment and the (new) pedagogic processes employed in the e-learning materials. (Cai et al. 2005: 26)

These findings illustrate the importance of taking major account of both the educational and cultural backgrounds of those involved in the programme, and using this knowledge as a firm baseline for the development of an appropriate and tailored induction programme and ongoing support mechanism.

The e-tutors played an important role in encouraging the participants to engage with learning, as well as in supporting them academically in subject matter. This was valued by the learners, especially in the early stages when they were new to the online learning. This ongoing support and adaptation by e-tutors is therefore critical in ensuring successful participation; by monitoring the trainees' progress, e-tutors were able to intervene and adapt as appropriate. However, this increased the workload for the e-tutors, and it risked reinforcing participants' dependence on the e-tutors and the sense of the teacher as the sole 'authority'— which mitigates against the student-centred, independent philosophy underpinning the project. One avenue to explore in the future is how new social technologies might be used to address this issue of e-tutor workload versus providing support for students. In particular, in what ways might these technologies be used to promote peer collaboration and support among the students? (cf. Hall et al. this volume, pp. 79–93; Joyes and Wang this volume, pp. 109–124.)

The approach adopted in the design of the *DEfT* modules mirrors that promoted by the Chinese MoE (Ministry of Education), who in their reforms on the national curriculum have called for more learner-centred learning. However, as this evaluation demonstrates, the reality on the ground is more complex. Learners involved in the programme were faced with new experiences on multiple levels — a new mode of learning (i.e. e-learning), studying in a new language (English), and a new approach to learning in the materials (student-centred, reflective and independent). Providing appropriate support and scaffolding for all of these is crucial, although it does raise questions as to whether trying to implement all of these changes at once is overambitious.

Linking theory to practice was identified as centrally important to the trainees. The e-tutors discovered that:

The most satisfying discussions we had revolved around sharing our classroom experiences. Firstly, exchanges of this kind facilitated a more personal relationship between the tutors and participants, and between participants themselves. Secondly, in terms of teachers sharing ideas to improve classroom practice, it provided a good way of offering suggestions, of 'trouble-shooting' and of reinforcing a collaborative climate. (Cai et al. 2005: 78)

This was not surprising, as only by doing this could they improve their teaching which, after all, was the main reason they participated in the study. The e-tutors strongly recommended that the learning materials should be developed in a way to be "a blend of theoretical input and practical activities" (Cai et al. 2005: 25).

Overarching findings

The project was seen as having provided a very good opportunity for the university staff in both countries to get to know each other, to share ideas and resources for developing online courses in the Chinese context, and to engage in intercultural collaboration. The experience reinforces the central argument made in this chapter that e-learning developments need to be implemented through an ongoing process of co-modification and joint construction. e-Learning requires more than front-loaded design and production of fixed e-learning commodities that can be imposed on learners and expected to meet their needs. Personally, all interviewees felt that, by participating in the project, they had gained valuable experience of developing courses through international collaboration, which was helpful for their career development. One interviewee actually declared that, "*eChina-UK* made my life more meaningful!" Mutual understanding was emphasized by one interviewee who stated that "we also have a long history in distance education like the UK . . . we are not going to give up all of our standards. Rather, we want the UK University to get to know the reality of distance education in China and find ways of being compatible with UK standards in such a project." The opportunity to learn from the practice of both traditions was seen as a key strength of the project.

There was belief held by one interviewee that there are some global pedagogic principles underlying online learning. Therefore, this kind of collaboration is a very useful experience "which can be used to develop all sorts of different traditional courses, degree courses and vocational training courses and so on". He further indicated that teachers and students should benefit, or should have already benefited, from this kind of communication and exchange of ideas across different countries and cultures. One interviewee argued for the importance of adopting a co-modified approach, stating: "I believe there are common things we can share and communicate not just knowledge, but ways of thinking and emotions. We are so pleased to have had this opportunity. So I think we should try our best to continue."

What might the global pedagogical principles underlying online learning consist of? The findings from the evaluation of this project identify a number of core issues associated with developments of this kind. Firstly, that understanding of the local context is crucial and that this understanding should be reflected in the materials developed *and* the support provided during delivery — both in the initial induction and ongoing support. Secondly, that development should be achieved through a process of co-modification rather than commodification — with joint construction of meaning and explicit understanding of the positions of those involved in the development. Thirdly, there is a need to take account of wider societal and technological changes, such as the changing nature of knowledge and the emergence of new affordances through new technologies (Conole and Dyke 2004): the creation and accessing of knowledge, and new forms of communication and collaboration. In particular, the three trends from individual to social, from information to communication, and from passive to active participation outlined at the beginning of this chapter need to be built into the design and development of these kinds of initiatives.

Conclusion

This chapter has argued that, in order to make most effective use of e-learning, it is important to take account of the wider contextual factors which are now influencing the nature and direction of education. In a chapter which provides an overview of the impact of policy directives on practice, Conole (forthcoming) illustrates the relationship between the wider contextual factors which affect education and the resultant key drivers, using specific examples of policy and related practice drawn from a series of international case studies (Figure 15.2, p. 248). This diagram shows how wider societal factors translate into specific drivers, which are then appropriated at a national level into policy directives which drive resultant practice. It shows how policy directives in different countries result in very different approaches being adopted on the ground, ranging from economic imperatives in the United States, through to those with more of a social and inclusion agenda in the developing countries, and demonstrates that these policy directives are intimately linked to the specific needs and cultural influences of the different countries. In this chapter and elsewhere in this book, the impact of policy directives in China are made clear, demonstrating the ways in which the major policy reforms and associated rhetoric are being implemented on the ground.

This chapter has demonstrated that modern education is influenced by a range of external influences and sits within a wider, constantly changing complex society. e-Learning has the potential to address many of the requirements of modern education and maximize the potential affordances of new technologies. However, e-learning developments cannot and should not occur in isolation. They need to be developed with an understanding of this complex context, and successful e-learning initiatives need to take account of this, as well as be aware of the local, cultural micro-contexts. This dual approach, we argue in this chapter, is best achieved by adopting a co-modified, shared enterprise approach to development, which includes continued reflection and evaluation on the processes, so that lessons can be learned for future developments. This is an interesting and challenging time for education in China and the role that e-learning might play. Programmes like *eChina-UK* provide valuable insights into the complexity of working on initiatives of this kind, and illustrate the factors that are needed in order to ensure successful implementation that will meet the vision of the future of education in China as instantiated in the government policy rhetoric and programmes of reform.

Context

Globalization, dynamic environment, information and networked society, changing social norms and values

Drivers   *widening participation, e-learning, access and inclusion, economic developments*

workforce development, lifelong learning, quality assurance

Policy	Practice
UK: 15 ICT recommendations (NCIHE, 97) 'let 1000 flowers bloom'	UK: TLTP project, CTI network, HE Academy, JISC ICT programmes
EU: Framework programmes; vision — significant impact across all aspects of society	EU: EUMEDIS — developing ICT in the Mediterranean region, IST programme#
US: Fragmented policy, driven by individual and commercial imperatives	US: Education/industry partnerships, learning as commodity, open courseware initiative
Australia: Learning for knowledge society	Australia: From roll out to mainstreaming partnerships
China: Government directed, Open access and massification	China: Sino-UK e-China programme, developing ICT across country, education for all
Africa: Leading from behind	Africa: African Virtual University

Impact: *local culture vs. global hegemony, urban vs. rural, commercial vs. government, funding models, complexity and change management, changing roles and structure, conflicting demands, risks and consequences, dissemination and impact, evaluation and reflection*

Figure 15.2   Drivers, Policy, Practice and Impact in e-Learning

Editor's Afterword:
Outstanding Issues

This book has mainly focused on the issues, insights and achievements of the initial *eChina-UK* projects that took place from 2003 to 2005. At the end of those projects, we were all deeply aware that the process of developing mutual understanding and of achieving innovative developments in e-learning was only just beginning. We felt that we had particularly more to learn in the following areas:

- in developing a deeper understanding of the pedagogic beliefs and perspectives that are held by the joint project members and that inform the design and delivery of our e-learning materials;
- in dealing with scalability issues for courses that are designed to be interactive and that stress the importance of collaborative learning;
- in identifying scalable and reproducible ways of training e-learning tutors, so that they can provide the support that is needed for effective online learning.

As a result, the *eChina-UK Programme* moved into a second phase. A further set of projects was approved, and at the time of writing, these projects are being implemented. Information on these new projects and the insights that emerge from them will be made available, in due course, on the *eChina-UK* website: http://www.echinauk.org/.

Notes

CHAPTER 1

1. 教育部关于印发《关于加强高等学校本科教学工作提高教学质量的若干意见》的通知 [Notification from the MoE: A few points re strengthening the teaching of university undergraduates, and raising the quality of teaching]. Available in Chinese at http://www.pgzx. edu.cn/upload/files/zxwd/jg20014.pdf [Accessed 7 August 2006]. For a brief description in English, see Zhou 2006: 96.
2. For a description in English of the scheme, see http://www.core.org.cn/en/resourses_project/ chinaocw.htm, and for a list of courses developed so far, see http://www.core.org.cn/cn/jpkc/ index_en.html [Both accessed 8 August 2006]

CHAPTER 2

1. 1 RMB = 0.125447 USD in August 2006.
2. Altogether 26: Tsinghua University, Peking University, Renmin University, Beijing Normal University, Beijing Jiaotong University, Beijing Post and Communications University, Beijing Institute of Technology, Beijing Foreign Studies University, North Eastern University, North East Agriculture University, Tianjin University, Shandong University, Shanghai Jiaotong University, Fudan University, Tongji University, South East University, Sun Yat-sen University, Zhejiang University, Wuxi Light Industry University, Sichuan University, Xian Jiaotong University, and CUBT.
3. Altogether 5: Beijing University of Chinese Medicine, Communication University of China, Beijing Language and Culture University, Hua Zhong Normal University, and Lanzhou University.
4. Zhejiang University, Bejing University of Aerospace and Astronomy (BUAA), Northeast Finance University, Xian Jiaotong University, Beijing Jiaotong University etc.
5. School-to-school communication through the Internet.
6. For more information (in Chinese), see http://www.wljy.cn/cms/ [accessed 8 August 2006].
7. For more information, see http://www.chinaedu.net/english/ (in English) or http://www.prcedu. com/ (in Chinese).

CHAPTER 3

1. This study is part of the key project (02JAZJD740004) funded by the Ministry of Education, People's Republic of China.

2. I have drawn a sharp distinction between e-learning and e-education, or between online learning and online education (between 网上学习 and 网络教育). I regard learning as the learner's behaviour, whereas education is a social/political system that enables learners to learn. In China, the two are treated indiscriminately both in conception and in practice. This is a fallacious act.

3. 1 RMB = 0.125447 USD in August 2006.

4. The term environment is used as a technical term, as defined by Gibson (1986: 7), referring to "the surroundings of those organisms that perceive and behave". To Gibson, "the words *animal* and *environment* make an inseparable pair. Each term implies the other. No animal could exist without an environment surrounding it. Equally, although not so obvious, an environment implies an animal ... to be surrounded" (Gibson 1986: 8).

CHAPTER 4

1. The MoE's aim is that:
   • by the end of 2007, 70 percent of all primary school teachers should have a three-year diploma or a bachelor's degree, and that by 2010 all primary school teachers should have at least a diploma;
   • by the end of 2007, 50 percent of all junior high school teachers should have a bachelor's degree and by 2010 all junior high school teachers should have at least a bachelor degree;
   • by 2010 a certain [unspecified] proportion of senior high middle school teachers should have a master's degree.
   (See [in Chinese] http://www.cutech.edu.cn/%5Cjiaoyuxinxihua%5C000014.asp and http://www.cau.edu.cn/jwc/wenjian/006.htm; both last accessed 11 December 2006.)

2. The core UoN team comprised: Dr Carol Hall (project director), Dr Gordon Joyes (project manager), Dr Ian McGrath (academic director, UoN-BFSU), Dr Barbara Sinclair (academic director, UoN-BNU), Dr Kevin Caley (learning technologist), Mr Quang Luong (flash designer). In keeping with the collaborative nature of the project, the new curriculum materials illustrated here were scripted by Dr McGrath and Ms Zehang Chen (BNU); those on grammar were designed by Ms Ann Smith (CELE, UoN) and Dr Barbara Sinclair (UoN).

3. Although registration was limited to teachers with regular access to online facilities, use was also made of print materials and CDs, and online coursework was complemented by face-to-face tutorial meetings at a local learning support centre.

4. A fuller description of this series of activities can be found in McGrath (2006).

CHAPTER 6

1. For more information on CULP, the Cambridge University Language Programme, see http://www.langcen.cam.ac.uk/develop/res_dev.php?c=2 and http://www.langcen.cam.ac.uk/develop/res_dev.php?c=14 [both accessed 8 August 2006].

2.   Learning Management System (or LMS) is a software package that enables the management and delivery of learning content and resources to students. Most LMS systems are Web-based, to facilitate 'anytime, anywhere' access to learning content and administration.

3.   Definition taken from Collins Cobuild English Language Dictionary.

4.   IELTS (the International English Language Testing System) is a worldwide recognized standardized exam of English language proficiency used to screen overseas applicants to UK universities and colleges. For further information, see http://www.ielts.org/.

5.   Further details on CUTE are available in the Case Study section of the eChina-UK website: http://www.echinauk.org/.

CHAPTER 10

1.   It is impossible to identify precisely the number of people who participated, because members varied in the extent to which they were involved. For the interviews for this research, we focused on the members who worked for the project for over three months.

2.   This course was aimed at middle school teachers who are non-specialists in English, and so much of the final courseware needed to be in Chinese.

3.   For a description in English of the scheme, see http://www.core.org.cn/en/resourses_project/chinaocw.htm, and for a list of courses developed so far, see http://www.core.org.cn/cn/jpkc/index_en.html [both accessed 8 August 2006].

4.   http://www.rae.ac.uk [accessed 25 May 2007].

CHAPTER 11

1.   Two other modules were developed for this project by staff at the University of Manchester and at BNU.

2.   Examples of the Unit 1 materials can be seen on the eChina-UK website: http://www.echinauk.org/cases/sheffield/materials.htm [accessed 14 August 2006].

CHAPTER 12

1.   The full team on the UK and China sides consisted of a large number of people. The full list can be found on the eChina-UK website, http://www.echinauk.org/cases/deft.php/.

2.   The preparation of the Sheffield materials was undertaken separately and is discussed in McConnell et al. this volume.

3.   Basic education refers to public education for students aged between three and eighteen years and covers kindergarten, primary and junior, middle and senior high schools.

4.   See also http://www.elearning.ac.uk/features/translation [accessed 9 August 2006] for another attempt at getting teachers talking to technicians.

5.   Engeström (n.d.) explicates these elements as follows:"In the model, the subject refers to the individual or sub-group whose agency is chosen as the point of view in the analysis. The object refers to the 'raw material' or 'problem space' at which the activity is directed and which is molded and transformed into outcomes with the help of physical and symbolic, external and

internal mediating instruments, including both tools and signs. The community comprises multiple individuals and/or sub-groups who share the same general object and who construct themselves as distinct from other communities. The division of labor refers to both the horizontal division of tasks between the members of the community and to the vertical division of power and status. Finally, the rules refer to the explicit and implicit regulations, norms and conventions that constrain actions and interactions within the activity system". http://www.edu.helsinki.fi/activity/pages/chatanddwr/activitysystem/ [accessed 9 August 2006]

6. Vygotsky's first generation considered only the subject, instruments and objects; to this were added rules, community and division of labour. In the third generation we see two different activity systems working on a 'potentially shared object'.

7. The other three principles are: (1) "that a collective, artefact-mediated and object-oriented activity system, seen in its network relations to other activity systems, is taken as the prime unit of analysis"; (2)" . . . the multi-voicedness of activity systems. An activity system is always a community of multiple points of view, traditions and interests"; (3) ". . . historicity. Activity systems take shape and get transformed over lengthy periods. Their problems and potentials can only be understood against their own history."

8. When the project started, the school was known as the School of Networked Education. It later became the School for Continuing Education and Teacher Training (SCETT), and Huang Ronghuai became head of the School of Educational Technology.

9. See http://moodle.org [accessed 9 August 2006].

10. He was also the head of technical support group prior to the reorganization of the school.

CHAPTER **14**

1. The cited currency unit here and thereafter is RMB yuan (1 RMB = US$0.125447 in August 2006).

2. The Self-study HE Examination system allows "self-taught students to take examinations that lead to a junior college diploma. It was a government initiative in the early 1980s to 'open up schooling avenues' for the learning public and encourage citizens to turn themselves into well-educated members of society through self-study. After twenty or so years of trial and error, the HE examinations for the self-taught have emerged as one of the most popular educational activities in China" (Zhou 2006: 187).

3. 'Regular institutions of higher learning' refer to those funded directly by the state.

4. The '211 Project' is a governmental initiative which aims to strengthen about 100 top institutions of HE and key disciplinary areas as a national priority for the twenty-first century. It has three major components: the improvement of overall institutional capacity, the development of key disciplinary areas, and the development of the technical support services (such as CERNET and the Modern Equipment and Facilities Sharing System, MEFSS) in HE. For further details see http://www.edu.cn/20010101/21852.shtml/ [accessed 30 May 2006].

5. Under a central government program started in 1998 called the '985 Project', 10 of China's leading universities were given special three-year grants in excess of 1 billion RMB (US$124 million) for quality improvements. Peking and Tsinghua universities, the top two ranked institutions in mainland China, each received 1.8 billion RMB. These grants were awarded in

addition to special financial support provided by the '211 Project', a separate program aimed at developing 100 quality universities for the twenty-first century. In 2004, the second phase of the '985 Project' was launched and the number of universities under its purview was enlarged to 30. (http://www.atimes.com/atimes/China_Business/HB18Cb05.html)

6. For further details see 国家创新体系（大学）框架基本形成，《中国教育报》2006年1月9日第1版 [The framework of the national innovation system (university) takes shape. *China Education News*, 9 January 2006, p. 1.]

7. Internet users are defined by the CNNIC as 'any Chinese citizen who spends at least 1 hour on the Internet weekly'.

8. Zhao Qinping, Vice Minister of Education, delivered a speech at the 2004 annual meeting for curators of e-Learning Education Institution entitled "Strive hard to promote educational informationization", 2 February 2004.

9. For a description in English of the scheme, see http://www.core.org.cn/en/resources_project/chinaocw.htm, and for a list of courses developed so far, see http://www.core.org.cn/cn/jpkc/index_en.html [both accessed 8 August 2006].

10. Architecture and Reference [China e-Learning Technological Standard-1 (CELTS-1)]; Standard of technical terms (CELTS-2), Meta-data standard of learning objects (CELTS-3), Specification for Rule-Based XML Binding Techniques (C ELTS-4), IMS Content Packaging Information Model (CELTS-9), etc. More can be found from the website of the China e-Learning Technology Standardization Committee, http://www.celtsc.edu.cn/680751c665875e93/folder.2006-04-03.8417036039/ [accessed 20 June 2006].

CHAPTER **15**

1. See http://www3.open.ac.uk/media/fullstory.aspx?id=7354&filter=general for a press release and further information.

2. For more information see http://oci.open.ac.uk/ [accessed 9 August 2006].

3. Derived from the Greek word *dromos* meaning 'running'.

4. For more information see the MoE website: http://www.moe.edu.cn/english/index.htm [accessed 9 August 2006].

References

CHAPTER 1

Chen Z. (2006) The influence of Chinese culture on trainees' online behaviours in a teaching training course. Paper presented at the Fifth International Conference on Networked Learning, Lancaster University, 10–12 April. Available at http://www.networkedlearningconference.org.uk/abstracts/ Spenceroatey.htm [accessed 20 July 2006].

CNNIC [China Internet Network Information Centre] (2006) 17th Statistical Survey Report on the Internet Development in China. Available at http://www.cnnic.net.cn/en/index/0O/02/index. htm [accessed 18 July 2006].

Fielden, J. (2006) Internationalisation and leadership — What are the issues? Paper presented at the Leadership Summit, Leadership and the Development Challenges of Globalisation and Internationalisation, 25–26 January, The Leadership Foundation, London.

HEFCE [Higher Education Funding Council for England] (2002) Circular Letter No. 14/2002. Available at http://www.hefce.ac.uk/pubs/circlets/2002/cl14_02.htm [accessed 20 July 2006].

HEFCE [Higher Education Funding Council for England] (2005) HEFCE Strategy for e-learning. Available at http://www.hefce.ac.uk/pubs/hefce/2005/05_12/ [accessed 21 July 2006].

Jin L. and Cortazzi, M. (2006) Changing practices in Chinese cultures of learning. *Language, Culture and Curriculum*, 19(1): 5–20.

Li L. (2004) *Education for 1.3 Billion. On 10 Years of Education Reform and Development.* Beijing: Foreign Language Teaching and Research Press/Pearson Education.

MoE [Ministry of Education] (2001) *Curriculum Development and Teaching Requirements for Schools.* Beijing: Ministry of Education. [In Chinese]

MoE [Ministry of Education] (2003) *Curriculum Development and Teaching Requirements for English in Colleges.* Beijing: Ministry of Education. [In Chinese]

Zhou J. (2006) *Higher Education in China.* Singapore: Thomson.

CHAPTER 2

ChinaEdu (2003)网络教育让谁受益[Who gets the benefit from online education?]. Available at http://www.prcedu.com/bulletin/release/8/340.htm [accessed 8 July 2006].

China Education and Research Network (2000) China distance education, 中国远程教育，论网络高等教育现状及其发展趋势[Discussing the situation and future trends of e-learning in higher education]. Available at http://www.edu.cn/20020517/3026149.shtml [accessed 7 August 2006].

China Invest Consultation Net (2006) 中国网络教育产业投资和分析报告 [Chinese e-learning education industry analysis and investment consultation report]. Beijing. Available at http://www.ocn.com.cn/reports/2006122wangluojy.htm [accessed 4 December 2006].

CNNIC (2005) 今天"你"用互联网平台做什么？[What did 'you' use the Internet for today?]. Available at http://s.sogou.com/say?md=viewTopic&messageid=6709073&name=%CB%D1%CB%F7%D2%FD%C7%E6&forumid=112 [accessed 8 July 2006].

Ding Xin（丁新）(2005) 中国远程教育发展的分析和推断 [Analysis and conclusion of Chinese distance education development]. Available at http://wenjuan210.bokee.com/3923127.html [accessed 4 December 2006].

Ding Xingfu （丁兴富）(2002) 远程教育研究 [Research on distance education]. Beijing: Beijing Capital Normal University Press.

Dong Guan Learning (2006) 专家在线谈网络教育的作用 [Expert online discussion of e-learning operations]. Beijing. Available at http://www.dglearn.net/showall.asp?id=16&dba=qzgsdb [accessed 4 December 2006].

Expert Group (2003), 2003年度全国现代远程教育试点高校网络教育学院年报检工作报告 [Examining the 2003 annual working report of e-learning in pilot universities]. Beijing: MoE.

Garrison, D. (1989) *Understanding Distance Education: A Framework for the Future.* New York: Routledge.

Huang Y.（黄勇）(2004) 专家在线网络教育的作用[Action of online education by experts] 101 Web School. Available at http://www.jxue.com [accessed 22 February 2007].

Internet Report (2006) 互联网报告：1500万人使用网络教育 [15,000,000 people use the Internet for learning]. Available at http://www.jyb.com.cn/cm/cmsj/t20060719_25560.htm [accessed 4 December 2006].

iResearch (2003)中美网络远程教育的差别 [Differences in e-learning in higher education between China and USA]. Available at http://www.netbig.com/eduol/ch2/04/02/1802.htm [accessed 4 December 2006].

iResearch (2004)中国教育信息化投资情况 [Chinese educational investment information]. Available at http://e.chinabyte.com/busnews/216483943904444416/20041027/1868968.shtml [accessed 4 December 2006].

iResearch (2005) 中国网络教育用户规模发展情况 [Scale of Chinese e-learners]. Report of 27 June 2005. Available at http://www.360doc.com/showWeb/0/0/92485.aspx [accessed 4 December 2006].

iResearch (2006a) 2005 年中国网络教育用户选择网络教育的主要因素 [Main factors why Chinese e-learners chose e-learning in 2005]. Available at http://iresearch.com.cn/html/online_education/detail_views_id_32874.html [accessed 4 December 2006].

iResearch (2006b) 2005年中国网络教育本专科生在校生数达到265万人[The number of Chinese e-learning transfer students in 2005 reached 2,650,000]. Available at http://iresearch.com.cn/html/online_education/detail_views_id_26815.html [accessed 4 December 2006].

Kang F.（康飞宇）(2003) e-Learning in China: Recent History and Current Situation. Paper presented at the First eChina-UK Workshop, 15–16 December, University of Cambridge. Available at ://www.echinauk.org/" http://www.echinauk.org/ [accessed 8 July 2006].

Liu Y. （刘英）(2005) e-Learning in China. Paper presented at the second Sino-UK e-Learning Workshop, 21–23 March at Beijing Foreign Studies University, Beijing, China.

MoE (1999a) 深化教育改革，全面推进素质教育－第三次全国教育工作会议文件汇编 [Concerning educational reform: Deepening and enhancing quality education] Beijing: Higher Education Publishing Company.

MoE (1999b) Looking toward the twenty-first century education promotion action plan. In MoE, *Concerning Educational Reform: Deepening and Enhancing Quality Education,* pp. 339–356. Beijing: Higher Education Publishing Company.

MoE (2006) 学习贯彻十六大精神开创教育改革发展新局面 [Learning implemented through the Sixteenth Big Report and opening New prospects in Education Reform Development] Beijing: China Education and Research Network. Available at http://www.edu.cn/20060111/3170018. shtml [accessed 27 February 2007].

Rao P. P. (1999) Open universities in SAARC region: Possibilities for institutional collaborations. In Ding X. (ed.) (1999) Open and distance education system and models facing the 21st century's information and learning societies. *Proceedings of the 13th Annual Conference of AAOU,* 14–17 October 1999, Volume 2, pp. 445–448. Central Radio and TV University, Beijing.

State Council (1999) 面向21世纪教育振兴行动计划4号档 [Education promoting action towards the 21st century: document number 4] State Council, China. Available at http://www.cau.edu. cn/jwc/wenjian/006.htm.

Yuan J. （袁纪）(2003) 网络教育网谁受益？ [Who benefits from e-learning?] Beijing: Distance Education, China Education and Research Network. Available at http://zjnews.zjol.com.cn/ 05zjnews/system/2005/06/16/006137057.shtml [accessed 7 August 2006].

Yang M. （杨霖霏）(2005) 远程教育期待新的突破 [Distance education expects new breakthroughs] Beijing: 6th edition, China Renshibao. Available at ?articleID=1284" http:// www.rensb.com/showarticle.php?articleID=1284 [accessed 8 July 2006].

Zhang Y. （张尧学）(2004a) 高校网络教育调查与思考 [Research and consideration of e-learning in universities]. Beijing: China distance education (data information). Available at http://www. chinaonlineedu.com/info/news_special.asp?id=4932 [accessed 7 August 2006].

Zhang Y. （张尧学）(2004b) 现代中国远程教育：挑战不容回避 [Chinese modern distance education: Challenges that cannot be avoided]. Beijing. 5 November 2004, 3rd edition, China Education News. Available at http://www.zhaoxuexiao.com/wangshangjiaoyu/Show_News.asp? newsId=1106 [accessed 27 February 2007].

CHAPTER **3**

Chapelle, C. A. (2000) Is networked-based learning CALL? In M. Warschauer and R. Kern (eds.) *Network-based Language Teaching: Concepts and Practice,* pp. 204–228. Cambridge: Cambridge University Press.

Chapelle, C. A. (2001) *Computer Applications in Second Language Acquisition: Foundations for Teaching, Testing and Research. Cambridge*: Cambridge University Press.

Gibson, J. J. (1986) *The Ecological Approach to Visual Perception*. London: Lawrence Erlbaum Associates.

Gu Y. (2005a) 教育生态学模型与网络教育 [An ecological model of education and online education] 《外语电化教学》 *Computer-assisted Foreign Language Education,* 4: 3–8.

Gu Y. (2005b)网络教育的基本理念、现存问题与发展方向 [Online education in China: problems and solutions] 《高校现代远程教育创新与实践文集》 *Innovation and Practice in China's Higher Distance Education* (special edition), 1: 64–75.

Gu Y. (2005c) (ed.) *Initial Exploration of Online Education.* Vol. 2. Beijing: Foreign Language Teaching and Research Press.

Gu Y. (2006) An ecological model of e-learning in Chinese context. *Studies in Continuing Education*, 28 (2): 99–119.

Gu Y., Hall, C., McGrath, I. and Sinclair, B. (2005) Developing resources for MA in e-ELT. In Y. Gu (ed.) *Initial Exploration of Online Education*, Vol. 2, pp. 23–42. Beijing: Foreign Language Teaching and Research Press

Gu Yueguo, Hall, C. and Hall, E. (2006) *Using the Computer in ELT: Technology, Theory and Practice.* Beijing: Foreign Language Teaching and Research Press.

Kern, R. and Warschauer, M. (2000) Introduction: Theory and practice of network-based language teaching. In M. Warschauer and R. Kern (eds.) *Network-based Language Teaching: Concepts and Practice*, pp. 1–19. Cambridge: Cambridge University Press.

Lynch, M. M. (2002) *The Online Educator: A Guide to Creating the Virtual Classroom.* New York: Routledge.

Mayer, R. E. (2001) Multimedia Learning. Cambridge: Cambridge University Press.

Odell, A. (1986) Evaluating CALL software. In G. Leech and C. N. Candlin (eds.) *Computers in English Language Teaching and Research*, pp. 61–77. London: Longman Group.

Shearer, R. (2003) Instructional design in distance education: an overview. In M. G. Moore and W. G. Anderson (eds.) *Handbook of Distance Education*, pp. 275–286. Hillsdale, NJ: Lawrence Erlbaum Associates.

Skinner, B. F. (1958) Teaching machines. *Science*, 128: 969–977.

Skinner, B. F. (1968) *The Technology of Teaching.* New York: Appleton-Century-Crofts.

Szymanski, R. A., Szymanski, D. P. and Pulschen, D. M. (1995) *Computers and Information Systems.* London: Prentice Hall.

Windeatt, S. (1986) Observing CALL in action. In G. Leech and C. N. Candlin (eds.) *Computers in English language Teaching and Research*, pp. 79–97. London: Longman Group.

CHAPTER **4**

Bandura, A. (1977) *Social Learning Theory.* Englewood Cliffs, NJ: Prentice Hall.

Berry, J.W. (1979) Culture and cognitive style. In A. J. Marsella, R. G. Tharp and T. J. Ciborowski (eds.) *Perspectives on Cross-cultural Psychology*, pp. 123–146. New York: Academic Press.

Chan V. (2001) Readiness for learner autonomy: What do our learners tell us? *Teaching in Higher Education*, 6(4): 505–518.

Chen Z. and Joyes, G. (2005). Evaluation of the pilot in Beijing. School of Education, University of Nottingham. Available at http://www.echinauk.org/papers/reports/reports.php [accessed 10 July 2006].

Cotterall, S. (1995) Readiness for autonomy: Investigating learner beliefs. *System*, 23(2): 195–205.

Dam, L. (1995) *Learner Autonomy 3: From Theory to Classroom Practice.* Dublin: Authentik.

Dickinson, L. (1992) *Learner Autonomy 2: Learner Training for Language Learning.* Dublin: Authentik.

Dickinson, L. and Carver, D. (1980) Learning how to learn: Steps towards self-direction in foreign language learning in schools. *ELT Journal*, 35: 1–7.

Ellis, G. and Sinclair, B. (1989) *Learning to Learn English: A Course in Learner Training: Teacher's Book*. Cambridge: Cambridge University Press.

Flavell, J. H. (1987) Metacognition and motivation as effective determinants of learning and understanding. In F. Weinert and R. Kluwe (eds.) *Metacognition, Motivation and Understanding*, pp. 21–29. Hillsdale, NJ: Lawrence Erlbaum.

Freire, P. (1972) *Pedagogy of the Oppressed*. Harmondsworth: Penguin.

Gomes de Matos, F. (1986) A gap in ESL pedagogy: learners' rights. *TESOL Newsletter* XX: 9.

Hofstede, G. (2001) *Culture's Consequences. Comparing Values, Behaviors, Institutions and Organizations across Nations*. Thousand Oaks: Sage.

Holec, H. (1981) *Autonomy and Foreign Language Learning*. Oxford: Pergamon.

Hsu W. C. (2005) Representations, constructs and Practice of Autonomy via a Learner Training Programme in Taiwan. Unpublished PhD thesis, University of Nottingham.

Kolb, D. (1976) *Learning Style Inventory*. Boston, MA: McBer.

Lave, J. and Wenger, E. (1990) *Situated Learning: Legitimate Peripheral Participation*. Cambridge: Cambridge University Press.

Little, D. (1995) Learning as dialogue: The dependence of learner autonomy on teacher autonomy. *System*, 23(2): 175–182.

Little, D. (1996) Freedom to learn and compulsion to interact: Promoting learner autonomy through the use of information systems and information technologies. In R. Pemberton, E. S. L. Li, W. W. F. Or and H. D. Pierson (eds.) *Taking Control: Autonomy in Language Learning*, pp. 203–218. Hong Kong: Hong Kong University Press.

Littlewood, W. (1981) *Communicative Language Teaching: An Introduction*. Cambridge: Cambridge University Press.

McGrath, I. (2000) Teacher autonomy. In B. Sinclair, I. McGrath and T. Lamb (eds.) *Learner Autonomy, Teacher Autonomy: Future Directions*, pp. 100–110. Harlow: Longman in association with the British Council.

McGrath, I. (2001) Self-evaluating future teachers. Paper presented at the International Learning in Education Conference, 13 December 2001, Hong Kong.

McGrath, I. (2006) Designing e-learning to support professional development. *International Journal of Learning*, 12(4): 43–54.

Mercer, N. (1995) *The Guided Construction of Knowledge*. Clevedon, Avon: Multilingual Matters.

Moskowitz, G. (1978) *Caring and Sharing in the Foreign Language Class: A Sourcebook of Humanistic Techniques*. Boston, MA: Heinle and Heinle.

[National Curriculum for English]l 国家英语课程标准 (2001) Beijing: Beijing Normal University Press.

Nunan, D. (1988) *The Learner-Centred Curriculum: A Study in Second Language Teaching*. Cambridge: Cambridge University Press.

O'Malley, J. M. and Chamot, A. U. (1990) *Learning Strategies in Second Language Acquisition*. Cambridge: Cambridge University Press.

Pask, G. (1976) Styles and strategies of learning. *British Journal of Educational Psychology*, 46: 128–148.

Pattison, P. (1987) *Developing Communication Skills*. Cambridge: Cambridge University Press.

Pennycook, A. (1997) Cultural alternatives and autonomy. In P. Benson and P. Voller (eds.) *Autonomy and Independence in Language Learning*, pp. 35–53. Harlow: Longman.

Pierson, H. (1996) Learner culture and learner autonomy in the Hong Kong Chinese context. In R. Pemberton, E. S. L. Li, W. W. F. Or and H. D. Pierson (eds.) *Taking Control: Autonomy in Language Learning*, pp. 49–58. Hong Kong: Hong Kong University Press.

Renshaw, P. (1992) The sociocultural theory of teaching and learning: implications for the curriculum in the Australian context. Paper presented at the Australian Association of Research in Education and the New Zealand Association of Research in Education (AARE/NZARE) Joint Conference, Deakin University, Geelong, Victoria, 22–26 November, 1992. Available at http://webpages. charter.net/schmolze1/vygotsky/renshaw.html [accessed 11 July 2006].

Rinvolucri, M. (1984) *Grammar Games: Cognitive, Affective and Drama Activities for EFL Students*. Cambridge: Cambridge University Press.

Rogers, C. (1969) *Freedom to Learn*. Columbus, OH: Charles E. Merrill.

Sinclair, B. (forthcoming, a) Multiple voices: Negotiating pathways towards teacher and learner autonomy. In T. Lamb and H. Reinders (eds.) *Selected Papers from The Scientific Commission on Learner Autonomy*. Amsterdam: John Benjamins.

Sinclair, B. (forthcoming, b) The teacher as learner: Developing autonomy in an interactive learning environment (or: Do you want your hub nodes more web-like?). In R. Pemberton and S. Toogood (eds.) *Autonomy in Language Learning: Maintaining Control*. Hong Kong: Hong Kong University Press.

Smith, R. (2000) Starting with ourselves: Teacher-learner autonomy in language learning. In B. Sinclair, I. McGrath and T. Lamb (eds.) *Learner Autonomy, Teacher Autonomy: Future Directions*, pp. 111–117. Harlow: Longman in association with the British Council.

Tudor, I. (1993) Teacher roles in the learner-centred classroom. *ELT Journal*, 47: 22–31.

Vygotsky, L. (1978) *Mind in Society*. Cambridge, MA: Harvard University Press.

Wang T. (2004) Learner support and tutor support in web-based degree programs in tertiary-level English education in China. In Y. Gu (ed.) *Exploring Online Education*, pp. 30–59. Beijing: Foreign Language Teaching and Research Press. Available at http://www.echinauk.org/, see under Papers and publications [accessed 8 August 2006].

Wenden, A. (1987) Conceptual background and utility. In A. Wenden and J. Rubin (eds.) *Learner Strategies in Language Learning*, pp. 3–14. London: Prentice Hall.

Wenden, A. (1991) *Learner Strategies for Learner Autonomy*. London: Prentice Hall.

Willing, K. (1988) *Learning Styles in Adult Migrant Education*. Adelaide: National Curriculum Resource Centre.

CHAPTER 5

Altman I. and Taylor, D. (1973) *Social Penetration: The Development of Interpersonal Relationships*. New York: Holt, Rinehart and Winston.

Asch, S. E. (1946) Forming impressions of personality. *Journal of Abnormal and Social Psychology*, 41: 258–290.

Beard, C. and Wilson, P. (2002) *The Power of Experiential Learning: A Handbook for Trainers and Educators*. London: Kogan Page.

Berger, C. (1987) Communicating under uncertainty. In M. Roloff and G. Miller (eds.) *Interpersonal Processes: New Directions in Communication Research*, pp. 39–62. Newbury Park, CA: Sage.

Chen Z. (2006) The Influence of Chinese Culture on Trainees' Online Behaviours in a Teacher Training Course. Paper presented at the Fifth International Conference on Networked Learning, Lancaster University 10–12 April. Proceedings available at: http://www. networkedlearningconference.org.uk/abstracts/pdfs/03Chen.pdf [accessed 12 July 2006].

Goleman, D. (1996) *Emotional Intelligence*. London: Bloomsbury.

Gu, Y., Hall, C., Sinclair, B. and McGrath, I. (2005) Developing Resources for MA e-ELT. In *Exploring Online Education (Contd.)*, pp. 23–42. Beijing: Foreign Language Teaching and Research Press.

Hall, C. (2003) The emotional development curriculum. In G. Hornby, C. Hall and E. Hall (eds.) *Counselling Pupils in Schools*, pp. 55–68. London: RoutledgeFalmer.

Jourard, S. (1971) *The Transparent Self*. New York: Van Nostrand Reinhold.

Joyes, G. (2006) When pedagogy leads technology. *International Journal of Technology, Knowledge and Society*, 17(1): 33–41.

Kelly, G.A. (1955) *The Psychology of Personal Constructs*, Vols. 1 and 2. New York: Norton.

Kolb, D.A. (1984) *Experiential Learning*. Englewood Cliffs, NJ: Prentice-Hall.

Kruger, J., Epley, N., Parker, J. and Ng, Z-W. (2005) Egocentrism over e-mail: can we communicate as well as we think? *Journal of Personality and Social Psychology*, 89 (6): 952–936.

Lambe, P. (2002) Confidence counts: What users want from e-learning. Straits Knowledge article. Available at http://greenchameleon.com/thoughtpieces/confidence.pdf [accessed 16 July 2006].

Lewis, D. and Allen, B. (2005) *Virtual Learning Communities: A Guide for Practitioners*. Maidenhead: Open University Press.

Linley, P. A. and Joseph, S. (Eds) (2004) *Positive Psychology in Practice*. New Jersey: John Wiley and Sons Inc.

Liu, N. F. and Littlewood, W. (1997) Why do many students appear reluctant to participate in classroom learning discourse? *System*, 25 (3): 371–384.

Maslow, A. (1954) *Motivation and Personality*. New York: Harper and Row.

McConnell, D. (2006) *E-learning Groups and Communities of Practice*. Maidenhead: Open University Press.

McCrae, R. (2000) Emotional intelligence from the perspective of the five-factor model of personality. In L R. Bar-On and J. D. A. Parker (eds.) *The Handbook of Emotional Intelligence*, pp. 263–276. San Francisco, CA: Jossey Bass.

McPherson, N. and Nunes, M.B. (2004) The failure of a virtual social space (VSS) designed to create a learning community: lessons learned. *British Journal of Educational Technology*, 35 (3): 305–321.

Rogers, C. R. (1961) *On Becoming a Person: A Therapist's View of Psychotherapy*. Boston: Houghton Mifflin.

Rovai, A. A. P. (2002) A preliminary look at the structural differences of higher education classroom communities in traditional and ALN [asynchronous learning network] courses. *Journal of Asynchronous Learning Networks*, 6(1): 41–56. Available at http://www.aln.org/publications/jaln/v6n1/v6n1_rovai.asp [accessed 11 July 2006].

Salmon, G., (2005) *E-tivities. The Key to Active Online Learning*. London: RoutledgeFalmer.

Sclater, M. and Bolander, K. (2004) Factors influencing students' orientation to collaboration in networked learning. In P. Goodyear, S. Banks, V. Hodgson and D. McConnell (eds.) *Advances in Research on Networked Learning*, pp. 175–203. Boston: Kluwer Academic Publishers.

See, H. K. P., Hall, C. and Hall, E. (1998) Changes in the attitudes of Hong Kong teachers and their students following an experiential counselling skills training course. *Asian Journal of Counselling*, 5(1): 1–11.

Seligman, M.E.P. (2003) Positive psychology: fundamental assumptions. *The Psychologist*, 16: 126–127.

Thurston, A. (2005) Building online learning communities. *Technology, Pedagogy and Education*, 14(3): 353–369.

Wallace, P. (1999) *The Psychology of the Internet*. Cambridge: Cambridge University Press.

CHAPTER 6

Achacoso, M. (2003) Evaluating technology and instruction: literature review and recommendations. Online report published by the University of Texas. Available at http://www.utexas.edu/academic/mec/LiteratureReview.pdf [accessed 7 August 2006].

Alexander, S. (2004) Opinion piece: Pedagogy and practice. *Australian Flexible Learning Community*, 2001–2004. Available at http://community.flexiblelearning.net.au/GlobalPerspectives/content/article_6966.htm [accessed 11 July 2006].

Bax, S. (2003) CALL — past, present and future. *System*, 31: 13–28. Available at http://www.iateflcompsig.org.uk/media/callpresentpastandfuture.pdf [accessed 7 August 2006].

BECTA (2004) Research into the use of ICT and e-learning for work-based learning in the skills sector. Literature review commissioned by the British Educational Communications and Technology Agency (BECTA). Available at www.becta.org.uk/page_documents/research/wbl_literature_review.doc [accessed 7 August 2006].

Chapelle, C. (2004) Learning through online communication: Findings and implications from second language research, 13 November 2004, pp. 1–22. The University of York. Available at http://www.wun.ac.uk/elearning/seminars/seminars/seminar_one/papers/chapelle.pdf [accessed 11 July 2006].

CIEL Project (2000) Supporting independent language learning: Development for learners and teachers. Guide to good practice published online by the Subject Centre for Languages, Linguistics and Area Studies. Available at http://www.lang.ltsn.ac.uk/resources/goodpractice.aspx?resourceid=1410 [accessed 7 August 2006].

Colburn, C. (1998) Online strategic interaction: ESL role-playing via internet relay chat. *The Internet TESL Journal*, IV(6): June. Available at http://iteslj.org/Articles/Colburn-SI_on_IRC/ [accessed 11 July 2006].

Conole, G. (2003) Learning technology standards in a networked society. Paper presented at the CETIS (The Centre for Educational Technology Interoperability Standards) Pedagogy Forum. Available at http://www.cetis.ac.uk/members/pedagogy/files/ppt5Networked_GC.ppt [accessed 7 August 2006].

Garrett, N. (1991). Technology in the service of language learning: Trends and issues. *Modern Language Journal*, 75(1): 74–101.

Gerbic, P. (2005) Chinese learners and computer mediated communication: Balancing culture, technology and pedagogy. Paper presented at ASCILITE (Australian Society for Computers in Learning in Tertiary Education) Conference, 4–7 December, Brisbane, Australia 2005. Available at http://www.ascilite.org.au/conferences/brisbane05/blogs/proceedings/27_Gerbic.pdf [accessed 7 August 2006].

González, V., Chen C. and Sanchez, C. (2001) Cultural thinking and discourse organizational patterns influencing writing skills in a Chinese English-as-a-foreign-language (EFL) learner. *Bilingual Research Journal,* 25(4): 418–442. Available at http://brj.asu.edu/v254/pdf/ar11.pdf [accessed 7 August 2006].

HEFCE (2005) HEFCE (Higher Education Funding Council for England) strategy for e-learning. Available at http://www.hefce.ac.uk/pubs/hefce/2005/05_12/ [accessed 7 August 2006].

Hymes, D. (1974) *Foundations in Sociolinguistics.* Philadelphia, PA: University of Pennsylvania Press.

Lamping, A. (2004) BBC/LSC Get talking: Blended language learning. Published by the BBC (British Broadcasting Company). Available at http://www.bbc.co.uk/languages/tutors/blended_learning/blended_learning_report.pdf [accessed 7 August 2006].

Lapadat, J.C. (2002) Written interaction: A key component in online learning. *Journal of Computer Mediated Communication,* 7(4): Online. Available at http://jcmc.indiana.edu/vol7/issue4/lapadat.html [accessed 7 August 2006].

Larsen-Freeman, D. and Long, M. (1991) *An Introduction to Second Language Acquisition Research.* New York: Longman Inc.

Lee, L. (2004) Learners' perspectives on networked collaborative interaction with native speakers of Spanish in the US. *Language Learning and Technology,* 8(1): 83–100. Available at http://Llt.Msu.Edu/Vol8num1/Lee/Default.Html [accessed 11 July 2006].

Maor, D. (2004) Pushing beyond the comfort zone: Bridging the gap between technology and pedagogy. Paper presented at ASCILITE (Australian Society for Computers in Learning in Tertiary Education) Conference, 5–8 December, Perth. Available at http://www.ascilite.org.au/conferences/perth04/procs/maor.html [accessed 7 August 2006].

Mayes, T. and de Freitas, S. (2004) Review of e-learning theories, frameworks and models. *JISC e-Learning Models Desk Study.* Available at http://www.jisc.ac.uk/uploaded_documents/Stage%202%20Learning%20Models%20(Version%201).pdf [accessed 11 July 2006].

McLoughlin, C. (2002) Learner support in distance and networked learning environments: Ten dimensions for successful design. *Distance Education,* 23(2): 149–162. Available at http://www.educationarena.com/educationarena/sample/sample_pdfs8/CDIE23_2a.pdf [accessed 7 August 2006].

Mitchell, N. (2003) Where is e-learning now? The training foundation. Available at http://www.trainingfoundation.com/articles/default.asp?PageID=1681#e-Learning%20-/ [accessed 11 July 2006].

MoE (2001) 教育部关于印发《关于加强高等学校本科教学工作提高教学质量的若干意见》的通知 . [Notification from the MoE: A few points re strengthening the teaching of university undergraduates, and raising the quality of teaching]. Available in Chinese at http://www.pgzx.edu.cn/upload/files/zxwd/jg20014.pdf [accessed 7 August 2006].

Warschauer, M. (2000) Online learning in second language classrooms: An ethnographic study. In M. Warschauer and R. Kern (eds.) *Network-Based Language Teaching: Concepts and Practice*, pp. 41–58. New York: Cambridge University Press.

Warschauer, M. (2004) Technological change and the future of CALL. In S. Fotos and C. Brown (eds.) *New Perspectives on CALL for Second and Foreign Language Classrooms*, pp. 15–25. Mahwah, NJ: Lawrence Erlbaum Associates. Draft copy of paper available at http://www.gse. uci.edu/faculty/markw/future-of-CALL.pdf [accessed 7 August 2006].

CHAPTER 7

Andreassen, E. F. (2000) Evaluating how students organise their work in a collaborative teleLearning scenario: An activity theoretical perspective. Unpublished Master's Thesis, University of Bergen. Available at http://www.ifi.uib.no/docta/dissertations/andreassen/index.htm [accessed 13 July 2006].

Berns, T. (2004) Usability and user-centred design, a necessity for efficient e-learning! *International Journal of the Computer, the Internet and Management*, 12(2): 20–25.

Brook, C. and Oliver, R. (2004) Online learning communities: Exploring the impact of group size on community development. Paper presented at the Ed-Media Conference, 21–26 June 2004, Lugano, Switzerland.

Campbell, A., Ammann, R. and Dieu, B. (2005) Elgg — A personal learning landscape. *Teaching English as a Second of Foreign Language — EJ*, 9(2): Online. Available at http://tesl-ej.org/ ej34/m1.html [accessed 13 July 2006].

Cao W. (2004) Resource development and provision. In Y. Gu (ed.) *Exploring Online Education*, pp. 9–29. Beijing: Foreign Language Teaching and Research Press. Available at http://www. echinauk.org/ [accessed 8 August 2006].

Chan, C. (2001) Promoting learning and understanding through constructivist approaches for Chinese learners. In D. Watkins and J. Biggs (eds.) *Teaching the Chinese Learner: Psychological and Pedagogical Perspectives*, pp. 181–203. Hong Kong: Hong Kong University Press.

Draper, S., Brown, M. I., Henderson, F. P. and McAteer, E. (1996) Integrative evaluation: An emerging role for classroom studies of CAL. *Computers and Education*, 26 (1–3): 17–32.

Duggleby, J., Howard, J. Butler, K. Williams, L., Cooke, M., Cotton, C., Schmoller, S. (2002) JISC effective online tutoring guidelines: The Sheffield College. Available at http://www.jisc.ac.uk/ techlearn_etutor.html [accessed 13 July 2006].

Engeström, Y. (1987) Learning by expanding: An activity-theoretical approach to developmental research. Helsinki, Orienta-Konsultit. Available at http://communication.ucsd.edu/MCA/Paper/ Engestrom/expanding/toc.htm/ [accessed 13 July 2006].

Festinger, L. (1957) *A Theory of Cognitive Dissonance*. Stanford, CA: Stanford University Press.

Godwin-Jones, R. (2003) Emerging technologies. Blogs and wikis: Environments for on-line collaboration. *Language Learning & Technology*, 7(2): 12–16. Available at http://llt.msu.edu/ vol7num2/emerging/ [accessed 13 July 2006].

Goodyear, P. (2001) Effective networked learning in higher education: Notes and guidelines. Centre for Studies in Advanced Learning Technology, Lancaster University.

Goodyear, P., Salmon, G., Spector, M., Steeples, C., and Tickner, S. (2001) Competences for online teaching: A special report. *Educational Technology, Research and Development*, 49(1): 65–72.

Gould, J. D. and Lewis, C. (1983) Designing for usability — Key principles and what designers think. Conference for Human-computer Interaction. 24–29 April 1983.

Jonassen, D. and Rohrer-Murphy, L. (1999) Activity theory as a framework for designing constructivist learning environments. *Educational Technology Research and Development,* 47(1), 61–79.

Joyes, G. (2006a) Sharing effective learning design processes versus labelling the pedagogy? Position paper for the online conference, Innovating eLearning 27–31 March 2006: Transforming Learning Experiences, Theme 1: Designing for Learning. Available at http://www.echinauk.org/ [accessed 4 December 2006].

Joyes, G. (2006b) When pedagogy leads technology. *International Journal of Technology, Knowledge and Society*, 17(1): 33–41.

Joyes, G. and Fritze, P. (2006) Valuing individual differences within learning: from face-to-face to online experience. *International Journal of Teaching and Learning in Higher Education* 17(1): 33–41. Available at http://www.isetl.org/ijtlhe/pdf/IJTLHE13.pdf [accessed 12 July 2006].

Joyes, G. and Chen Z. (2006) Researching an on online teacher education course. Paper presented at the Asia TEFL Conference, November 2005, Beijing.

Kukulska-Hulme, A. and Shield, L. (2004) Usability and pedagogical design: Are language learning websites special? Paper presented at the Ed-Media Conference, June 2004, Lugano, Switzerland. Available at http://www.aace.org/DL/index.cfm?fuseaction=ViewPaper&id=16072 [accessed 13 July 2006].

Laurillard, D. (1993). *Rethinking University Teaching*. London: Routledge.

Leont'ev, A. N. (1981) *Problems of the Development of Mind*. Moscow: Progress Publishers.

Lewis, D. and Allen, B. (2005) *Virtual Learning Communities: A Guide for Practitioners*. Milton Keynes: Open University Press.

Lisewski, B. and Joyce, P. (2003) Examining the five stage e-moderating model: Designed and emergent practice in the learning technology profession. *Association for Learning Technology Journal*, 11(1): 55–66.

McConnell, D. (2000) *Implementing Computer-supported Cooperative Learning.* Second edition. London: Kogan Page.

Merrill, D. (2003) First principles of instruction. *Educational Technology Research and Development*, 50(3): 43–59.

Mwanza, D. (2001) Where theory meets practice. A case for an activity theory based methodology to guide computer system design. In H. Michitaka (ed.) *Proceedings of INTERACT 2001: Eighth IFIP TC 13 International Conference on Human–Computer Interaction*, pp. 342–349. IOS Press: Oxford.

Mwanza, D. (2002) Conceptualising work activity for CAL systems design. *Journal of Computer Assisted Learning*, 18 (1): 84–92.

Nardi, B. A. (ed.) (1996). *Context and Consciousness: Activity Theory and Human-Computer Interaction*. Cambridge, MA: MIT Press.

Oliver, R. and Herrington, J. (2001) *Teaching and Learning Online: A Beginner's Guide to eLearning and e-Teaching in Higher Education*. Perth, Western Australia: Centre for Research in Information Technology and Communications, Edith Cowan University.

Redfern, S. and Naughton, N. (2002) Collaborative virtual environments to support communication and community in Internet-based distance education. *Journal of Information Technology Education*, 1(3): 201–211. Available at http://jite.org/documents/Vol1/v1n3p201-211.pdf [accessed 13 July 2006].

Russell, D.R. (2002) Looking beyond the interface: Activity theory and distributed learning. In R. M. Lea and K. Nicoll (eds.) *Distributed Learning: Social and Cultural Approaches to Practice*, pp. 64–88. London: Routledge Falmer.

Salmon, G. (2000) *E-Moderating, the Key to Teaching and Learning Online*. London: Kogan Page.

Taylor, J. C. (2001) *Fifth Generation Distance Education*. Higher Education Series Report No. 40, Department of Education Training and Youth Affairs, Australia.

Vygotsky, L. S. (1978) *Mind in Society: The Development of Higher Psychological Processes*. Cambridge, MA: Harvard University Press.

Wang T. (2004) Learner support and tutor support in web-based degree programs in tertiary-level English education in China. In Y. Gu (ed.) *Exploring Online Education*, pp. 30–59. Beijing: Foreign Language Teaching and Research Press. Available at http://www.echinauk.org/ [accessed 8 August 2006].

Watkins, D. and Biggs, J. (eds.) (2001) *Teaching the Chinese Learner: Psychological and Pedagogical Perspectives*. Hong Kong: Hong Kong University Press.

CHAPTER **8**

Advanced Distributed Learning (ADL) (2004) Sharable Content Object Reference Model (SCORM (r)) 2nd Edition Overview, 2004. Available at http://www.adlnet.org [accessed 12 July 2006].

Beck, K. (2005) *EXtreme Programming eXplained: Embrace Change*. Harlow, Essex: Addison Wesley.

Brewster, E., Cavaleri, N., King, A. and Zähner, C. (2005) CUTE (Chinese University Teachers Training in English): Pedagogy in practice. Paper presented at *CRIDALA 2005 (Conference of the Centre for Research in Distance and Adult Learning), 20–22 June 2005*, The Open University Hong Kong.

Vygotsky L. S. (1978) *Mind in Society*. Cambridge, MA: Harvard University Press.

Vygotsky, L. S. (1986) *Thought and Language*. Cambridge, MA: MIT Press.

Wells, G. (1999) *Dialogic Inquiry: Towards a Sociocultural Practice and Theory of Education*. Cambridge: Cambridge University Press.

CHAPTER **9**

Biggs, J. (1996) Enhancing teaching through constructive alignment. *Higher Education*, 32(3): 347–364.

Biggs, J. (1999) *Teaching for Quality Learning at University*. Buckingham: OU Press/SRHE.

Bonk, C. J. (2001) *Online Teaching in an Online World*. Bloomington, IN: Courseshare.com

Cao W. (2004) Resources development and provision a descriptive picture of tertiary level degree programmes in English language education in China. In Y. Gu (ed.) *Exploring Online Education*, pp. 9–29. Beijing: Foreign Language Teaching and Research Press. Available at http://www.echinauk.org/ [accessed 4 December 2006].

Cao W. (2005) Dropouts of web-based degree programmes: When and who. *Journal of China Distance Education*, 11a.

Chen Z. and Joyes, G. (2005) eChina-UK project report: University of Nottingham and Beijing Normal University evaluation report of the pilot in Beijing. Available at http://www.echinauk.org/papers/reports/reports.php/ [accessed 12 July 2006].

Conole, G. (2003) Research questions and methodological issues. In J. Seale (ed.) *Learning Technology in Transition: From Individual Enthusiasm to Institutional Implementation,* pp. 129–146. Heereweg, NL: Swets and Zeitlinger.

Conole, G. and Dyke, M. (2004) What are the affordances of information and communication technologies? *ALT-J,* 12(2): 13–124.

Dam, L. (1995) *Learner Autonomy 3: From Theory to Classroom Practice.* Dublin: Authentik.

Daniel, J. (1996) *Mega Universities and Knowledge Media.* London: Kogan Page.

DfES (2005a) Department for Education and Skills 5-year strategy for learners and children. Available at http://www.dfes.gov.uk/publications/5yearstrategy/ [accessed 12 July 2006].

DfES (2005b) Department for Education and Skills E-strategy — harnessing technology: transforming learning and children's services. Available at http://www.dfes.gov.uk/publications/e-strategy/ [accessed 12 July 2006].

Gibbs, G. (2003) The future of student retention in open and distance Learning. In A. Gaskell and A. Tait (eds.) *The Future of Open and Distance Learning. Collected Conference Papers,* pp. 37–48. The 10th Cambridge International Conference on Open and Distance Learning in association with The Commonwealth of Learning. Cambridge: The Open University in the East of England.

Gibson, J. J. (1979) *The Ecological Approach to Visual Perception.* Boston, MA: Houghton Mifflin.

Green, H., Facer, K., Rudd, T., Dillon, P. and Humphreys, P. (2005) The personalisation and digital technologies report. Available at http://www.nestafuturelab.org/research/personalisation.htm [accessed 12 July 2006].

Greeno, J. (1998) The situativity of knowing, learning and research. *American Psychologist,* 53: 5–26.

Gu Y. (2003) Online education: Nature and status in China. In 《中国远程教育》 [*Chinese Distance Education*], No. 4.

HEFCE (2004) Effective Practice with e-Learning: A good practice guide in designing for learning. Available at http://www.jisc.ac.uk/index.cfm?name=publications [accessed 10 August 2006].

Huang R. and Zhou Y. (2006) Designing blended learning focused on knowledge category and learning activities. In C. J. Bonk and C. R. Graham (eds.) *Handbook of Blended Learning: Global Perspectives, Local Designs,* pp. 296–310. San Francisco, CA: Pfeiffer Publishing.

Joyes, G. and Fritze, P. (2006) Valuing individual differences within learning: From face-to-face to online experience. *International Journal of Teaching and Learning in Higher Education,* 17 (1): 33–41. Available at http://www.isetl.org/ijtlhe/pdf/IJTLHE13.pdf [accessed 12 July 2006].

Keller, J. M. (1983) Motivational design of instruction. In C. Reigeluth (ed.) *Instructional Design Theories and Models,* pp. 383–434. Hillsdale, NJ: Erlbaum.

Kennewell, S. (2001) Using affordances and constraints to evaluate the use of information and communications technology in teaching and learning. *Journal of Information Technology for Teacher Education,* 10(1–2): 101–116.

Laurillard, D. (1994) How can learning technologies improve learning? *Law Technology Journal*, 3 (2): Online. Available at http://www.warwick.ac.uk/ltj/3-2j.html/ [accessed October 2004].

Laurillard, D., Stratfold, M., Luckin, R., Plowman, L. and Taylor, J. (2000) Affordances for learning in a non-linear narrative medium. *Journal of Interactive Media in Education*, 2(2): 1–19.

McConnell, D. (2000) *Implementing Computer-Supported Cooperative Learning*. Second edition. London: Kogan Page.

Mitchell, P. D. (2000) The impact of educational technology: A radical reappraisal of research methods. In D. Squires, G. Conole and G. Jacobs (eds.) *The Changing Face of Learning Technology*, pp. 51–58. Cardiff: University Wales Press.

O'Donoghue, J. and Singh, G. (2001) A study of social-learning networks of students studying an on-line programme. Paper presented at the International Conference on Advanced Learning Technologies (ICALT), 6–8 August 2001, Madison, WI.

Redfern, S. and Naughton, N. (2002) Collaborative virtual environments to support communication and community in Internet-based distance education. *Journal of Information Technology Education*, 1(3): 201–211. Available at http://jite.org/documents/Vol1/v1n3p201-211.pdf [accessed 12 July 2006].

Russell, T. (1999) *The No-Significant Difference Phenomena*. Chapel Hill, NC: North Carolina State University.

Spratt, M. (1999) How good are we at knowing what learners like? *System*, 27: 141–155.

Timmis, S., O'Leary, R., Weedon, E., Harrison, C. and Martin, K. (2004). Different shoes, same footprints? A cross-disciplinary evaluation of students' online learning experiences: Preliminary findings from the SOLE project. *Journal of Interactive Media in Education* (*Designing and Developing for the Disciplines* Special Issue), 2004 (13). Available at http://www-jime.open. ac.uk/2004/13/ [accessed 12 July 2006].

Wang T. (2004) Learner support and tutor support in web-based degree programs in tertiary-level English education in China. In Y. Gu (ed.) *Exploring Online Education*, pp. 30–59. Beijing: Foreign Language Teaching and Research Press. Available at http://www.echinauk.org/ [accessed 4 December 2006].

EDITOR'S INTRODUCTION TO SECTION 4

Canney Davison, S. and Ward, K. (1999) *Leading International Teams*. Maidenhead, UK: McGraw Hill.

Engeström, Y. (2001) Expansive learning at work: Toward an activity theoretical reconceptualization. *Journal of Education and Work*, 14(1): 133–156.

Maznevski, M. L. (1994) Understanding our differences: Performance in decision-making groups with diverse members. *Human Relations*, 47(5): 531–552.

CHAPTER 10

Canney Davison, S. and Ward, K. (1999) *Leading International Teams*. Maidenhead, UK: McGraw Hill.

de Dreu, C. (2002) Team innovation and team effectiveness: The importance of minority dissent and reflexivity. *European Journal of Work and Organizational Psychology*, 11(3): 285–298.

DiStefano, J. and Maznevski, M. (2000) Creating value with diverse teams in global management. *Organizational Dynamics*, 29(1): 45–63.

HEFCE (2002) e-University: Invitation to express interest in a project to develop in-service teacher training programmes for teachers in China. HEFCE Circular Letter, 14/2002. Available at http://www.hefce.ac.uk/pubs/circlets/2002/ [accessed 8 August 2006].

Janssens, M. and Brett, J. (1997) Meaningful participation in transnational teams. *European Journal of Work and Organizational Psychology*, 6(2): 153–168.

Maznevski, M. L. (1994) Understanding our differences: Performance in decision-making groups with diverse members. *Human Relations*, 47(5): 531–552.

Maznevski, M., and Chudoba, K. (2000) Bridging space over time: Global virtual team dynamics and effectiveness. *Organization Science*, 11(5): 473–492.

Polzer, J., Milton, L. and Swann, W. (2002) Capitalizing on diversity: Interpersonal congruence in small work groups. *Administrative Science Quarterly*, 47: 296–324.

Spencer-Oatey, H. and Tang M. (2006) International teamworking and e-learning design. Paper presented at the Fifth International Conference on Networked Learning, Lancaster University 10–12 April. Available at http://www.networkedlearningconference.org.uk/abstracts/pdfs/03Spencer.pdf [accessed 8 July 2006].

West, M. (2002) Sparkling fountains or stagnant ponds: An integrative model of creativity and innovation implementation in work groups. *Applied Psychology: An International Review*, 51 (3): 355–424.

CHAPTER 11

Banks, S., Lally, V. and McConnell, D. (2003) *Collaborative e-learning in Higher Education: Issues and Strategies*. University of Sheffield SPIE publication.

Banks, S., Lally, V., Liu B. and McConnell, D. (2006) Intercultural e-Learning: Reflections on developing a collaborative approach to pedagogy and educational technology in a Sino-UK context. Paper presented at the Fifth International Conference on Networked Learning, Lancaster University, 10–12 April. Available at http://www.networkedlearningconference.org.uk/abstracts/Spenceroatey.htm [accessed 6 August 2006].

Barab, S., Thomas, M., Dodge, T., Goodrich, T., Carteaux, B., and Tuzum, H. (2002) Empowerment design work: Building participant structures that transform. Available at http://inkido.indiana.edu/research/onlinemanu/papers/icls_2002.pdf [accessed 6 August 2006].

Boekaerts, M. and Simons, P. R. J. (1995) *Leren en instructie: psychologie van de leerling en het leerproces* [Learning and instruction: The psychology of the learner and his learning process]. Assen: Dekker and Van de Vegt.

Brown, J. S., Collins, A. and Duguid, P. (1989) Situated cognition and the culture of learning. *Educational Researcher*, 18 (1): 32–42.

Burnard, P., Arthur, D. and Wang Z. (1999) A report of the development of a Chinese and British education initiative. *Journal of Psychiatric and Mental Health Nursing*, 6(5): 391–392.

Cao W., Wang T. and Tang J. (2005). Tertiary-level online English language education in China: tensions and implications, Parts 1, 2 and 3. Papers presented at the Second Sino-UK e-Learning Workshop, 21–23 March, Beijing Foreign Studies University, Beijing, China. PowerPoint presentations available at http://www.echinauk.org/. See Papers and Publications, Workshop 2 Day 3 [accessed 6 August 2006].

De Laat, M. and Lally, V. (2003) Complexity, theory and praxis: Researching collaborative learning and tutoring processes in a networked learning community. *Instructional Science (Special Issue on Networked Learning)*, 31(1–2): 7–39.

Dillenbourg, P. (ed.) (1999) *Collaborative Learning: Cognitive and Computational Approaches.* Amsterdam: Pergamon.

Ding, X. (2005) A framework for research and development in the Sino-UK e-learning project for higher education. Paper presented at the Second Sino-UK e-Learning Workshop, 21–23 March, Beijing Foreign Studies University, Beijing, China. PowerPoint presentation. Available at http://www.echinauk.org/. See Papers and Publications, Workshop 2 Day 3 [accessed 6 August 2006].

Duffy, T. M. and Jonassen, D.H. (1992) Constructivism: New implications for instructional technology. In T. M. Duffy and D. H. Jonassen (eds.) *Constructivism and the Technology of Instruction: A Conversation*, pp. 1–15. Mahwah, NJ: Lawrence Erlbaum Associates.

Goldstein, L. S. (1999) The relational zone: The role of caring relationships in the co-construction of mind. *American Educational Research Journal*, 36(3): 647–673.

Goodyear, P., De Laat, M. and Lally, V. (2006) Using pattern languages to mediate theory-praxis conversations in design for networked learning. *ALT-J, Research in Learning Technology*, 14 (3): 211–223.

Huang R. and Zhou Y. (2005) Designing blended learning focused on knowledge category and learning activities. Case studies from Beijing Normal University. In C. J. Bonk and C. R. Graham (eds.) *Handbook of Blended Learning: Global Perspectives, Local Designs*, pp. 296–310. San Francisco, CA: Pfeiffer Publishing.

Koschmann, T. (1999) Toward a dialogic theory of learning: Bakhtin's contribution to understanding learning in settings of collaboration. Paper presented at the Computer Supported Collaborative Learning Conference, 12–15 December, Stanford University.

Lave, J. (1988) *Cognition in Practice*. Cambridge: Cambridge University Press.

Lave, J. (1996) Teaching, as learning, in practice. *Mind, Culture, and Activity*, 3(3): 149–164.

Lave, J. and Wenger, E. (1991) *Situated Learning: Legitimate Peripheral Participation.* Cambridge: Cambridge University Press.

Levine, J. M., Resnick, L. B. and Higgins, E. T. (1996) Social foundations of cognition. *Annual Review of Psychology*, 44: 585–612.

Ling, S. C. (1990) The effects of group cultural composition and cultural attitudes on performance. Unpublished PhD thesis, University of Western Ontario, London, ON.

Maznevski, M. L. (1994). Understanding our differences: Performance in decision-making groups with diverse members. *Human Relations*, 47(5): 531–552.

McConnell, D. (2000) *Implementing Computer-Supported Cooperative Learning.* Second edition. London: Kogan Page.

McConnell, D. (2006) *E-Learning Groups and Communities.* Maidenhead: SRHE/Open University Press.

McLeod, P. L. and Lobe, S. A. (1992) The effects of ethnic diversity on idea generation in small groups. In L. R. Jauch and L. C. Wall (eds.) *Academy of Management Annual Meeting Best Papers Proceedings*, pp. 227–231. Briarcliff Manor, NY: Academy of Management.

Moll, L. C., Tapia, J. and Whitmore, K. P. (1993) Living knowledge: The social distribution of cultural resources for thinking. In G. Salomon (ed.) *Distributed Cognitions: Psychological and Educational Considerations*, pp. 139–163. Cambridge: Cambridge University Press.

Ngor, A. (2001) The prospects for using the Internet in collaborative design education with China. *Higher Education*, 42(1): 47–60.

Pi, L. S. (ed.) (1998) *Knowledge Category and Objective Instruction: Theory and Practice*. Shanghai: East China Normal University Press.

QAA (2001) Subject review report, University of Sheffield, Education (Q391/2001). Quality Assurance Agency for Higher Education (UK). Available at http://www.qaa.ac.uk/reviews/reports/subjectLevel/q391_01.pdf [accessed 6 August 2006].

Resnick, L. B. (1991) Shared cognition: Thinking as social practice. In L. B. Resnick, J. M. Levine and S. D. Teasley (eds.) *Perspectives on Socially Shared Cognition,* pp. 1–20. Arlington VA: American Psychological Association.

Salomon, G. and Perkins, D. N. (1998) Individual and social aspects of learning. *Review of Research in Education*, 23: 1–24.

Sfard, A. (1998) On two metaphors for learning and the dangers of choosing just one. *Educational Researcher*, 27(2): 4–13.

Smith, J. B. (1994). *Collective Intelligence in Computer-based Collaboration*. Mahwah, NJ: Lawrence Erlbaum Associates.

Van Boxtel, C., Van der Linden, J. and Kanselaar, G. (2000) Collaborative learning tasks and the elaboration of conceptual knowledge. *Learning and Instruction*, 10(4): 311–330.

Vygotsky, L. S. (1962) *Thought and Language* (translated by E. H. a. G. Vakar). Cambridge, MA: MIT Press.

Vygotsky, L. S. (1978) *Mind in Society: The Development of Higher Psychological Processes* (translated by V. J.-S. M. Cole, S. Scribner and E. Souberman). Cambridge MA: Harvard University Press.

Wegerif, R., Mercer, N. and Dawes, L. (1999) From social interaction to individual reasoning: An empirical investigation of a possible socio-cultural model of cognitive development. *Learning and Instruction*, 9(6): 493–516.

Wertsch, J. V. (1991) A sociocultural approach to socially shared cognition. In L. B. Resnick, J. M. Levine and S. D. Teasley (eds.) *Perspectives on Socially Shared Cognition*, pp. 85–100. Arlington VA: American Psychological Association.

You, Y. (1993) What can we learn from chaos theory? An alternative approach to instructional systems design. *Educational Technology Research and Development*, 41 (3): 17–32.

CHAPTER 12

Centre for Activity Theory (n.d.) Cultural historical activity theory. Available at http://www.edu.helsinki.fi/activity/pages/chatanddwr/chat/ [accessed 1 June 2006].

Conole, G., Carusi, A., de Laat, M. and Darby, J. (2006) What can we learn from the demise of the UKeU? Evaluation of the lessons learnt. Paper presented at the Fifth International Conference on Networked Learning, 10–12 April, Lancaster University. Available at http://www.networkedlearningconference.org.uk/abstracts/connole.htm [accessed 14 July 2006].

Engeström, Y. (2001). Expansive learning at work: Toward an activity theoretical reconceptualization. *Journal of Education and Work*, 14(1): 133–156.

Engeström, Y., Miettinen, R., and Punamaki, R.-L. (1999) *Perspectives on Activity Theory.* Cambridge: Cambridge University Press.

Forrester, G. and Motteram, G. (2004) The Fujian Pilot. Preliminary Report. Available at http://www.echinauk.org [accessed 14 July 2006].

Forrester, G., Motteram, G. and Liu B. (2006) Transforming Chinese teachers' thinking, learning and understanding via e-learning. *Journal of Education for Teaching,* 32(2): 197–212.

Goldrick, S. and Wang Y. (2005) Instructional design issues in developing a collaborative e-learning programme. Paper presented at CRIDALA 2005 (Conference of the Centre for Research in Distance and Adult Learning in Asia), 20–22 June 2005, The Open University of Hong Kong, Hong Kong.

Holliday, A. (1999) Small cultures. *Applied Linguistics,* 20: 237–264.

Lambert, P. (2003) Promoting developmental transfer in vocational teacher education. In T. Tuomi-Grohn and Y. Engeström (eds.) *Between School and Work: New Perspectives on Transfer and Boundary Crossing,* pp. 233–254. London: Pergamon.

Lamont, M. and Molnar, V. (2002) The study of boundaries in the social sciences. *Annual Review of Sociology,* 28: 167–195.

Schön, D. (1983) *The Reflective Practitioner: How Professionals Think in Action.* London: Temple Smith.

Star, S. L. and Griesmar, J. R. (1989) Institutional ecology, 'translations' and boundary objects: Amateurs and professionals in Berkley's Museum of Vertebrate Zoology 1907–39. *Social Studies of Science,* 19: 387–420.

Wenger, E. (1998) *Communities of Practice: Learning, Meaning and Identity.* Cambridge: Cambridge University Press.

CHAPTER 13

Casey, J. (2004, updated April 2006) Intellectual Property Rights (IPR) in Networked e-Learning. A Beginner's Guide for Content Developers. Joint Information Systems Committee (JISC) report. Available at http://www.jisclegal.ac.uk/publications/johncasey_1.htm [accessed 17 July 2006].

China Britain Business Council [CBBC] (2004) Intellectual Property Rights in China: Risk Assessment, Avoidance Strategy and Problem Solving. The UK China IPR Forum. Available at http://www.cbbc.org/initiatives/ipr_forum/china_ipr_gl.pdf [accessed 17 July 2006].

HEFCE [Higher Education Funding Council for England] (2003) Intellectual Property Rights in e-Learning Programmes: Report of the Working Group. Available at http://www.hefce.ac.uk/Pubs/HEFCE/2003/03_08.htm [accessed 20 July 2006].

HEFCE [Higher Education Funding Council for England] (2006) Intellectual Property Rights in e-Learning Programmes: Report of the Working Group. Available at http://www.hefce.ac.uk/pubs/hefce/2006/06_20/ [accessed 20 July 2006].

JISC [Joint Infrastructure Systems Committee] (2005) e-Learning Series. Available at http://www.jisclegal.ac.uk/publications/e-learningseries.htm [accessed 17 July 2006].

McSherry, C. (2001) *Who Owns Academic Work? Battling for Control of Intellectual Property.* Cambridge, MA: Harvard University Press.

MoE [Ministry of Education] (1999) The Provisions of Intellectual Property Protection and Management in the University. Beijing, Third Order in 1999.

MoE [Ministry of Education] (2003) Regulations of the People's Republic of China on Chinese-Foreign Cooperation in Running Schools. State Council. English translation available at http://www.moe.edu.cn/english/laws_r.htm [accessed 20 July 2006].

MoE [Ministry of Education]/The National Intellectual Property Bureau (2004) Certain opinions on further enhancing the intellectual property work in the university. Beijing. No 4.

Oppenheim, C. (2004) Recent Changes to Copyright Law and their Implications for HE and FE. Report for Joint Information Systems Committee — Legal Information Service. http://www. jisclegal.ac.uk/publications/copyrightcoppenheim.htm [accessed 20 July 2006].

Stamatoudi, D. Q. and Torresmans, P. L. C. (2000) *Copyright in the New Digital Age: The Need to Redesign Copyright.* London: Sweet and Maxwell.

State Intellectual Property Office (2001) Copyright Law of the People's Republic of China. Beijing. Translated version available at http://www.sipo.gov.cn/sipo_English/flfg/bmgz/200204/ t20020416_33876.htm [accessed 20 July 2006].

Strathern, M. (2004) *Commons and Borderlands: Working Papers on Interdisciplinarity, Accountability and the Flow of Knowledge.* Oxford: Kingston Publishing.

Williamson, A., Kennedy, D. M., McNaught, C. and DeSouza, R. (2003) Issues of intellectual capital and intellectual property in educational software development teams. *Australian Journal of Educational Technology*, 19(3): 339–355. Available at http://www.ascilite.org.au/ajet/ajet19/ williamson.html [accessed 17 July 2006].

Withers, K. (2006) *Intellectual Property and the Knowledge Economy.* Report for the Institute for Public Policy Research, London. Available at http://www.ippr.org.uk/ecomm/files/ intellectual_property.pdf [accessed 20 July 2006].

CHAPTER **14**

Chen L. (2003–04) China: ICT use in Education. UNESCO meta-survey on the use of technologies in Education in Asia and the Pacific 2003–4. Available at http://www.unescobkk.org/fileadmin/ user_upload/ict/Metasurvey/CHINA.PDF [accessed 14 July 2006].

Chen S. (陈上仁) (2005) 我国区域高等教育发展失衡及其解决对对策研究 [Imbalances of regional development in China's higher education and their solution]. 《中国高教研究》[China Studies on Higher Education], 3: 38–41.

China's Distance Education: Opportunities and Challenges (n. d) 中国远程教育面临的机遇与挑战。Available at http://www.isnet.org.cn/ASP/proxuhome/XUWEB2/ziliao/forum/main/ chinese/10.doc/ [accessed 30 May 2006].

CNNIC [China Internet Network Information Center] 中国互联网络信息中心(2006)第17次《中国互联网络发展状况统计报告》The 17th Statistical Survey Report on the Internet Development in China. Available at: http://news.xinhuanet.com/it/2006-01/18/content_4067043. htm. Available in English at http://www.cnnic.net.cn/en/index/0O/02/index.htm [accessed 14 July 2006].

Jiao K.（焦科）(2006)高校教育信息化建设与应用水平调查 [A survey of the construction and application of educational informationization in China's institutions of higher learning]《中国教育报》[China Education Newspaper]. 2006年6月14日 [14 June 2006]. Available at http://www.chinaonlineedu.com/info/news_special.asp?id=10142 [accessed 18 June 2006].

Li Z.（李志民）(2005)探索教育资源建设新模式，全面提升教育信息化应用水平 [Exploring new models of building educational resources and enhancing an overall application of educational informationization]. 2005年8月 [August 2005] Available at http://www.edu.cn/20050803/3145534.shtml/ [accessed 30 May 2006].

MoE (Ministry of Education of the People's Republic of China)（教育部）(1998)面向21世纪教育振兴行动计划 [Action scheme for invigorating education towards the 21st century (ASIE)]. 1998年12月24日. Available at http://www.moe.edu.cn/edoas/website18/info3337.htm [accessed 29 May 2006].

National Bureau of Statistics of China（中华人民共和国国家统计局）(2004)中国统计年鉴，2004年9月 [China statistics yearbook, September 2004]. 北京：中国统计出版社 [Beijing: China Statistics Publishing House].

World Conference on HE (1998) Declaration. Available at http://portal.unesco.org/education/en/ev.php-URL_ID=7152&URL_DO=DO_TOPIC&URL_SECTION=201.html [accessed 30 May 2006].

Wu Q.（吴启迪）(2005) 中国高等教育信息化发展与展望 [China's higher education: development and outlook]. 2005年5月 [May 2005]. Available at http://www.kongzhi.cn/News/newscontent.asp?idg=20203 [accessed June 14, 2006].

Xu M. and Li X.（徐明祥·李兴洲）(2001)构建我国终身教育体系的难点及对策[Constructing a lifelong learning educational system: Problems and countermeasures]. 教育研究 [*Education Research*], 3: 38–41.

Yang C.（杨昌江）(2005) 基础教育均衡发展及其策略 [The balanced development of basic education and its strategies]. 河北教育 [Hebei Education] 2005年第14–6期[2005, Nos. 14–16].

Zhang J.（张婧）(2005)中国教育发展面临四大挑战 [The four challenges China faces in educational development].半月谈[Banyuetan], 8: 26–28.

Zhang W.（张伟远）(2005)现代远程教育与亚洲教育变革 [Modern distance learning and Asian educational reform].《中国远程教育》[China Distance Education] 7(1): 71–75.

Zhang X.（张尧学）(2005)高等教育面临哪些挑战 [What are the challenges higher education faces?].《中国教育报》[China Education Newspaper] 2005年9月15日第5版 [15 September 2005: 5].

Zhao G.（赵国栋）(2004)关天中国、美国和日本高等教育信息化发展的比较研究：ACCS研究项目介绍 [A comparison of ICT in higher education among China, U.S.A & Japan: introduction to ACCS project].《比较教育研究》[Comparative Education Review] 2004年第2期（总第期165）165(2)]

Zhou, Ji (2006) *Higher Education in China*. Singapore: Thomson Learning.

Zong H.（宗河）(2006) 国家创新体系（大学）框架基本形成 [The national collegiate innovation system framework takes shape.《中国教育报》[China Education Newspaper] 2006年1月9日第1版。[9 January 2006: 1].

CHAPTER 15

Beck, U. (1992) *Risk Society. Towards a New Modernity.* Sage: London.

Brown, P. and Lauder, H. (1992) *Education for Economic Survival: From Fordism to Post-Fordism?* London: Routledge.

Bush, V. (1945) As we may think. *The Atlantic Monthly.* Available at http://www.theatlantic.com/ doc/194507/bush [accessed 24 March 2006].

Cai, C., G. Conole, et al. (2005). Evaluation report of Worldwide Universities Network (WUN) Consortium eChina-UK Project. Available at http://www.echinauk.org/. See Papers and Publications, Reports [accessed 17 July 2006].

Carr-Chellman, A. (Ed.) (2005) *Global Perspectives on e-Learning: Rhetoric and Reality.* Sage: London.

Castells, E. (1996) *The Rise of the Network Society. The Information Age: Economy, Society and Culture Vol. I.* Oxford: Blackwell.

Castells, M. (2001) *The Internet Galaxy: Reflections on the Internet, Business and Society.* Oxford University Press: Oxford.

Conole, G. (2005) What impact are technologies having and how are they changing practice? In I. McNay (ed.) *Beyond Mass Higher Education: Building on Experience, The Society for Research into Higher Education*, pp. 81–95. Milton Keynes: Open University Press/McGraw-Hill Education.

Conole, G. (forthcoming) An international comparison of the relationship between policy and practice in e-learning. In R Andrews and C. Haythornthwaite (eds.) *Handbook of e-Learning Research.* London: Sage.

Conole, G. and Dyke, M. (2004). What are the affordances of information and communication technologies? *ALT [Association for Learning Technology] Journal*, 12(2): 113–124.

Conole, G. and Oliver, M. (2007) *Contemporary Perspectives in e-Learning Research: Themes, Tensions and Impact on Practice.* Oxford: RoutledgeFalmer.

Conole, G., Oliver, M. and White, S. (2007) The impact of e-learning on organisational roles and structures. In G. Conole and M. Oliver (eds.) *Contemporary Perspectives in e-Learning Research: Themes, Methods and Impact on Practice,* pp. 69–81. Oxford: RoutledgeFalmer.

Conole, G., Smith, J. and White, S. (2007) A critique of the impact of policy and funding. In G. Conole and M. Oliver (eds.) *Contemporary Perspectives in e-Learning Research: Themes, Methods and Impact on Practice*, pp. 38–54. Oxford: RoutledgeFalmer.

Conole, G., De Laat, M., Dillon, T. and Darby, J. (2006) 'LXP: The learner experience of e-learning — final project report', at http://www.jisc.ac.uk/media/documents/programmes/ elearning_pedagogy/lxp%20project%20final%20report%20dec%2006.pdf [accessed 26 May 2007].

Cook, J., White, S., Sharples, M., Sclater, N. and Davis, H. (2007) The design of learning technologies. In G. Conole and M. Oliver (eds.) *Contemporary Perspectives in e-Learning Research: Themes, Methods and Impact on Practice*, pp. 55–68. Oxford: RoutledgeFalmer.

Council of European Union (2002) Council resolution on lifelong learning. *Official Journal of the European Communities.* C163: 1–3. Available at http://europa.eu.int/eur-lex/pri/en/oj/dat/2002/ c_163/c_16320020709en00010003.pdf [accessed 17 July 2006].

Creanor, L., Trinder, K., Gowan D., and Howells, C. (2006) 'LEX: The learner experience of e-learning — final project report,' at http://www.jisc.ac.uk/uploaded_documents/ LEX%20Final%20Report_August06.pdf [accessed 26 May 2007].

DfEE (1998) The Learning Age. A renaissance for a new Britain. Government Green Paper. Available at http://www.lifelonglearning.co.uk/greenpaper/ [accessed 17 July 2006].

DfES (2004) Towards a unified e-learning strategy. Available at http://www.dfes.gov.uk/consultations/ conResults.cfm?consultationId=774 [accessed 21 July 2006].

DfES (2005) DfES e-Learning Strategy: Harnessing Technology — Transforming Learning and Children's Services. Available at http://www.dfes.gov.uk/publications/e-strategy [accessed 17 July 2006].

Drucker, P. (1994) Knowledge work and knowledge society: The social transformation of this century. 1994 Edwin L. Godkin Lecture. Transcript available at http://www.ksg.harvard.edu/ifactory/ ksgpress/www/ksg-news/transcripts/drucklec.htm.

Dyke, M. (2001) Reflective learning and reflexive modernity as theory practice and research in post-compulsory education. Unpublished PhD Thesis, Educational Studies, University of Surrey.

Dyke, M (2006) The role of the 'other' in reflection, knowledge formation and action in a late modernity. *International Journal of Lifelong Education*, 25(2): 105–123.

Dyke, M., Conole, G., Ravenscroft, A. and de Freitas, S. (2007) Learning theory and its application to e-learning. In G. Conole and M. Oliver (eds.) *Contemporary Perspectives in e-Learning Research: Themes, Methods and Impact on Practice,* pp. 82–97. Oxford: RoutledgeFalmer.

Giddens, A. (1991) *The Consequences of Modernity*. Polity Press: Cambridge.

Giddens, A. (2000) *Runaway World: How Globalization Is Reshaping Our Lives*. New York: Routledge.

Government of Ireland (2003) The Progress Report on the New Connections Action Plan. Dublin, Ireland: Government Publications Office.

Henkel, M (2000) *Academic Identities and Policy Change in Higher Education*. London: Jessica Kingsley.

Jochems, W., Van Merrienboer, J. D. and Koper, K. (2004) *Integrated e-Learning: Implications for Pedagogy, Technology and Organization*. Oxford: RoutledgeFalmer.

Kearns, P. (2002) Towards the connected learning society. An international overview of trends in policy for information and communication technology in education. Available at http://www. dest.gov.au/NR/rdonlyres/7AC0E17C-C0C6-4BE3-9017-88CA7B983D42/1916/ TowardstheConnectedLearningSociety.pdf [accessed 17 July 2006].

Kuhn, T. S. (1996) *The Structure of Scientific Revolutions*. Chicago/London: University of Chicago Press.

Land, R. (2006) Networked learning and the politics of speed: A dromological perspective. Paper presented at the Fifth International Conference on Networked Learning, Lancaster University, 10–12 April. Available at http://www.networkedlearningconference.org.uk/abstracts/Land.htm [accessed 17 July 2006].

Lash, S. and Urry, J. (1994) *Economics and Signs and Space*. London: Sage.

Mayes, T. and de Freitas, S. (2004) Review of e-learning frameworks, models and theories, JISC e-learning models desk study. Available at http://www.jisc.ac.uk/uploaded_documents/ Stage%202%20Learning%20Models%20(Version%201).pdf [accessed 17 July 2006].

Nobles, D. (2001) Digital diploma mills: the automation of higher education. *First Monday*, online. Available at http://www.firstmonday.org/issues/issue3_1/noble/#author [accessed 21 July 2006].

OECD [Organization for Economic Co-operation and Development] (1996) *Lifelong Learning for All*. Paris: OECD.

Oliver, M., Roberts, G., Beetham, H., Ingraham, B., Dyke, M. and Levy, P. (2007), Knowledge, society and perspectives on learning technology. In G. Conole and M. Oliver (eds.) *Contemporary Perspectives in e-Learning Research: Themes, Methods and Impact on Practice*, pp. 27–37. Oxford: RoutledgeFalmer.

Oliver, R. (2005) Quality assurance and e-learning: blue skies and pragmatism. *ALT-J [Association for Learning Technology — Journal]*, 13(3): 173–187.

QAA [Quality Assurance Agency] (2004) Code of practice for the assurance of academic quality and standards in higher education? Section 2: Collaborative provision and flexible and distributed learning (including e-learning). Available at http://www.qaa.ac.uk/academicinfrastructure/codeOfPractice/default.asp [accessed 17 July 2006].

Raymond, E. (1999) The cathedral and the bazaar. *Knowledge Technology and Policy*, 12(3): 23–49.

Salomon, G. (ed.) (1993) *Distributed Cognitions: Psychological and Educational Considerations*. Cambridge: Cambridge University Press.

Seale, J. (2005) Editorial and articles in Special Issue on Accessibility, *ALT-J [Association for Learning Technology — Journal]*, 14(1).

Selwyn, N. and Gorard, S. (2003) Reality bytes: Examining the rhetoric of widening educational participation via ICT. *British Journal of Educational Technology*, 34(2): 169–181.

UNESCO (n.d.) ICT in education: China. Available at http://www.unescobkk.org/index.php?id=1374 [accessed 17 July 2006].

Weller, M. (2007) Beyond the VLE. In M. Weller (ed.) *Virtual Learning Environments: Effective Deployment and Use*, pp. 29–42. Oxford: RoutledgeFalmer.

Index